Mentoring the Mentor

Studies in the
Postmodern Theory of Education

Joe L. Kincheloe and Shirley R. Steinberg
General Editors

Vol. 60

PETER LANG
New York • Washington, D.C./Baltimore
Bern • Frankfurt am Main • Berlin • Vienna • Paris

Mentoring the Mentor

A Critical Dialogue with
Paulo Freire

Edited by Paulo Freire
with James W. Fraser, Donaldo Macedo,
Tanya McKinnon, and William T. Stokes

PETER LANG
New York • Washington, D.C./Baltimore
Bern • Frankfurt am Main • Berlin • Vienna • Paris

Library of Congress Cataloging-in-Publication Data

Mentoring the mentor: a critical dialogue with Paulo Freire/
edited by Paulo Freire with James W. Fraser, Donaldo Macedo,
Tanya McKinnon, and William T. Stokes.
p. cm. —(Counterpoints: vol. 60)
Includes bibliographical references.
1. Freire, Paulo. 2. Education—Philosophy. 3. Critical pedagogy. I. Freire,
Paulo. II. Series: Counterpoints (New York, NY); vol. 60.
LB880.F732M46 370'.1—dc20   97-1382
ISBN 0-8204-3798-0
ISSN 1058-1634

Die Deutsche Bibliothek-CIP-Einheitsaufnahme

Mentoring the mentor: a critical dialogue with Paulo Freire/
edited by Paulo Freire with James W. Fraser, Donaldo Macedo,
Tanya McKinnon, and William T. Stokes.
– New York; Washington, D.C./Baltimore; Bern; Frankfurt am Main;
Berlin; Vienna; Paris: Lang.
(Counterpoints; Vol. 60)
ISBN 0-8204-3798-0
NE: GT

Cover design by James F. Brisson.

Cover photo of Paulo Freire by Jane Cook, for Lesley College.

The paper in this book meets the guidelines for permanence and durability
of the Committee on Production Guidelines for Book Longevity
of the Council of Library Resources.

Printed in the United States of America.

Mentoring the mentor

TABLE OF CONTENTS

BEANS AND BEAUJOLAIS

Joe L. Kincheloe, Series Editor

I have always been put off by people who are "star struck," who fawn in the presence of celebrity. Maybe it comes from my egalitarian Appalachian cultural roots where we didn't "bow down to nobody"—I'm not sure. Working in a field where brushes with celebrities are virtually non-existent, such concerns are generally irrelevant. I suppose Paulo Freire is the closest thing education has to a celebrity. Known and loved (or not) throughout the world, Paulo commands a presence unequaled by anyone who calls himself or herself an educator. Thus, Paulo presents me with a rare opportunity to enjoy a brush with a celebrity and whenever I'm around him, contrary to my nature, I fawn. This book, however, does not fawn. Indeed, the essays included here range from appreciative to highly critical—all engaging Freire's work seriously.

Recently, Shirley and I had lunch with Paulo and his wife, Nita, in their home in São Paulo. I was thrilled to see how Paulo's house was furnished, the artwork displayed on his walls, the office where he writes, the books in his library, etc. As he and Nita showed us around, I was an over-eager ethnographer making mental notes for future reference. I was even fascinated by the Xerox machine in his office—he has one just like me, my thoughts exclaimed.

My star-struckness finds its roots in the role Paulo played in my life long before I had ever met him. As an aspiring teacher in my early twenties, I had an inarticulated, immature vision of a proto-critical pedagogy. For me, reading *Pedagogy of the Oppressed* was not merely a lesson in politics and pedagogy but a personal affirmation that I was not alone with my intuitions and passions. Thus, Paulo's life took on major importance for an isolated Tennessee boy with hopes for a voice in the larger conversation about issues of schooling and justice. Freire's life showed me that my aspirations were possible.

As I continued my ethnography of Paulo's home, these thoughts about his role in my life for the last twenty-five years dominated my consciousness. I studied his face, his gentle countenance, his passionate responses to Shirley and my questions about a variety of issues. I contemplated the irony of my actually being with someone so influential in my life who, in 1971 seemed so many light-years away from my academically isolated Tennessee microcosm. My ethnographic and autobiographical analyses were interrupted by Nita's announcement that lunch was ready. Paulo had a speaking engagement later that afternoon and we knew lunch would be relatively brief.

We sat down to a bounteous spread of food. As I watched Paulo, his attention focused on the rice and brown beans. This was his culinary passion dating back to childhood. The cook brought the rest of the dishes into the dining room, but Paulo saw them only as side dishes to the rice and beans. I had a similar relation to brown beans—a staple of poor Appalachians who would eat them with cornbread several times a week. I told Paulo and Nita about how much I loved beans and how many I would eat at one sitting. "I have never tasted anything better," he told me. Upon opening a bottle of Beaujolais, Paulo filled our glasses. The juxtaposition of the beans and Beaujolais struck us as funny and we drank a toast to them.

The humor behind the toast involved the contradiction between the brown beans and the Beaujolais—a contradiction that reflected both of our lives and bound us together. We had both come from the poorest sections of our countries: Paulo from northeast Brazil and me, from the southern Appalachians. Just as we both loved beans, we loved and appreciated the people and places we had left behind. We both had dreamed of something else, something unexperienced—something not unlike the sophistication of the Beaujolais. We had both played our dreams in the same defiant way, refusing to give up the beans once we tasted the wine.

My mental structuring of the bean and wine transubstantiation ritual (a critical pedagogical transubstantiation?) was interrupted by Paulo and Nita's cook mistaking me for Peter McLaren—my hair's not that long, I thought. Brought back into the material reality of my location, I traded loving looks with Shirley. She knew how profound a conversation with Paulo Freire regarding our mutual love of beans was for me.

I write this simply to express what an honor it is for me to write a series editor's preface for a book about the pedagogy and person of Paulo Freire. My hope is that this volume will be as nourishing as the brown beans and Beaujolais we shared in São Paulo. These chapters explore many different themes in Paulo Freire's work, represent authors from many different historical, racial, gendered, and class positions. Yet in that variety a spread of intellectual nourishment is offered which should help readers move forward in their own role as engaged and passionate, democratic teachers.

INTRODUCTION

Paulo Freire
James W. Fraser
Donaldo Macedo
Tanya McKinnon
William T. Stokes

As its title indicates, *Mentoring the Mentor* is designed to create—in written form—a critical dialogue between Paulo Freire and a range of scholars and practitioners who have felt the impact of his work. Our goal in this volume is truly critical engagement—voices of criticism and voices of appreciation, voices of questions, concerns and uncertainty as well as voices that reflect the sure touch of Freire's impact. And finally, we include a response from Paulo Freire to the major themes that have emerged in the other chapters. The purpose of presenting this range of voices is to invite the reader into the dialogue, not as an observer, but as an activate participant. As Freire says in the concluding chapter of this work:

> The pitfall of a linguist is to believe that writing words is freezing them in time. Writing fixes the force of the orality in time, but the reader, in engaging with that force, is continually reinventing and redialoguing.

If readers of this volume are able to take Freire at his word, if *Mentoring the Mentor* can lead to a process of "continually reinventing and redialoguing," then the enterprise will be a success and the impact of the dialogue on those who struggle for more democratic forms of schools and society will be significant.

The dialogue that led to *Mentoring the Mentor* began in July 1991 at a four-day conference held at Lesley College in Cambridge, Massachusetts, to honor Paulo Freire and to create the opportunity to engage with him in a critical examination of his work and its relevance to the struggle for democratic schools in the North American context. The conference was attended by sixty scholars, teachers, community workers, and students from the region and around the country—all committed to critical dialogue with Freire and with each other. The conference organizers were clear that it is only through the rigorous intellectual interrogation of practice and ideas about practice that education can maintain its liberatory commitment. Lesley College, a small institution whose mission includes teacher education and progressive educational practices, provided the space and the resources to permit us to meet together and engage in extended, serious conversation, during which all participants had the opportunity to speak with Paulo Freire and to listen to each other and to the perspectives of others across disciplinary domains and across the borders of race, gender, nationality, language, and class positions. At the conclusion of the conference, we were left with the challenge of living out the truth of the words that were shared and the energy of the dialogue as a site of knowledge production. This book was born out of the decision to sustain that critical dialogue—in writing—between Paulo Freire and the fifteen contributing authors.

Our dialogue continued when Freire returned to Boston as a guest lecturer at Northeastern University in 1994. And finally, the dialogue came full circle when three of the editors met in the summer of 1996 in Paulo Freire's study overlooking the city of São Paulo, Brazil. We gathered as three friends and colleagues to continue the process of responding to the chapters that have been assembled for this volume. The goal of that meeting, and of the volume itself, is to find ways to continue and expand the dialogue that is represented in these chapters. Our goal is not to complete the dialogue, for no dialogue worth its salt is ever complete. Rather the dialogue presented here is part of a continuing process of reading the word and the world within the context of a commitment to the expansion of human and democratic opportunities for all people.

It is not our intention in this volume to contribute to the proliferation of summaries and secondary texts that attempt to appropriate, explain, or—in some cases—domesticate Freire's work into a "method." Rather, we write in order to reengage in a critical dialogue with Paulo Freire and his texts, and by writing allow others to join in the conversation in which respect and critique are understood to be inseparable. In this way, Paulo Freire serves as a mentor to chapter authors and readers alike, yet in his own engaging with the text, he is also mentored by the other voices.

Freire has written elsewhere that "it is absolutely fundamental, however, that an author be criticized not on the basis of what is said about him or her, but only after an earnest, devoted competent reading of the actual author."[1] Such a reading must serve as the beginning point for this volume or any other attempt to engage Freire or any other serious thinker. This book began out of the reality that all of us first met Freire through *Pedagogy of the Oppressed* or one of his many other texts. Our first engagements were thus as readers. Subsequently most of us who wrote these chapters have met and spoken with Freire at times during the past twenty-five years, either during the four days at Lesley College or the subsequent gatherings at Northeastern University and elsewhere. Some of us have worked closely with him, others continue to know him primarily through his written work. Whatever the specific form of the encounter, we have sought participation in a critical dialogic practice that is created when there is genuine conversation as people face each other with respect and a commitment to speaking and listening seriously. Now we wish to continue that dialogue in writing. There are other collections addressing Freire's work and engaging his ideas, but this volume differs. We seek here to merge the oral and literate critical discourses—to write, yes, but to write so as to merge with talking, in a sense of immediacy of engagement, despite the actuality of the delay experienced between first writing and only later, perhaps much later, reading what others, including Paulo Freire, have written also. In one essay in the volume, this relation of oral discourse to written texts is problematized explicitly. James Gee asks to what degree does the act of publishing something freeze it and remove it from dialogue, remove it from the conversation in which the mutual engagement of participants as agents in production of meanings take place. This volume engages this contradiction directly.

The title of this volume, *Mentoring the Mentor*, illustrates the purpose of the work. It is in both the appreciation for Paulo Freire and in the critique of Paulo Freire contained in these chapters that Freire's work is continued and expanded. Since the early 1970s Freire himself has been calling for a process of reinventing Paulo Freire in the North American context, or in any other context where he himself has not worked or is not currently working. He repeats this call in his response in this volume. No one is more adamant than Freire himself in insisting that he has not developed a set of methods that can be used in any context. On the contrary, what Freire has done is to provide a framework for thinking about education—a framework in which the process of human liberation is at the very center of the enterprise—but a framework that also demands the continuing "reinvention of Freire" in real and specific human cultural and historic educational contexts.

We title this volume *Mentoring the Mentor: A Critical Dialogue with Paulo Freire*, in order to assert again our understanding of teaching and learning as a serious engagement between subjects who in collaboration are agents of their own learning. Paulo Freire has been a mentor to all the contributors to this volume. He has probably been one to many who will come to it as readers. And, as the conference that began the project was intended to honor him, this volume also honors his work, but does so by being able to engage critically with that work, as exemplified especially in the essays by Peter Murrell, Michelle Fine, Gloria Ladson-Billings, Anita Sheth and George Dei, and Asgedet Stafanos. In all the essays, problems are posed and critical interrogations of Freire's work are offered.

Freire has examined the contradictions in the relations between educators and students, between mentors and those who are mentored. Traditional pedagogy, in the simplest terms, operates from the position that the teacher or mentor is presumed to know and the learner to "know not" and therefore the teacher must transfer or export knowledge to the learner, who "receives" learning in a manner that denies the validity of the ontological and epistemological productions of the learner and the learner's community. This is an authoritarian, manipulative, "banking" pedagogy, which negates the possibility of democracy and distorts the lived experiences of the learners who are silenced and denied the opportunity to be authors of their own histories.

The second option is that of the uncritical idealist who celebrates the spontaneous acquisition of critical insight, but who denies that the learner may also internalize the ready-made categories of domination and subordination, and do so at an age or from a position where mechanisms of resistance are least available and who become more dehumanized participants in their own subordination. The romanticization of the student, sometimes done most inappropriately in the name of Paulo Freire, has led too many educators to abandon their responsibility for bringing the best that they have to the teaching-learning process. The result has been too many instances of miseducation from which supposedly idealistic educators have excused themselves from any degree of responsibility.

Freire is quite clear in his rejection of both banking education and uncritical idealism. In reflecting on the authority of the teacher he insists, "The teacher's authority...is indispensable to the development of the learner's freedom. What may frustrate the process is the abuse of authority by the teacher, which makes him or her authoritarian, or the emptying of authority, which leads to permissiveness."[2] The third option is thus that "we need neither authoritarianism not permissiveness, but democratic substance."[3] A critical educator must be prepared to intervene, to dialogue, to offer his or her skills and insights, but never through the banking approach. "What is ethically required of progressive educators is that, consistent with their democratic dream, they respect the educands, and therefore never manipulate them" and also that the progressive educator "never cancels, crushes or hinders the development of the educand's thinking."[4] The term "educand" challenges the objectification of the student as the passive receiver of the lessons provided by the teacher. The educand occupies the position of agent, of cognizing subject. As such the learner is not subordinate to the teacher or mentor, but a participant in a dialogic exploration toward knowing and understanding. Moreover, knowledge is understood to be socially constructed in the negotiation of experience with other knowers (including educators and mentors). As a humanist, Freire makes the metaphysical commitment to freedom, to the ontological necessity to become more fully human which requires a critical pedagogy that reveals, unveils and challenges, by respecting the educands as subjects who can transform present realities and "write" their future into existence.

The essays in this volume raise questions and challenges to Freire in order to open a dialogue within which he can respond and engage with us. We hope that the result will both model and advance the kind of critical dialogue that is so badly needed in education today. This book seeks to present a model wherein intellectuals, as both scholars and as students—as teacher and learners, as mentors and mentees, may be exposed to criticism, respond to it, and thereby continue to "make the road by walking."

The sixteen chapters offer a wide diversity of themes that interweave and appear in somewhat different forms in various places throughout the volume. This introduction will, of necessity, underrepresent that complexity, but may offer the reader a guide to our efforts.

We begin, in the chapter by Macedo, with an examination of a tendency, at least in North America, to "tame" Freire and reduce his work to a "method." Macedo argues for an "anti-method" pedagogy—that is, that there is no contextless Freireian method that can be used as a template for liberatory education in São Paulo, Eritrea, or Boston. A critical pedagogy is not a matter of process and procedures, but of goals and actions, that is possibilities for transformation and liberation. Related themes are raised throughout the volume, especially in the chapters by Frankenstein, Stokes, and Seiber.

In the North American context, the specific workings of racism, the social construction of "white" and "black," and the conditions of immigration and linguistic minority status require context-specific theory and practice. These themes are raised especially in relation to "layered identities" and who "speaks"—who is silenced and who speaks for whom. Tarule's and Fine's letters to Freire raise the questions of identity and position, and these are taken up by Murrell, McKinnon, and Scapp who examine the relations of teachers and learners both within and across the boundaries of racial, cultural, and linguistic differences. They examine the many ways educators can silence their students even as they declare their intention to "liberate the oppressed" students. The chapters by Ladson-Billings, and Sheth and Dei elaborate on these themes and provide powerful challenges to conceptions of race and oppression in Freire's writings and those of other contributors to theories or critical pedagogy. Stefanos extends questions of sexism (raised also by Tarule, Fine, McKinnon, and others) and feminism beyond the North American context in case studies of liberatory pedagogies in Eritrea and Guinea Bissau.

Chapters by Fraser, Stokes, and Seiber draw from specific personal and professional experiences in Freire's life to explore topics as diverse as humility and love, theory and praxis, and the exercise of power in positions of educational leadership and the preparation of the next generation of educational leaders. Theories of literacy and possibilities of genuine liberatory discourse are problematized by Gee, as noted earlier. And McLaren's analysis of pedagogy, postmodernism, and the politics of race joins all the themes in a critical interrogation and construction of theory and its relation to liberatory praxis.

All of us, and especially Paulo Freire, are intensely conscious that the dialogue presented here, as with any single dialogue, must remain partial. We have not sought to exhaust the possibilities of answers, but rather end our conversation leaving open the possibility that the readers of this book will ask new questions and be engaged in new ways of searching for probable answers. By remaining conscious that we do not provide definitive answers we keep our dialogue alive in testimony that there is an incompleteness to both questions and answers that should be framed and reframed according to the challenge of new and multiple contexts.

We hope this book achieves its purpose and extends the conversation by inviting more participants into a critical dialogue with others who are committed to the investigation and transformation of the conditions of marginalization, subordination, and oppression that distort the humanity of all teachers and learners. It is our hope that this volume will contribute to the generation of pedagogies of possibility.

REFERENCES

1. Freire, Paulo, *Pedagogy of Hope: Reliving Pedagogy of the Oppressed* (New York: Continuum, 1995), p. 76.

2. Freire, Paulo, *Letters to Christina: Reflections on My Life and Work* (New York: Routledge, 1996), p. 163.

3. *Pedagogy of Hope*, p. 113.

4. *Ibid.*, pp. 80 and 117.

CHAPTER ONE

AN ANTI-METHOD PEDAGOGY
A Freirian Perspective

Donaldo Macedo

As the capitalist "banking model" of education generates greater and greater failure, many liberal and neoliberal educators are looking to Paulo Freire's pedagogy as an alternative. No longer can it be argued that Freire's pedagogy is appropriate only in Third World contexts. For one thing, we are experiencing a rapid Third Worldization of North America where inner cities resemble more and more the shantytowns of the Third World, with a high level of poverty, violence, illiteracy, human exploitation, homelessness, and human misery. The abandonment of our inner cities and the insidious decay of their respective infrastructures, including their schools, makes it very difficult to maintain the artificial division between the First World and the Third World. It is just as easy to find Third Worldness in the First World inner cities as it is to discover First World opulence in the oligarchies in El Salvador, Guatemala, and within many other Third World nations. The Third Worldization of the North American inner cities has also produced large-scale educational failures that have created minority student dropout rates from 50 percent in the Boston public schools to over 70 percent in larger metropolitan areas like New York City.

Against this landscape of educational failure, conservative educators, by and large, have recoiled in an attempt to salvage the status quo and contain the "browning" of America. These conservative educators have attempted to reappropriate the educational debate and to structure the educational discourse in terms of competition and privatization of schools. The hidden curriculum of the proposed school privatization movement consists of taking resources from poor schools that are on the verge of bankruptcy to support private or well-to-do schools. Private school choice is only private to the degree that it generates private profit while being supported by public funds. What is rarely discussed in the North American school debate is that public schools are part and parcel of the fabric of any democratic society. In fact, conservative educators fail to recognize that a democratic society that shirks its public responsibility is a democracy in crisis. A society that equates for-profit privatization with democracy is a society with confused priorities. A democratic society that falsely believes, in view of the savings and loan debacle and the Wall Street scandals, for example, that quality, productivity, honesty, and efficiency can be achieved only through for-profit privatization is a society that displays both an intellectual and ethical bankruptcy of ideas. If we follow the line of argument that "private" is best, we should once again consider Jack Beaty's question: "Would we set up a private Pentagon to improve our public defense establishment?"[1] Would private-is-best logic eradicate the ongoing problems in the military that range from rampant sexual harassment, payment of over $600 for a toilet seat, to billions for airplanes that don't fly? Most Americans would find the privatization of the Pentagon an utter absurdity, claiming a national priority for a strong defense. Instead of dismantling public education further, I believe we should make it a national public priority. I would also contend that the safeguarding of our democracy rests much more on the creation of an educated smart citizenry than on the creation of smart bombs.

In contrast to the market notion of school reform in the United States, many liberal and neoliberal educators have rediscovered Freire as an alternative to the conservative domestication education that equates free-market ideology with democracy. Part of the problem with some of these pseudocritical educators is that, in the name of liberation pedagogy, they reduce Freire's leading ideas to a method. According to Stanley Aronowitz, the North American fetish for method has allowed Freire's philosophical ideas to be "assimilated to the prevailing obsession of North American education, following a tendency in all human and social sciences, with methods—of verifying knowledge and, in schools, of teaching, that is, transmitting knowledge to otherwise unprepared students."[2]

This fetish for method works insidiously against adhering to Freire's own pronouncement against the importation and exportation of methodology. In a long conversation I had with him about this issue he said: "Donaldo, I don't want to be imported or exported. It is impossible to export pedagogical practices without reinventing them. Please, tell your fellow American educators not to import me. Ask them to recreate and rewrite my ideas."

Freire's leading ideas concerning the act of knowing transcend the methods for which he is known. In fact, according to Linda Bimbi, "the originality of Freire's work does not reside in the efficacy of his literacy methods, but, above all, in the originality of its content designed to develop our consciousness"[3] as part of a humanizing pedagogy. According to Freire, "a humanizing education is the path through which men and women can become conscious about their presence in the world. The way they act and think when they develop all of their capacities, taking into consideration their needs, but also the needs and aspirations of others."[4]

With that said, why is it that some educators, in their attempt to cut the chains of oppressive educational practices, blindly advocate for the dialogical model, creating, in turn, a new form of methodological rigidity laced with benevolent oppression—all done under the guise of democracy with the sole purpose that it is for your own good. Many of us have witnessed pedagogical contexts in which you are implicitly or explicitly required to speak, to talk about your experience as an act of liberation. We all have been at conferences where the speaker is chastised because he or she failed to locate himself or herself in history. In other words, he or she failed to give primacy to his or her experiences in addressing issues of critical democracy. It does not matter that the speaker had important and insightful things to say. This is tantamount to dismissing Marx because he did not entrance us with his personal lived-experiences.

The appropriation of the dialogical method as a process of sharing experiences is often reduced to a form of group therapy that focuses on the psychology of the individual. Although some educators may claim that this process creates a pedagogical comfort zone, in my view it does little beyond making the oppressed feel good about his or her own sense of victimization. In other words, the sharing of experiences should not be understood in psychological terms only. It invariably requires a political and ideological analysis as well. That is, the sharing of experiences must always be understood within a social praxis that entails both reflection and political action. In short, it must always involve a political project with the objective of dismantling oppressive structures and mechanisms.

This overdose of experiential celebration that characterizes some strands of critical pedagogy offers a reductionist view of identity and experience within, rather than outside, the problematics of power, agency, and history. By overindulging in the legacy and importance of their respective voices and experiences, these educators often fail to move beyond a notion or difference structured in polarizing binarisms and uncritical appeal to the discourse of experience.[5] For this reason, they invoke a romantic pedagogical mode that exoticizes lived experiences as a process of coming to voice. By refusing to link experiences to the politics of culture and critical democracy, these educators reduce their pedagogy to a form of middle-class narcissism. On the one hand, the dialogical method provides the participants with a group therapy space for stating their grievances and, on the other hand, it offers the educator or facilitator a safe pedagogical zone to deal with his or her class guilt.

By refusing to deal with the issue of class privilege, the pseudo-critical educator dogmatically pronounces the need to empower students, to give them voices. These educators are even betrayed by their own language. Instead of creating pedagogical structures that would enable oppressed students to empower themselves, they paternalistically proclaim, "We need to empower students." This position often leads to the creation of what I call literacy and poverty pimps to the extent that, while proclaiming the need to empower students, they are in fact strengthening their own privileged position.

The following example will clarify my point: a progressive colleague of mine who had been working with me in a community-based literacy project betrayed her liberal discourse to empower the community when one of the agencies we work with solicited my help to write a math literacy proposal for them. I agreed and welcomed the opportunity. One of my goals is to develop structures so that community members and agencies can take their own initiative and chart their own course, thus eliminating the need for our continued presence and expertise. In other words, our success in creating structures so that community members empower themselves rests on the degree to which our presence and expertise in the community are no longer necessary because community members have acquired their own expertise, thus preventing a type of neocolonialism.

When my colleague heard about the math literacy proposal she was reticent but did not show outward opposition. However, weeks later, when she learned that the community-based math literacy grant I was writing with the community members competed with our own university-based proposal, which was designed to provide literacy training to community members, my colleague reacted almost irrationally. She argued that the community agency that had written the math literacy grant did not follow a democratic process in that it had not involved her in the development of the grant. A democratic and participatory process in her view referred to the condition that community action needed to include her, this despite the fact that she is not a member of the particular community the math literacy grant was designed to serve. Apparently, in her mind, one can be empowered so long as the empowerment does not encroach on the "expert's" privileged, powerful position. This is a position of power designed to paternalistically empower others.

When I pointed out the obvious ideological contradictions in my colleague's behavior, her response was quick, aggressive, and almost automatic: "I'll be very mad if they get their proposal and we don't get ours." It became very clear to me that my colleague's real political commitment to the community hinged on the extent to which her "expert" position remained unthreatened. That is, the literacy "expert," do-gooder, antiestablishment persona makes sure that his or her privileged position within the establishment as an antiestablishment "expert" is never absorbed by empowered community members.

It is this colonizer, paternalistic attitude that led this same colleague to pronounce publicly, at a major conference, that community people don't need to go to college because, since they know so much more than do members of the university community, there is little that the university can teach them. While making such public statements, this colleague was busily moving from the inner city to an affluent suburb, making sure that her children attend better schools.

A similar attitude emerged in a recent meeting to develop a community-university relationship grant proposal. During the meeting a liberal white professor rightly protested the absence of community members in the committee. However, in attempting to valorize the community knowledge base, she rapidly fell into a romantic paternalism by stating that the community people knew much more than the university professors and that they should be invited to come to teach us rather than we teaching them. This position not only discourages community members from having access to the cultural capital from which these professors have benefited greatly but it also disfigures the reality context that makes the university cultural capital indispensable for any type of real empowerment. It also smacks of a false generosity of paternalism that Freire aggressively opposes:

> The pedagogy of the oppressed animated by authentic humanism (and not humanitarianism) generously presents itself as a pedagogy of man. Pedagogy which begins with the egoistic interests of the oppressors (an egoism cloaked in the false generosity of paternalism) and makes of the oppressed the objects of its humanitarianism, itself maintains and embodies oppression. It is an instrument of dehumanization.[6]

The paternalistic pedagogical attitude represents a middle-class narcissism that gives rise to pseudocritical educators who are part of the same instrumentalist approach to literacy they claim to renounce. The instrumentalist approach to literacy does not only refer to the goal of providing readers who meet the basic requirements of our contemporary society as proposed by conservative educators. Instrumentalist literacy also includes the highest level of literacy through disciplinary specialism and hyperspecialization. Pseudocritical educators are part of this latter term of instrumentalist literacy to the extent that they reduce Freire's dialogical method to a form of specialism. In other words, both the instrumentalist literacy for the poor in the form of a competency-based skill-banking approach, and the highest form of instrumentalist literacy for the rich acquired through the university in the form of professional specialization, share one common feature: they both prevent the development of critical thinking that enables one to read the world critically and to understand the reasons and linkages behind the facts. The instrumentalist approach to literacy, even at the highest level of specialism (including method as a form of specialism) functions to domesticate the consciousness via a constant disarticulation between the reductionistic and narrow reading of one's field of specialization and the reading of the universe within which one's specialism is situated. This inability to link the reading of the word with the world, if not combated, will further debilitate already feeble democratic institutions and the unjust asymmetrical power relations that characterize the hypocritical nature of contemporary democracies. At the lowest level of instrumentalist literacy a semiliterate reads the word but is unable to read the world. At the highest level of instrumental literacy achieved via specialization, the semiliterate is able to read the text of his or her specialization but is ignorant of all other bodies of knowledge that constitute the world of knowledge. This semiliterate specialist was characterized by Ortega y Gasset as a "learned ignoramus." That is to say, "he is not learned, for he is formally ignorant of all that does not enter into his specialty; but neither is he ignorant, because he is a 'scientist' and 'knows' very well his own tiny portion of the universe."[7]

Because the "learned ignoramus" is mainly concerned with his or her tiny portion of the world disconnected from other bodies of knowledge, he or she is never able to relate the flux of information so as to gain a critical reading of the world. A critical reading of the world implies, according to Freire, "a dynamic comprehension between the least coherent sensibility of the world and a more coherent understanding of the world."[8] This explains the inability, for example, of medical specialists in the United States who have contributed to a great technological advancement in medicine to understand and appreciate why over 30 million Americans do not have access to this medical technology and why we still have the highest infant mortality rate in comparison to other developed nations.

Finally, I end this chapter by proposing an anti-method pedagogy that refuses the rigidity of models and methodological paradigms. The anti-method pedagogy forces us to view dialogue as a form of social praxis so that the sharing of experiences is informed by reflection and political action. Dialogue as social praxis "entails that recovering the voice of the oppressed is the fundamental condition for human emancipation."[9] The anti-method pedagogy also frees us from the beaten path of certainties and specialisms. It rejects the mechanization of intellectualism. In short, it calls for the illumination of Freire's leading ideas that will guide us toward the critical road of truth, toward the reappropriation of our endangered dignity, toward the reclaiming of our humanity. No one could argue more pointedly against reducing dialogue and problem posing to a mere method than Freire himself:

> Problem posing education is revolutionary futurity. Hence, it is prophetic.... Hence it corresponds to the historical nature of man. Hence it affirms men as beings who transcend themselves. Hence it identifies with the movement which engages men as being aware of their incompletion—an historical movement which has its point of departure, its subjects and its objective.[10]

The anti-method pedagogy not only adheres to Freire's view of education as revolutionary futurity, it also celebrates the eloquence of Antonio Machado's poem: "Cominante no hay camino, se hace el camino al andar." ("Traveler, there is no road. The road is made as one walks.")

REFERENCES

1. Beaty, Jack, *The Boston Globe*, August 14, 1992.

2. Aronowitz, Stanley, "Paulo Freire's Radical Democratic Humanism," in Peter McLaren and Peter Leonard, eds., Paulo Freire: A Critical Encounter (London: Routledge, 1993), p. 8.

3. Bimbi, Linda, cited in Moacir Gadotti, *Convite a Leitura de Paulo Freire* (São Paulo: Editora Scipione, 1989), p. 32.

4. Freire, Paulo, and Frei Betto, *Essa Escola Chamada Vida* (São Paulo: Atica, 1985), pp. 14-15.

5. Giroux, Henry, "The Politics of Difference and Multiculturalism in the Era of the Los Angeles Uprising," *Journal of the Midwest Modern Language Association* [in press.]

6. Freire, Paulo, *Pedagogy of the Oppressed* (New York: Continuum Publication, 1990), p. 39.

7. Ortega y Gasset, José, *The Revolt of the Masses* (New York: Norton, 1932), p. 112.

8. Freire, Paulo, and Donaldo Macedo, *Literacy: Reading the Word and the World* (South Hadley, Mass.: Bergin & Garvey, 1987), p. 131.

9. Aronowitz, Stanley, "Paulo Freire's Radical Democratic Humanism," p. 18.

10. Freire, Paulo, cited in Stanley Aronowitz, "Paulo Freire's Radical Democratic Humanism," pp. 11-12.

CHAPTER TWO

A LETTER TO PAULO FREIRE

Jill Mattuck Tarule

Dear Paulo Freire, My decision, as I sit down to pose some questions to you, is to do so in a letter form. It is not intended to be overly familiar—a worry that sprang up as I tried to decide the most respectful and appropriate way to address you (Paulo, too informal; Mr. Freire, too Euro-American; Sir, too formal...)—and, yet, to find a way to ensure that this "felt" more like dialogue than monologue, more like conversation than announcement. At first, when I was asked to write an outline for your perusal and response, I was aware that my mind does not construct thought in outlines, which led me to understand that what I want to dialogue with you about actually begins there, in the difference between those whose thinking organizes in outline and those whose thinking does not. A series of thoughts and questions began to flow from those ruminations. I realized that I welcomed an opportunity to dialogue with you about questions and issues emerging as I think about your work and connected and separate thinking, layered identities, and what all that means for the learners in our classrooms and communities. (I decided to use headings as slim mimicking of the outline form!)

Connected and Separate Thinking

My work with my colleagues Mary Belenky, Blythe Clinchy, and Nancy Goldberger emphasized epistemological development in women.[1] We describe five developmental positions, not necessarily sequential, that women learners aged sixteen to sixty bring to how they consider the core epistemological issues of what truth, knowledge, and authority mean to them. From this exploration, we identified women who have reached a level of sophisticated thought (procedural knowers) in which they understand that all these issues are negotiable and that there are procedures one uses to go about reasoning and analysis. But there were two significantly different sets of procedures. The Separate Knowers enjoy adversarial debate, believe that the self must be extracted from all considerations, and employ reasoning that achieves what we (at least in America) have conventionally defined as critical thinking: the capacity to be objective, distant, and abstract in one's thinking. They write outlines easily. In contrast, the Connected Knowers emphasize relationships in their analysis. They seek narrative conversation in lieu of debate, and often experience debate as personal attack; they look at ideas as relationally influenced by their and others' experience, by the author's experience, and they assert that the self cannot be abstracted from reasoning. Outlining, as a procedure, may well baffle the Connected Knower whose thoughts will not fall into neat, sequential chunks.

My first set of questions—of wonderings, really—emerge from positing that there are, at the very least, these two modes of analysis, of meaning-making, of knowing. It would suggest that there are at least two rather distinct routes to take in the movement toward what you have defined as consciousness (*conscientização*).[2] Core to the process of consciousness is the process of dialogue, as you have defined it, and a particular kind of dialogue that in response to a problem leads toward "the act of cognition which unveils reality" (p. 71). Yet, Connected and Separate Knowers engage in dialogue in rather different ways. Connected Knowers speak in a way that emphasizes what Tannen[3] has called "rapport"—a particular form of dialogue that is peppered with tag questions, with unfinished sentences as the speaker attempts to ensure that his or her colleagues in conversation are hearing and understanding his or her perspective and he or she theirs. In contrast, the Separate Knower's dialogue style emphasizes "report," a conversational approach that looks to deliver the idea in a complete form. Each are, I would argue, particular "acts of cognition" that may lead to rather different views of reality. Thus, the process of achieving consciousness may vary significantly, depending on what might be referred to as one's predilection in both dialogue and, hence, cognition.[4] At the very least, Connected Thinking may illuminate another epistemological strand and, as such, suggest that problem-posing, liberatory education will be differentially experienced by different learner/participants. It may also suggest that the content of the problems themselves will be perceived very differently, depending upon which approach—separate or connected—is emphasized.

An example of how this problem solving may be different, albeit an example drawn from a considerably less important issue than solidarity and community building, comes from an engineering student I interviewed. She was describing how unhelpful it was for her to try to dialogue with her Separate-Knower peer students as they prepared for an exam:

> The stuff [they] were spouting out before class, before the exam when we were all cramming together, was Greek to me and I thought I am absolutely going to fail this thing. Then I'd get in there and ace it…It's like they were keying in on different aspects totally than I was…I'm doing it my way and assimilate knowledge differently than they do…We could both go in from different perspectives and do identically on the same exam.

This student—a Connected Knower—describes her experience of finding herself wanting to use a different approach to solving the problem of preparing for the exam. She focuses on different aspects as she engages in an act of cognition. Other students have helped us to see that foregrounding relationships in both analysis and dialogue style leads the Connected Knower to focus on the particular rather than generalities. Less likely to move toward abstraction in analysis, the Connected Knower tends to maintain a sensitivity to contexts in which the particulars are embedded. Thus, while others may be attending to the more abstract ideas and the conclusions that emerge in dialogue, connected knowing balances attention to those ideas with attention to the ways they are being derived and to the relationships among the people constructing the ideas. As a result, Connected Knowers often experience the traditional educational environment as alien and alienating. They learn quickly that they do not speak the language of the discourse as it is proceeding.

Their way of speaking with its tentativeness as they seek rapport is not in the traditionally measured and careful language of the academy.

Rather than succumb to the majority form of discourse, these Connected Knowers may go mute while assuming that they are not different but dumb, not ill-matched for the discourse but ignorant and unable. Thus, the way that discourse is conducted—even in problem-solving approaches—produces for the Connected Knower this experience of disconnection and powerlessness. In this way, oppressive practices are unwittingly reproduced in the educational process, often most poignantly in those that claim to be liberating. This poses, I think, a fundamental contradiction in even the most liberating of educational practice.

I would be most interested in hearing your ideas about philosophical and ethical perspectives that could direct us toward ways to see and reconsider dialogue and the process of developing consciousness that incorporate differentiated ways of making meaning, differentiated epistemological approaches. I cast this in philosophical and ethical perspectives because what is needed is a way to address a diversity of styles or cognition. Connected and Separate Knowing may be only two examples of that potential diversity.

Layered Identities

Now nine or so years after first stumbling on the preceding ideas in our *Women's Ways of Knowing* work, it is clear that we were addressing a real dialectic that is only gender related, not gender specific. Moreover, male or female can no longer be understood as a simple dialectic. Rather, the complexity lies in the fact that we each have layered identities, comprised of a race, class, gender, ethnicity, physical ability, sexual partner preference, regional affiliation, and so forth. This leads, as many have observed, to multiple interpretations of what constitutes "reality" and to different positions and competing interpretations of oppressor and oppression within that reality.[5] I read much of your work, perhaps erroneously, as describing a singular "majority culture," dominant group and a singular oppressed group. This, too, seems dialectic or, perhaps a better term, bipolar.

It seems that when we try to base analyses of power and oppression on the exploration of the collective experience of individuals, trouble emerges. When experience is the basis for "revealing reality," and that experience is grounded in importantly different positions for interpretation, then profound dissonance emerges. Exploration does not then lead to "a common knowledge and solidarity based on sameness," but reveals, instead, "overlapping and multiple forms of oppression."[6] What is absent is the possibility for anyone—participant, leader, or teacher—to lay claim to a singular analysis of either oppression or oppressors. The complexity thus introduced seems to me to raise some significant questions.

> ∾ How can we develop ways to think about and to describe populations of learners that might avoid reproducing an underlying, "bipolar" assumption about power relations?

> ∾ Are there ways to reframe how one considers the educational context, process and intentions which would direct attention toward the complexity and contradictions that layered identities suggest?

Final Thoughts on Praxis

As I write, I am aware that based on the thinking previously delineated, I am currently feeling/thinking confused about next steps, about how to reforge a link between belief and action, theory and practice, assumption and assertion. It seems that there may be what I would consider a fairly dangerous trend afoot that leads in two directions. The first is a renewed emphasis on the individual as subject of his or her experience and thus toward a centering on subjective experience that appears to be cut adrift from the community and therefore is minimally connected to the wisdom, political processes, and any practices of that community—even the oppressive ones. The second is an extremely odd and pernicious discourse that I would characterize as a tenacious hold to the old dualities that results in truly bizarre arguments about who is more oppressed; what I call the "more oppressed than thou" arguments. Now, I am afraid, my questions grow even more general:

∾ What philosophical, reasoned trail of thought can provide a way out of these odd interpersonal and political backwaters so that we forge stronger links among the various perspectives in lieu of the regression to ever more clearly defined hierarchies and dualities?

∾ How do we conceptualize notions of community, discourse, and communal action in light of the fact of layered identities and multiple sources or forms of oppression?

∾ What do (or should we do) when, having taken this complexity into our consideration, we turn to issues of practice, particularly practice in educational environments?

I am extremely grateful for the opportunity to raise these ideas with you. As I close, I am struggling to not write long, Connected Knower paragraphs of apology for the potential murkiness of my thought, the lack of erudite references, the possibility that my language obscures, and so on. I will resist that and end by stating simply that I consider it an honor to have this chance to engage with you and with your ideas, ideas that have provided me with a significant source of knowing—a rudder—over the past three decades. Thank you.

Sincerely,

Jill Mattuck Tarule, Dean
University of Vermont
College of Education and
    Social Services
Burlington, Vermont

REFERENCES

1. Belenky, M., B. Clinchy, N. Goldberger, and J. Tarule, *Women's Ways of Knowing: The Development of Self, Voice, and Mind,* (New York: Basic Books, 1986).

2. Freire, P., *Pedagogy of the Oppressed* (New York: Seabury, 1971).

3. Tannen, D., *You Just Don't Understand: Women and Men in Conversation* (New York: Ballantine, 1990).

4. Tarule, J. M., "Voices in Dialogue: Collaborative Ways of Knowing" in N. Goldberger, J. Tarule, M. Clinchy, and M. Belenky, eds., *Knowledge, Power, and Difference: Essays Inspired by Women's Ways of Knowing* (New York: Basic Books, 1996).

5. Maher, F., and M. K. Tetreault, *The Feminist Classroom: An Inside Look at How Professors and Students Are Transforming Higher Education for a Diverse Society* (New York: Basic Books, 1994).

6. Weiler, K., "Freire and a Feminist Pedagogy of Difference," *Harvard Educational Review.* vol 61., no. 4. pp. 149-174 (November, 1991).

CHAPTER THREE

DIGGING AGAIN THE FAMILY WELLS
A Freirian Literacy Framework as Emancipatory Pedagogy for African-American Children

Peter C. Murrell, Jr.

There is no such thing as a neutral educational process. Education either functions as an instrument that is used to enculturate the young into the logic of the present system, or it is the means of dealing critically and creatively with reality to discover how to participate in the transformation of their world.

> Paulo Freire and D. Macedo
> *Literacy: Reading the Word and the World*

The proper starting point for the crucial debate about the prospects for black America is an examination of nihilism that increasingly pervades black communities. Nihilism is to be understood here not as a philosophic doctrine that there are no rational grounds for legitimate standards or authority; it is, far more, the lived experience of coping with a life of horrifying meaninglessness, hopelessness and (most important) lovelessness.

> Cornel West
> *Race Matters*

[A]n oppressed people cannot understand the nature of their oppression before they are inspired with hope and a vision of freedom that they desire. To understand the nature of their oppression, a people must first know who they are..."

> Reverend Effie Clark
> *Outstanding Black Sermons*

Introduction

The shattering of African-American civil society in urban communities is at hand. The urban communities where most of this nation's African-American children go to school are communities where few would choose to *live*. The glimpse of these communities given us by Alex Kotlewitz in his book *There Are No Children Here,* (4) and by Johnathan Kozol in his books *Savage Inequalities* (5) and *Amazing Grace* (6) attest to the conditions that rob even the heartiest children of their spirit and hope. More tragic than the fact that children live in dangerous and depressed conditions is the failure of schools to provide the means for positive change—education as the cultivation of young minds and spirits.

The education needed for African-American children in these urban communities cries out for the development of critical consciousness with a purpose, and with a moral and spiritual center. Education should provide that center from which children learn to contest the destruction of black urban communities, to resist the assault on cultural blackness, and to sustain the struggles for true democracy. As West points out in his book *Race Matters* (2), what happened in Los Angeles in April of 1992 was neither a race riot or a class rebellion, but "a multiracial, trans-class, and largely male display of justified social rage" (p. 1).

Historically, education (along with the black church) has been a major context of struggle for the cultivation of critical consciousness, self-determination, and positive identity on the part of African-Americans. Black Americans have persisted throughout American history in acquiring literacy and education as a means of survival and advancement as a people. Despite being segregated, many public schools in black communities in the south during the early decades of the twentieth century served children better than desegregated schools have since the Brown vs. Board of Education Supreme Court ruling in 1954.

Vanessa Siddle Walker (7) describes such an instance in her historiography of an all-black high school Caswell County, in rural North Carolina. Walker demonstrates how the esteem that the black community held for the school and for education, and the interdependency between the school and community, virtually guaranteed that graduates received a quality education. Then, more than now, black schools functioned to prepare African-American children to see the political realities of being black in America, to live with purpose and dignity in spite of (and to change) those realities. Then, more than now, the purpose of collective uplift was clearly manifest in the curriculum, policies, and practices of all-black schools. Then, more than now, African-American communities had teachers who taught the children with the same love and care as they did their own.

I am not, of course, suggesting a nostalgic return to segregated, all-black schools. The point here is that there is much worth recovering from the historical experiences and the cultural legacy of African-American education, as we grapple with contemporary issues of quality schooling for black children. The question is how do we re-insert essential qualities of education for the full development of African-American children in today's urban schools. What kind of education do African-American children need now? For that matter, what kind of education must any oppressed people have to "understand the nature of their oppression" and "know who they are"? What kind of education must any oppressed people have to "read the world" and to recognize, confront, and transform the structural inequalities and cultural politics responsible the oppressive, unhealthy and unsafe condition of their lives? In this essay I address these questions in light of the educational theory of Paulo Freire.

Since the time I first read *Pedagogy of the Oppressed* (8) some twenty years ago, I believed that that Freire provided answers to these questions—up until recently when this belief was dislodged. As I work with movements within African-American communities attempting to create their own schools as alternatives to failure of public schools systems, it occurs to me that few people in those communities even heard of Paulo Freire, much less explicitly applied his theory. Moreover, in these struggles I found little in our policies or practices that one would recognize as "Freirian."

Paulo Freire has had a profound influence on my thinking, and it is fair to say that *The Pedagogy of the Oppressed* changed my life. Yet, I found myself wondering why this theory of liberatory or emancipatory education was not more apparent in the work of building African-centered community schools that promoted development, self-agency and subjectivity in black children. I began to examine more deeply the applicability of the theory to promoting agency and critical-subjectivity in the education of black children.

What does Freirian theory have to say about liberatory education for African-American children in public schools? Whether it's from a Frierean perspective or not, what *does* constitute a working theory of liberatory education for African-American children, especially those who attend under-resourced urban public schools?

It is these last two questions I examine in this essay. My goal is to articulate the project for helping African-American children develop subjectivity and critical agency, and also articulate the relationship that Freirian theory has to that project. I will begin by first explaining what liberatory or emancipatory education means in the context of the African-American experience. Then I will examine the relevance and relationship Freirian theory has to the project of black emancipatory education. Finally, I will articulate five important themes for an critical Africanist pedagogy.

The Need for Emancipatory Education
for African-American Children

But can you expect teachers to revolutionize the social order for the good of the community? Indeed we must expect this very thing. The educational system in this country is worthless unless we accomplished this task.

> Carter G. Woodson
> *The Miseducation of the Negro*

In the midst of national conversations regarding how to improve increasingly diverse and under-resourced urban public schools, African-American children as a group are horribly served by public schools. In every major urban school system, African-American children, particularly males, fare dramatically less well than their European-American counterparts. They are disproportionately expelled, suspended, and relegated to special programs for the emotionally disturbed, learning disabled, and mentally retarded. They have dramatically higher drop-out rates, yet dramatically lower grade point averages and rates of matriculation. Half as many young African-American men go to college than a decade ago, but many more go to prison.

All indicators point to the inescapable fact that urban public schools in large metropolitan school systems simply do not work for African-American children. Can schooling for African-American children ever be more than institutional indoctrination into a social system and American culture that reproduces, reinforces and fortifies the devaluation of African-American people? Not without drastic reformulation of the purposes and ideologies of schools as they currently exist. The words of Carter G. Woodson are as cogent a response today as they were back in 1933:

> No systematic effort toward change has been possible, for, taught the same economics, history, philosophy, literature and religion which have established the present code of morals, the Negro's mind has been brought under control of the oppressor. The problem of holding the Negro down, therefore, is easily solved. When you control a man's thinking you do not have to worry about his actions. You do not have to tell him not to stand here or go yonder. He will find his "proper place" and will stay in it. He will go without being told. In fact, if there is no back door, he will cut one for his special benefit. His education makes it necessary. (9)

Woodson makes a subtle but critically important observation about public education for African-Americans that must be taken into account when visioning pedagogy for empowerment. It is the fact that the assault on cultural blackness is embedded in curriculum and practices of schools. It is not as though legions of white, culturally mainstream teachers in public schools purposely set out to destroy black culture, self-agency, and self-determination through policies and practices. Intended or not, however, this is precisely what is happening. The legacies of structured inequality and white supremacist logics continue unabated and unexamined in school curriculum, policies, and practices. Multicultural education notwithstanding, black people are, in the words of Woodson, "taught the same economics, history, philosophy, literature and religion" and essentially still taught their "proper place." Historian James Anderson states that:

> It is crucial for an understanding of American educational history, however, to recognize that within American democracy there have always been classes of oppressed people and that there have been essential relationships between popular education and the politics of oppression. *Both schooling for democratic citizenship and schooling for second-class citizenship have been basic traditions in American education...* [emphasis mine]. [B]oth were fundamental American conceptions of society and progress, occupied the same time and space, were fostered by the same governments, and usually were embraced by the same leaders. (10; p. 1)

It is a matter of historical record that black people in America experienced the "schooling as second class citizens" epistemology while being promised the "schooling for democracy" epistemology. But out of this experience a cultural heritage developed. Within the collective community and consciousness of black people in America, a distinct perspective on schooling, education and literacy has developed. A black epistemology of educational achievement has become embedded into the cultural heritage of African-Americans.

For example, the work of freed slaves building freedom schools in the era of Reconstruction is emblematic of this cultural heritage —specifically, the cultural values of self-determination, agency and self-study in education. The driving values of the movement during Reconstruction by black people to create their own schools, independent of white authority and government, were *self-agency* and *self-determination*. Similarly emblematic of this heritage are the movements of the free African-American community in Boston, Massachusetts in the early 1800s, who first created their own African public school, and later sought to integrate schools within the Boston school system that brought the school under bureaucratic oversight.

In the twentieth century, Woodson, among others, added to that foundation of black emancipatory education *critical consciousness:* the understanding that two epistemologies of education—schooling for second class citizenship and schooling for democracy—coexist in the fabric of American society, and that black people should make no mistake which was (and is) destined for them. It has long been a cultural value of African-Americans to acquire education and literacy (e.g., slaves learning to read under penalty of death), and it has been a difficult historical struggle for black people to acquire literacy as the means and ends to a critical political consciousness and full humanhood. Woodson stridently argued the importance of "cultural motifs of blackness"—self-determination, self-agency, self-knowledge—as determinants of the appropriate educational experience for African-American children.

The historian James Anderson recounts the epoch of African-American struggle for self-determination and agency in education in his book *The Education of Blacks in the South, 1860-1935.* The cultural motifs of "struggle for literacy," "self-agency," and civil rights he reveals in the period from Reconstruction to 1935 are much less apparent in the education of most African-American students in urban public schools today. Yet, an understanding of the educational experience of black people, or any historically oppressed group, is incomplete without an analysis of the institutions of white supremacy in educational policy that oppose this heritage.

It is beyond dispute that public schooling is an institution that functions as a socializing force in society, and that, for certain populations in the United States, functions to assimilate them. Social reproduction is one of several theories that provides an analysis of schooling as a mechanism to distribute power and to maintain social hierarchies. It asserts that schooling operates to maintain and replicate the undemocratic hierarchical social order—to reproduce disparities of wealth, cultural dominance, and unequal political relationships between groups and classes (cf. Bordieu and Passeron (11); Bowles and Gintis (12)).

To the extent that this occurs, emancipatory education for African-American children must then be fundamentally subversive—

as W. E. B. DuBois has argued. What needs to be subverted through emancipatory education are not governments and institutions, but rather the structures and practices of domination and oppression that reside within them. The project of reformulating the culture of schools in ways more responsive to people, neighborhoods and communities has found wide acceptance in contemporary writing on education (Bruner, 13), conceptions of mind (Shore, 14), and instructional practices (Delpit, 15). I advocate here the application of the idea to black emancipatory education.

Contemporary educational approaches are not up to the task of imbuing the cultivation of consciousness and identity development among black children for this kind of empowerment. At stake is whether education for African-American children in under-resourced urban communities will prepare them to successfully con-front the conditions that are destroying them—the meaningless, hopelessness, and lovelessness aptly described by West:

> The collapse of the meaning in life—the eclipse of hope and absence of love of self and others, the breakdown of family and neighborhood bonds —leads to the social deracination and cultural denudement of urban dwellers, especially children. We have created rootless, dangling people with little link to the supportive networks—family, friends, school—that sustain some sense of purpose in life. We have witnessed the collapse of spiritual communities that in the past helped Americans face despair, dis-ease, and death and that transmit through the generations dignity and decency, excellence and elegance. (2; p. 5)

The point here is that American public educational policy and thought, as it currently exists, is congenitally flawed with respect to providing an emancipatory educational experience for African-American children. Contemporary educational thought and policy neither take account of the cultural motifs of African-Americans nor do they address the conditions of their subjugation in American society. More serious is that the value system traditionally promul-gated in public schools is frequently at odds with many of the cul-tural values of African and African-American culture regarding edu-cational achievement. Competition, rugged individualism (i.e., "looking out for number one"), and materialism (i.e., rampant consumerism) to name a few, are alien to the cultural heritage of African-American achievement.

Contemporary educational theory and practice engenders an epistemology of schooling is based in an ideology[1] inimical to black subjectivity and self-agency. One aspect of this is the conflict of cultural values just mentioned. Contemporary educational theory and practice is based in a winners-losers, sort-and-select process that depends upon "losers" in order for the system to function—thus relegating to the bottom those who have been historically, culturally and politically defined as "losers." Another aspect of ideological conflict is the blind-eye bureaucracies have regarding its practices of cultural assault embedded in schooling. Not only does contemporary educational theory and practice offer little critique of the debasement of children of color, but school systems are among the biggest consumers of the tools and technologies (e.g., standardized tests, certain "packaged" curricula) contributing to that debasement.

The type of educational theory required for the critical democratic subversion described above can be found in the work of Paulo Freire, to which we turn in the following discussion. I will conclude the present discussion with the point that whatever the requirements are for liberatory education and an emancipation pedagogy in today's society, they are that much more urgent for African-American children. What remains to be done is to realize this theory in the *cultural praxis* of the classroom in a way that acknowledges the particular dimensions of domination emanating from cultural hegemony and racism as it relates to the development of African-American people.

African-American Emancipatory Education:
To Heal a People

Something vital is missing in our current struggle as Africans, continental and diasporic. We are missing a clear identity, a global view of ourselves, a view of ourselves in geopolitical context, and we suffer a lack of collective planning and effort to build our communities and to ensure our welfare....To see reality, to see our way, to revolt from oppression, is to heal a people. (18)

Asa G. Hilliard, III
To Heal a People

What form of education do we need to heal a people? To begin the discussion of the relationship between Freirian theory and emancipatory pedagogy for African-American children, I will briefly examine the requirements of an emancipatory pedagogy for African-American children.

To ward off the destruction of children's identity as black people, emancipatory pedagogy for African-American children must be re-created in contrast to the dominating and oppressive elements of popular culture as well as contemporary educational theory and practice. Children need intellectual tools for developing critical consciousness in order to develop a robust racial identity as well as a sense of self-agency and self-determination. For example, demonized media images of blackness and black people need to be interrogated as part of a curriculum of "reading the world." Too often African-American children are bombarded with negative images of blackness in the media—particularly television. The buffoon images of black people in so-called situation comedies, the stereotypical black man as street-hustler and criminal, and the prurient and degrading portrayal of disordered personal relationships on afternoon talk shows ought to be deconstructed and exposed for what they are—an assault on black cultural self-definition—so that these images do not become internalized by young people.

An emancipatory pedagogy must therefore expose the inadequacies and racist foundations of contemporary educational theories and practices while at the same time articulate a pedagogy which supports a *critical literacy* for "reading the world" among African-American children. I do not mean to suggest here that the project of liberatory education for African-American children is merely political action. The essence of a liberatory education project is the *cultivation of a consciousness* and the development of children's identities, as well as academic proficiencies.

I return now to the question: What does the Freirian theoretical framework offer to the project of liberatory education for African-American children in public schools? I have said that an emancipatory education ought to promote the development of the critical subjectivity (cultivation of consciousness) as well as an integrated and robust cultural identity. Emancipatory education for black children ought to promote the development of a sense of self-efficacy and self-agency so they critically interrogate the cultural, racial, political, and economic barriers to their full participation as citizens in a multicultural democracy. How would the Freirian framework fit this pedagogical project?

Black emancipatory pedagogy ought to provide the means to deconstruct and decode white supremacy as a *cultural phenomenon*[2] and racism as cultural imperialism (16). Racism is a social phenomenon that inscribes itself in practices (e.g., acts of violence, marginalization, exclusion, contempt, and exploitation) as well in the discourses and popular representations (e.g., demonized and buffoon-like representations of blackness in popular media) in America. Racism works as the decomposition of the cultural integrity of blackness.

As Hilliard observes (18, p. xxiv), the unpreparedness of black people to successfully repel expressions and institutions of white supremacy is not a matter of educational experience. He notes as an example Ellis Close's *Rage of a Privileged Class* documenting the laments of the "black middle class" at feeling betrayed by their continued experience of overt and covert white supremacy, despite having "played the game" and possessing Ivy League degrees.

Paulo Freire's literacy and pedagogy framework as articulated in *Pedagogy of the Oppressed* and *Pedagogy of the City*, provides some basis for realization of African-American emancipatory pedagogy. A Freirian theory views education as essential and integral to black people's continuing struggle for humanity in American society. In this view education is the practice of assisting people to find agency in, and responsibility for, the struggle for freedom. On this account emancipatory education does not merely take place at instructional sites we call schools, but is inextricably linked to political action and the responsibility that all of us have toward trying to realize a democracy that truly delivers on the promises of humanity for all.

It is important at this point to identify additional elements of Freirian theory relevant to emancipatory pedagogy for African-American children. To begin with, Freire provides a perspective of schooling as a societal process in which social groups both accept and reject mediations of power and interpretations of culture. Consider for example Paul Willis's ethnography *Learning to Labor* (20) in which he shows how the means by which young working class men resist and oppose the structures of schooling, rather than leading to their empowerment actually, ultimately consign, them to relative powerlessness because they become manual laborers (20). Structure and agency are brought together so that we always have access to seeing how practices of self-determination and self-agency by African-Americans shape and are shaped by the dominant and dominating "culture of school," that reflects the core values of American society. This is important because it enables us to move beyond a conception of African-American schooling as having only two polarities—assimilation or resistance.

A second relevant feature of Freirian theory to African-American emancipatory education—resistance to oppression as an educational principle. His theory situates the notions of human agency and racial oppression in a new problematic that politicizes the notions of race, culture, and power. The theory promotes a dialectical sensibility for interpreting how human beings both participate in and oppose structures of domination in public schooling. This is important because it enables us to understand resistance and opposition in terms broader than the limiting categories of overt political action—such as the civil rights movement and black nationalism. The resistance of African-Americans in schools is rooted in a variety of forms that may not necessarily be articulated in an ideological and cultural terrain. An example of this is rap music, which has only recently appeared in cultural analysis, as scholars have begun examining it as a discourse of protest and opposition from young African-Americans.

A third relevant feature of Freirian theory is the dialectical notion of culture that politicizes it. In this account literacy involves the ability to "read" culture as "text" for two moments of under-standing. The first of these is to critically read the ways that culture functions in the interests of the dominant market culture, America's popular culture. This would mean that a black emancipatory peda-gogy would incorporate the cultural texts of the social contexts of schooling in the curriculum. This would include, for example, the images, organizations of relationships and activities, and arrange-ments of space in schools. The second moment of the understand-ing for students to acquire through "reading culture as text" is that they are participants in the construction of culture, and that they can assume agency for the reinvention of culture, as well as the social and political practices that define a new common culture of radical democracy.

A fourth feature of Freirian theory relevant to a black emanci-patory pedagogy is the dialectical notion of critical consciousness, in which critical reflection and action are connected but separate moments of a dynamic process. The dynamic tension of these two moments in the process of becoming literate constitutes and is con-stituted by two aspects of emancipation: (1) individual emancipation resulting in a subjectivity where the learner is the subject rather than the object in the educational enterprise, and (2) collective emanci-pation resulting in African-American children having the tools of critical dialogue, thought, and action through which to transform themselves and their relationship to larger society.

A fifth constitutive element of Freirian theory for a black eman-cipatory pedagogy is his dialectical epistemology, where the objec-tive and the subjective are dialectically counterposed in the recon-stitution of what knowledge is, what knowledge is worthwhile, the purposes of education and the nature of worthwhile pedagogy. What is worth knowing on this account is not determined by its prominence in a standard curriculum or the literary canon. Rather, knowledge that is worthwhile is not received, but constructed for the revolution of the human spirit. In this account knowledge is not static and merely incorporated from texts in undigested fashion. Rather knowledge is socially constructed and does not exist apart from the social, historical, and political contexts in which it is constituted.

For Freire, acts of literacy are *praxis*, which is not merely the synthesis of theory and practice. Rather, the dialectal tension important to praxis is that between reflection and action that also transforms existence. Freire says that "Subjectivity and objectivity thus join in a dialectical unity producing knowledge in solidarity with action, and vice versa" (8; p. 20). It is the process by which the subjective and the objective come together, posed in the dialectal relationship that makes possible resolutions to the oppressor-oppressed contradiction.

The basis of this is in literacy—and the basis of literacy is "naming the world," the basic action for establishing intersubjectivity about that which can be objectively recognized and subjectively *cognized*. The generative and productive power of the word, *nomo*, the power to say one's own word is the power to *cognize* (I use this word purposely to connote "knowing in the original" in contrast to *recognize* or "to know again").

Freire's notion of literacy views the ways of being and knowing of oppressed people as the human knowledge appropriate and necessary for literacy learning. This use of knowledge is not only for the purpose of negotiating the codes of dominant society, but helping people reclaim their own voices, histories, and lives so that they "become empowered to fight for the necessary reinvention of the world" (8; p. 42).

Clearly, Freire's theory provides a framework for an Africanist emancipatory pedagogy. I turn now to the question of how the framework should be fleshed out to become a critical Africanist pedagogy for African-American children in contemporary schooling contexts.

Critical Africanist Pedagogy: Freirian Theory in Cultural Context

Central to our planning is to start from a clear understanding of our cultural reality, our history and our present conditions. We must design our future from the rich cultural base of our past, because no other beginning point makes sense.

Asa G. Hilliard, III
To Heal a People

A stumbling block in transforming a Freirian framework into a pedagogical plan is the negotiation of meaning among participants. Negotiating meaning is particularly difficult when parties occupy different cultural spaces, as is frequently the case when one is an African-American community and the other is a largely white, middle-class, and traditional educational establishment. When parties occupy different cultural realities, conflicts in ideology ought to be explicitly stated and negotiated.

Freire draws, in part, on foundations of Marxism and European class analysis. As we examine theory, it is important to remember that these foundations have also been instruments of domination to the extent that they fail as a *cultural analysis* of the *political role of culture*. It is not skin color or membership in a racial category of blackness that is under siege, but rather *blackness as a cultural reality*.

At the crux of ideological conflict is the fact that contemporary educational theory regarding the school achievement of black children has, historically, been at odds with the actual cultural values and beliefs African-Americans have culturally and collectively held regarding education. For example, while contemporary explanations of black underachievement in schools have always assumed diminished interest in, access to, and regard for education and literacy, the historical record of the African-American experience indicates otherwise (Anderson, 10). Historically, African-Americans have valued education as the major element of their struggle for citizenship, and as preparation for leadership.

What this means for the project of a black emancipatory pedagogy is that the participants in the project need to be culturally grounded—a fact that may spell a serious limitation for the Freirian framework. I will illustrate this possible limitation with a rendition of a biblical parable from a sermon given by Pastor James E. Leary entitled "Digging Again the Family Wells." Pastor Leary's narrative of Isaac in Genesis (Gen. 26: 6-18) is a metaphor not only for the struggle for black self-determination, but also for the problematic ideological negotiation between the black community and the wider community of educators. It is a compelling metaphor for the historical struggle for education among African-Americans.

In his sermon that Sunday, Pastor Leary likened the hard times experienced by Isaac, son of Abraham, to the oppression and hardship of black people in America. There were two other compelling metaphors in the sermon. One is the water of the wells, representing the wellsprings of knowledge, the font of cultural wisdom, and the spirit of the culture analogous to the KiSwahili term *asili,* coined by Marimba Ani (21). The wells constitute the other metaphor, representing the repositories for the sources of knowledge in a community, the collective knowledge and wisdom of a culture (e.g., the *griots,* the keepers of the oral tradition in a village).

The story begins with tragic circumstances. Isaac's grief over his father's death was exacerbated by the aggression of the Philistines and the threat of starvation due to a severe famine that plagued the land. The Philistines, upon Abraham's death, filled in the many wells he had dug where his tribe lived in the Gerar valley. Finally, the famine and the threats of the Philistines forced Isaac and his wife, Rebekah, to leave the land of his father and travel to the city of Gerar.

In Pastor Leary's sermon, the wells dug by Isaac's father, Abraham, were likened to the cultural heritage of African-Americans and the legacy of struggle for literacy and self-determination against oppression. There are a number of points in American history when African people have been cut off from cultural heritage—first through slavery and bondage, and later through attempts to derail black self-determination in the creation of independent black schools. The filling-in of the wells by the Philistines was a metaphor for the variety of attempts to erase the cultural legacies and distort the history of black people in America.

Currently, the filling-in of the wells represents the silencing of

African-American voices and the remaking of the images of black-ness in pejorative terms. Put another way, the filling-in of the wells represents all of the ways in which African-American people have been cut off from their rich cultural heritage by the many guises of racial oppression and cultural hegemony by the dominant culture in America, including the distortion of the participation of black people in the construction of America.

The wellsprings of African-American people—its vibrant culture, rich legacy, and deep history—had been filled with the soil of white supremacist ideology and master narratives invested in subordination of black people. Isaac's leaving the valley of his fathers represents the efforts of black people to find a definition of self in cultural motifs other than African or African-American collective experience and identity. In other words, leaving the valley of Gerar represents cultural assimilation into the mainstream popular American culture.

The story continues as Isaac and his beautiful wife, Rebekah, arrive in the city of Gerar and appear before Abimelech, king of the Philistines. Abimelech was, at first, benevolent to Isaac and his wife by extending protection to them. When the Philistine men of the city had asked Isaac about Rebekah as they entered the city, Isaac had replied that she was his sister, fearing that if he told the truth that they might kill him to get to her. But Abimelech, having seen them together from an upper window, discovered that they were man and wife. Upon questioning Isaac and learning of his fear, Abimelech extended his kingly benevolence by decreeing that anyone molesting Rebekah or Isaac would be put to death.

This, of course, symbolizes the tenuous relationship African-Americans as a people have had with power structures of society. Isaac was in good stead as long as Abimelech could assume the role of benefactor and protector, and on his own terms. Abimelech's decree, issued from a position of absolute power, is a metaphor for what historically has been the relationship between the African-American community and white liberals and supporters (and on occasion, I would add, radical and progressive educators) who extend their patronage, political support, and protection as long as there were no challenges to, or changes in, their custodial role in a position of power.

Isaac's crops in his first harvest were tremendous. He harvested a hundred times the grain he had sown and his flocks swelled with many more sheep and goats. Isaac's increasing wealth made the Philistines envious. Finally, Abimelech asked Isaac to leave because he had become too rich and powerful to live among them. Isaac, once again bereft, returned to the valley of Gerar, and began digging again the wells which his father Abraham had dug before him. In digging again the family wells that the Philistines had filled in, Isaac asserted his right to his heritage. He returned to restore what his father had accomplished and drew upon it as a resource to sustain him and his family through hardship and grief.

Just as Abimelech's benevolence toward Isaac waned as Isaac became wealthy and was no longer dependent and powerless, support for black agency from outside the community dissipates as black political agency is asserted from within the community (e.g., Ture and Hamilton, 22). A black emancipatory pedagogy similarly asserts the cultural heritage of African-Americans in the curriculum and schooling practices of public schools. A black emancipatory pedagogy returns us to the point at which we can work to restore what our people before us have accomplished in the struggle for freedom, equality, and human rights. After Isaac returned and dug again the family wells, he made peace with the many shepherd adversaries over the water from the wells and Abimelech himself came to Isaac to make peace.

Isaac's return and the resumption of the ways of his father and making peace with adversaries from a position of self-agency and self-determination completes the circle in this metaphor for an Africanist pedagogy and for the relationship between African-American and liberal educators in revisioning schooling for black children. The wider community, including white liberal, progressive, and radical educators, despite their emancipatory intentions, do not possess, nor have ready access to, the "family wells" of African culture.

The cultural meanings and motifs necessary for building a critical Africanist pedagogy for black children are not readily available to white Americans, in part because "whiteness" as a cultural field has been historically, shaped and defined in opposition to "blackness" (cf. Ignatiev, 23). For example, in her book *Playing in the Dark*, the novelist and critic Toni Morrison illustrates how white people's distortion of the black idiom in the dialogue created for black characters in literature and in popular media has historically been used to "establish difference, to reinforce class distinctions, and make distinct others' otherness" and to assert privilege and power (24).

Because "whiteness" has been constructed in oppositional contrast to "blackness," it is difficult for those who do not already share the cultural motifs of blackness to establish the intersubjectivity needed between learners and teachers in a Freirian literacy learning framework. Two things stand in the way of this intersubjectivity. One is the necessity of white people to critically interrogate and deconstruct their own racial identity in relation to practices of racial oppression and cultural hegemony. The other is to develop the cultural optic of African-Americans one needs to "dig again the family wells"—the process of recovering narratives and motifs that are the "dangerous memories" to racial oppression, cultural hegemony, and socioeconomic domination.

All of this is not to say that the steps white Americans must make to establish intersubjectivity in a black emancipatory pedagogy are impossible. However, these steps are preconditions that a theory of pedagogy must address, and they may constitute a strain on the agenda of an African-American community in the process of reconstituting a school for their children. Few white Americans critically deconstruct their whiteness, and fewer still (if any) can do this in connection with crafting a critical pedagogy for African-American children requiring "digging again the family wells" of African and African-American culture and political history.

The other themes in the parable include aspects of Africanist cultural heritage of creating humanhood out of inhuman treatment and lived experiences; Africanist wisdom, spirituality, and ethics as represented in oral traditions, narratives, and teachings of black people; and the Africanist legacy of confronting the perennial struggle of dual consciousness every African-American must face. The project must dig again the cultural frames of the Africanist heritage of *resilience* and *resistance* as the root themes of African-American cultural psychology. From a Freirian perspective, the centrality of African-American culture, critical consciousness, and ideology need not be *constructed out of critical discourse* as much as need to be *uncovered* and *"dug out."*

The "digging" metaphor described here is consistent with Freirian literacy learning and pedagogy in at least three senses. First is the sense of individuals awakening not so much to their oppression, as to their humanity. This awakening to humanity is central to the ideological foundation of education in Freire's formulation— education as the practice of freedom. This is the Freirian sense of emancipatory education as getting to the real meaning of one's lived experience as one who is oppressed in an unjust and undemocratic society—the sense of accurately "reading the world" for the purpose of transforming both self and society. This tradition is exemplified, for example, in the African principles of *Uji-Ba Maat* (see Addae, 25) and by the project of Martin Luther King, Jr., who read the world of racial oppression in terms of an opportunity for reaching a higher morality and ethics for both oppressor and oppressed.

The second sense the digging metaphor applies is that it urges an educational process of critique, questioning, and critical interpretation. Children should learn to "read the world" without losing sight of their cultural community as a source of knowing, understanding, and taking action.

The third sense is digging deeper to the meaning of blackness, past the distorted images of black people in the popular media, especially film and television. What makes this third sense important is that the agenda of struggling for our own image of ourselves and for humanity is precisely what Paulo Freire views as the purpose of education—the reformation of a democratic society in which all of us can have the freedom and opportunity to create knowledge from our own experience.

The question of whether a Freirian liberatory framework *can* empower African-American school children with critical consciousness is not really an issue. Rather, the important question concerns how well the framework supports the other two senses of digging— recovery of cultural knowing and the resistance to having our images of ourselves created by others—in cultural praxis of Americans of African descent. In the next section I will articulate more specifically what a project of Africanist critical literacy might be like, drawing upon Freire's ideas of critical literacy.

I conclude this discussion with a recapitulation of the themes that would need to be inserted in the Freirian literacy framework to create a critical pedagogy for African-American children. As West (2) says, the literacy framework must be one that:

> puts black doings and sufferings, not white anxieties and fears, at the center of discussion...one that look(s) to new frameworks and languages to understand our multilayered crisis and overcome our deep malaise...(one that) meets the need to generate new leadership...(one) that recognizes the possibilities for participation in political action while at the same time maintaining moments of self-agency and even black nationalism (p. 4).

This would entail taking seriously the intellectual, social, moral, and spiritual development of children in relation to academic achievement. It would mean rearranging the purposes of school so that rather than making slavish attempts to reach minimalist and meaningless goals (e.g., to score ever closer to the national average on standardized tests) children would be pushed to develop the ability to think critically and act morally. More importantly, the purpose of schooling would be viewed as the construction of a radical democracy for African-American children.

What must be prominent among the goals of an black emancipatory pedagogy seeking to formulate a radical democratic epistemology are the following: (1) a critical Africanist discourse for reinscribing definitions of African-American identity from the perspective of African-Americans; (2) an Africanist cultural agency—the reinsertion of the narratives recovering cultural motifs of African-American people; (3) the development of robust and integrated racial and cultural identity; (4) a pedagogy incorporating a "credible sense of political struggle" with authentic social and cultural critique; and (5) a continuous interrogation of the purpose of schooling in relation to their lived experience and broader society. Freire's *Pedagogy of the Oppressed* and the revisitation of that theory in *Pedagogy of the City* provide the framework for these five learning goals in a critical literacy.

Africanist Critical Literacy and Freire

> To be literate is to undertake dialogue with others who speak from different histories, locations, and experiences. Literacy is a discursive practice in which difference becomes crucial for understanding not simply how to read, write, or develop aural skills, but also to recognize that the identities of "others" matter as part of a broader set of policies and practices aimed at the reconstruction of democratic public life.
>
> Paulo Freire and Donaldo Macedo
> *Literacy: Reading the Word and the World*

The Freirian notion of critical literacy offers a framework making possible a critical Africanist discourse. It offers a lens, a language, a "shovel for digging" the cultural meanings of blackness from the perspective of black people themselves. Moreover, because Freire views culture in dialectical terms, his notion of literacy potentially offers African-American learners the discursive tools they need to undo the myths and transform the structures sustaining the oppressive social realities of racism and second-class citizenship. The pedagogical framework offers African-American children language for defining themselves as individuals and cultural beings.

On this account literacy is both a quality of human consciousness and a of abilities for interpreting the world in the broadest sense. The discursive practices in education would then incorporate those aspects of culture, oral and narrative tradition, and communicative styles of African-Americans. Freire would assert that ascription of differences that locate African-American dialect and language as inferior promotes powerlessness, as people become voiceless when denied the tools with which they make meaning, communicate, think, and act reflectively.

Let me provide a short illustration of how tenuous this critical consciousness is even among the most progressive of the wider community. Earlier this year I happened to hear a National Public Radio broadcast of the talk show "The Connection" with Christopher Lyden, who was having a conversation with Jonathan Kozol about his book *Amazing Grace*. At one point, Lyden asked him about the language of the children—whose voices are prominently foregrounded in the book. Now, Christopher Lyden, who is by almost anyone's account of the interview, a progressive and enlightened interviewer, sympathetic to the message of the book, said: "Oddly enough these kids do not speak a sort of ghetto-ese, they are not the lippy kids you associate with *Boyz 'n the Hood* or TV. And then he asked Jonathan Kozol: "Did you clean up the language or is this the way they talk?"

This question reveals the bias that many have who do not share the cultural space of urban African-American communities. Despite their progressive impulses, people who do not share the lives and experiences of the children Mr. Kozol was talking about are just that much more apt to be influenced by the manufactured media images of what "life in the ghetto" is like. Mr. Lyden expressed some initial disbelief in the articulate eloquence of the children's speech by asking whether Mr. Kozol had in any way "cleaned up the language" or whether he had selected from among many to get the most eloquent voices. Knowing that they lived in the South Bronx, Christopher Lyden did not expect to hear the dignity and incisiveness in the children's voices.

A Freirian critical literacy framework urges the interrogation of language—especially language attributed to an oppressed group by a dominant culture. His theory urges the interrogation of the street slang peppered with profanities depicted in many film and television representations of urban life, and urges an analysis of the extent to which the imagery is created for the purpose of othering, distancing, and making exotic the lives in urban communities. An Africanist critical pedagogy would require those with little experience in the cultural knowledge of African and African-American people to be particularly critically aware of exoticized representation of "blackness."

A critical literacy for all children must work toward promoting the sensibilities, skills, and knowledge necessary for critically interpreting experiences and resolving "dilemmas of belonging" as children move in and out of different cultural scenes between home and school. The additional educational agenda for African-American children is the development of a cultural and racial identity both to counter the hegemonic ascription of inferiority to their language, and to encourage literacy learning based upon their abilities to recover substantive meanings and motifs of blackness. Freire (17) writes: "We want a truly competent public-school system: one that respects the ways of being of its students, their class and cultural patterns, their values, their knowledge, and their language" (p. 36).

Developing an integrity of racial and cultural identity, which I will discuss in more detail in the last section, is an important educational outcome for African-American children that cannot be brought about without specifically addressing developmental psychology in a black cultural context. Part of this project is stewarding children into adulthood in ways not diminished by racist ideology. The other part of this project is promoting children's ability to "dig the family wells" and recover aspects of Africanist culture that not only develop consciousness and self-knowledge (via Africanist pedagogy) but that also create spaces for self-definition and credible resistance to the arbitrariness of dominant cultural forms (via Freirian pedagogy). Freire calls this *dialogic relation*—the incorporation of the student's world view into the educational process.

The narratives of all subordinate groups need to be recovered as what Henry Giroux has termed "dangerous memories" that rewrite and reinscribe the historical threads of community forged in resistance and struggle. This is "digging again the family wells." Recovering narratives as an act of collective self-definition is a crucial part of the reconstruction of African-American subjectivity. The project of rethinking schooling so as to invest African-American children with subjective agency is fundamentally a project of rearticulating and reinscribing the narratives representing cultural themes, community traditions, dialectical contradictions, and collective voice of African-American people.

The act of collective self-definition is a crucial part of the reconstruction of African-American subjectivity—a project complicated by class differences (cf. Gates and West, 26). Just as important are integrated and robust cultural and racial identity development. For this to happen, a critical literacy must include a politics of identity that allows African-Americans to develop racial and cultural identities that have not been predefined by the cultural optics of popular media. As bell hooks points out, the identity themes imposed from without and the themes inscribed in opposition to oppression are not the only ones important to the reconstruction of black subjectivity. She writes:

> Assimilation, imitation, or assuming the role of rebellious exotic other are not the only available options and never have been. This is why it is crucial to radically revise the notions of identity politics, to explore marginal locations as spaces where we can best become whatever we want to be while remaining committed to liberatory black liberation struggle. (27)

The project of rebuilding the culture of school so as to invest African-American children with subjective agency must address two problems, if it is to involve those from outside the African-American community. The first of these concerns how to create conditions in which African-American children reinscribe the narratives representing the cultural themes, community traditions, dialectical contradictions, and collective voice of African-American people. Put simply, how can children learn to affirmatively recognize themselves in their people when it is not *their people* who make up the school?

The second problem concerns how educators create the conditions under which African-American children can "explore marginal locations as spaces where they can best become whatever they want to be" and still be participants in the realization of multicultural democracy. As discussed previously, this is a cultural project that requires full cultural participation. The Freirian literacy framework offers only a partial answer to these problems. The realization of an Africanist critical pedagogy is endangered by the lingering toxicity of the ideological baggage that otherwise well-meaning educators bring, regardless of their liberatory intentions. Some examples are: unreflective multicultural education; building up of self-esteem with no consideration to agency and efficacy; special programming (e.g., "pull-out" in Chapter One), and palliative acknowledgments to diversity (e.g., *Basal Readers* with the faces colored in); unreflective, obligatory, and uninspired Black History month "celebration"; uncritical, hypertechnological "learning styles" classroom technologies.

Freire asserts that critical analysis and the insertion of narratives need to be centered with the people who are oppressed. This is an important aspect of his theory, and also the point that limits applicability to the theory to the project. To develop an Africanist critical literacy in public schools, the pedagogical must become very political. An example of Africanist critical literacy would examine the resurgence of interest and awareness of Malcolm X and the commodification of his image and domestication of his ideas. Malcolm X has resurfaced as an image that has been domesticated and legitimated and openly marketed as a commodity in the form of T-shirts, X-caps, and other items. It is no accident that his rhetoric and his meaning have been left out of the image making.

What could children critically read in this received image of Malcolm X? From a "deeper read"—such as allowing children to read, hear, and understand his actual words through recordings and texts of his speeches—they might discover what the struggle of black people in America is all about. From the perspective of an emancipatory educational project, children might recognize the hegemonic impact of stripping the rendered and received images of Malcolm X of all vestiges of revolutionary content. From a "deeper read" children might understand the political uses of language and symbols, such as reducing Malcolm X to a single phrase—"by any means necessary." It would be instructive for black children to notice which symbols are marketed and which are ignored. In the case of the Malcolm X paraphernalia, it seems as though the marketers went right for the phrase with the greatest revolutionary possibilities as the target, resulting in the distortion, desensitization to, and domestication of its original meaning.

Reinserting Malcolm as he *actually was* is the pedagogical action of a black emancipatory education making the pedagogical political, and the political pedagogical. This is particularly important in the critical "identity work" children undergo. It is necessary for African-American children to understand hegemonic force in relation to "blackness" if they are to develop robust and integrated identities. It is important for them to consider the selective survival of only certain themes of Malcolm's discourse in the image-making: (1) the anti-Muslim (that is that anti-"black Muslim") theme, and (2) the "white-people-aren't-devils-after-all" theme. It is not that either one of these is a misrepresentation of what Malcolm X said, or of the political place he occupied before his assassination. Rather, it is that these themes occur together in the constructed image of Malcolm, mediated by the hegemonic intent to stem the current of mounting black resistance—in the form of Louis Farrakhan's organization of black Muslims.

The Freirian framework does not specifically address racial polarization, nor does it account for the interests and agency of African-Americans apart from the wider movement of emancipatory practices. Realizing a Freirian framework would require a critical classroom "discourse of difference" that articulates the lived-experiences of children who are marginalized in their school environments on the bases of race, ethnic-membership, and culture. Realizing a Freirian framework would also require insertion of those cultural motifs of blackness important to the formation of integrated racial and ethnic identities. This will be addressed presently.

We have discussed the first of the five themes—(1) *critical Africanist discourse*—at length. In the remaining portion of this essay I will articulate the remaining four themes I propose for a critical Africanist pedagogy. These themes are: (2) *cultural agency*—a critical Africanist discourse for reinscribing definitions of African-American identity from the perspective of African-Americans and reinserting the narratives recovering cultural motifs of African-

American people; (3) *cultural/racial identity*—development of robust and integrated racial and cultural identity; (4) *critical pedagogy*—a pedagogy incorporating a "credible sense of political struggle" with authentic social and cultural critique; and (5) *critical consciousness*—a continuous interrogation of the purpose of schooling in relation to the lived experiences of African-American children and broader society.

Cultural Agency in an Africanist Critical Pedagogy

> Through an understanding of hegemony and cultural invasion, critical bicultural educators can create culturally democratic environments where they can assist students to identity different ways that domination and oppression have an impact on their lives. Through a process of dialogue, all students can examine and compare together the content of historical texts with their own cultural and personal histories and come to understand their role as social agents in society. (28)

> Antonia Darder
> *Culture and Power in the Classroom:*
> *A Critical Foundation for Bicultural Educators*

The manner in which the dominant ideologies of popular American culture have influenced the Africanist consciousness has been documented in scholarly research, represented in literature, and conventionally understood by many African-Americans. Powerful expressions of how Africanist consciousness and culture have been shaped in opposition to the negative imagery of blackness created by the dominant ideology have been important themes in African-American studies, art, literature, social science, and popular culture.

The learning goal of cultural agency can be supported by "digging again the family well" for the oppositional cultural motif central to the Africanist consciousness. Africanist counters to negative images of blackness exist in literature, of which Ralph Ellison's *Invisible Man* and Richard Wright's *Native Son* are examples; in cinema, of which John Singleton's *Boyz 'n the Hood* and Spike Lee's *Do the Right Thing* and *Get on the Bus* are examples; and in rap music such as Public Enemy's *You Can't Trust Us*. These are but a few of the articulations of the struggle for Africanist self-definition in the face of the attempts by the dominant mainstream culture to define blackness through pejorative symbols, imaginal representations, and myths regarding African-Americans. These articulations need to be "dug" in the project of critical literacy.

The most fundamental aspects of Africanist critical consciousness for assuming cultural agency, therefore, are a *redefinition* of blackness removed from the backdrop of white supremacy and a *synthesis* of contradictory meanings and impulses emanating from the historical dilemma of otherness black people face in America. The willingness to engage in this sort of critical discourse on the part of white educators, regardless of their revolutionary impulses, is an issue independent of whether they operate out of a Freirian liberatory framework. The task for a critical Africanist pedagogy is to help black children acquire literacy not only out of their own lived experience, but from their cultural heritage as well, while at the same time making possible intersubjectivity with members of the wider non-African-American community.

What this would mean in practice is that teachers and curriculum planners would need to constantly interrogate the meanings represented in both curriculum and school routines that support, foster, or perpetuate racist ideologies. It would also mean that school planners and developers would need to articulate a vision of what schooling is for, when it comes to poor African-American children. Because of differing world views, white and black educators may be expected to respond differently to the question: For poor black children, what should schools be for? An Africanist critical pedagogy would provide the framework for bringing different views together in the common enterprise of revising curriculum and schooling practices.

An educational program designed to invest African-American children with a sense of subjectivity, promote academic achievement, and support personal development must have a critical discourse on *literacy* and *difference* from an Africanist perspective. According to Freire, students need to be able to uncover and decode their own lived realities in order to be able to fully comprehend the relations of dominance and power that exist outside their experience. Pedagogically, this process is assisted by the recovering narratives both as extensions of their own experience and as "dangerous memories" that contradict the white supremacist logics that support the structures of their domination. This could be done through literature and literacy learning from a Freirian perspective.

Let me illustrate this last point with a situation I experienced a couple of years ago when I was observing one of my student teachers in an urban, under-resourced fifth-grade classroom having a portfolio conference with one of her students, an African-American boy. They were talking about the contents of his "written responses to writers" section in his language arts portfolio. The fifth graders in the class were asked to include in their writing portfolios three book reviews on novels they selected from an "assigned" set provided by the teacher, and then they were to make three additional selections on their own from an "open selectives" list.

Now, this young white student teacher had done a superb job of composing a reading list of multicultural children's literature for both the "assigned" list, and the "open selectives" list. However, this young man, having chosen all African-American writers from the "assigned" list now proposed to read and report on three more for his "selectives." The student teacher gently tried to persuade the young man to select from among some of the Asian, Puerto Rican, and Native American literature she had skillfully placed on her "open selectives" list. The young man was adamant in his three additional selections, all by the same African-American author, Mildred Taylor. In a final attempt to coax the young man she said "After all, we're a multicultural school here at Horace Mann. There are all these other cultures to learn about." The young African-American boy retorted emphatically, "I *know*, Miz L. But I'm not *multi*. I'm *black*!"

This anecdote makes several points in regards to the problems identified in the preceding text—the insertion of narratives and the formation of robust racial and cultural identity. The first is that in reading about the authentic experiences of black people, this child was doing more than acquiring historical knowledge of the American south during the depression years. I submit that there is critical identity work going on here.

By pursuing the continuing saga of Cassie Logan in the sequence of Mildred Taylor novels, this African-American boy was not merely acquiring literacy skills, but was also fulfilling the essential developmental task of discovering himself and whom he strives to become. He sees glimpses of himself—and perhaps who he'd like to become—by identifying with a black family in their struggles against racial oppression and adversity—glimpses that have profound meaning for him as he works through the same issues for himself. This is the power of literature and narrative to help children gain a new world view, but it's also the power of critical literacy to help children make sense of their own world view in relation to the injustices in our society.

The second crucial point illustrated by the anecdote concerns the conception of cultural pluralism engendered by his remark, which might be rephrased as something like; "I prefer *black*-cultural education to *multi*-cultural education just now, thank you!" This is the sentiment of a child choosing to explore his own cultural frame before entering another. The remark points to a critique many writers have made about the *practice* of multicultural education: the goal of gaining other perspectives and world views is very difficult to reach when one is unaware and unreflective about one's own cultural and racial identity. Hence, we might better reach goals of multicultural education by *cultural education* in the Freirian sense —where people first deeply understand their own culture and cultural identity in social, historical, and political context *before* they proposed to teach or learn *about* other cultures in an unexamined and uncritical way.

A third point to be made about this anecdote is the importance of an authenticated history of black people in America. That is to say, it is an important collective memory for African-Americans to realize that the fruits of democracy were not enjoyed by everyone nor at the same time. Historically, the discourse of democratic struggle for African-Americans overlays these democratic principles of equality and justice with the cultural themes of resistance, self-determination, racial self-definition, and the collective economic, social, and political advance of African-American people. The democratic value of *equality* has historically meant something different for black Americans than it has for white Americans. The "life, liberty and pursuit of happiness" that white Americans *pursued* and assumed as a right, African-Americans *struggled for* as a political goal. These differences make a difference in the meanings embedded in culture, collective ethos, and consciousness of African-American people.

The subjectivity of the African-American child is promoted by three ideas developed as themes throughout the curriculum of a Africanist critical pedagogy. First is the idea that literacy has always operated as both an *action* and a *symbol* in the collective experience of African-Americans in America, acquiring capabilities for reading, writing, and interpreting *symbolized power*, as for example when African slaves risked death in the attempt to learn to read and write. Second, literacy has been the *basis of oppression*, as for example the inception of literacy tests at the election polls in the post-Reconstruction south as a primary means of disenfranchising African-American voters. Third, literacy has been the means of *collective resistance to domination*, as for example the emergence of the black press such as Frederick Douglass' *The Defender*.

These themes—*literacy as power, literacy as the basis of oppression, and literacy as resistance to domination*—represent more that simply a reinsertion the Africanist presence in "master narratives" of American history, but additionally, establish for African-American children the purposes of literacy that are linked to the historical, political, and social construction of racism. black children may then experience reading, writing, and thinking as acts of liberation for themselves and African-American people. They may learn to see reading as a way of discovering the power of one's own mind, as Malcolm X did in prison; or a way of transcending paralyzing trauma, as did Maya Angelou; or a way of defining oneself in confining role restrictions from both the black community and white authority, as did Richard Wright; or a discovery and assertion of basic personhood, as did Frederick Douglass in his narrative of slave experience.

Identity Development in Africanist Critical Pedagogy

DuBois (29) wrote about the issue of bicultural identity as "dual consciousness"—as an intrapersonal conflict never fully resolved, but that nonetheless is a transformative element in the consciousness of every black American. His dual consciousness is a dialectical lens providing "double vision" through which to continuously resolve "dilemmas of belonging" that African-American youngsters continually face in school. For example, Fordham and Ogbu (30) have described cultural inversion among academically talented high school students in Washington D.C., who avoided expression of characteristics they associated with "acting white." Unfortunately, these characteristics, rather than being merely "white behavior," were behaviors associated with academic success—like class participation, complying with teacher requests, and turning in homework.

The oppositional cultural markers that are taken on by African-American students may diminish their ability to negotiate the social and cultural demands of their schooling environment. They also create both interpersonal conflict (e.g., rejection by white peers, sanctions by teachers and administrators for "bad" behavior), and intrapersonal conflict as they struggle with the choice between not "selling out" on the one hand, and academic success on the other.

A critical pedagogy for African-American children must work toward promoting the sensibilities, skills, and knowledge necessary for critically interpreting experiences and resolving dilemmas of belonging as they learn and grow among others. Developing a *critical identity of resilience* is an important educational outcome for African-American children that cannot be brought about without specifically addressing the developmental psychology of African-American children in light of the historical and political context of racism in society. One of the ways is to redefine the received notions of blackness and turn them on their heads, as was done by Louis Farrakhan in the example earlier.

Africanist critical pedagogy is a way to invest children with the ability to analyze race and racism with regard to identity. Children could be given the opportunity to confront normative whiteness and interrogate whiteness as an ethnic category (cf. Ignatiev, 23; Roediger, 31). This kind of analysis would expose the constructed category of ethnic whiteness as the implicit, unnamed norm against which the "Africanist Other" is pejoratively defined by white America. A critical discourse of race and pedagogy must analyze how normative whiteness colonizes definitions of the normal and the other.

One example concerns a prevalent image of black males and the image of the unredeemability of any young black people who have on any occasion run afoul of the law. The truth is that it is not difficult for a young black man to slip into the category of "unredeemability" given, for instance, the frequency and regularity with which black men are stopped by police. But in the address at Malcolm X College, Louis Farrakhan presented an interesting perspective that turns on its head the cultural optic of "unredeemability" based upon running afoul of the law. He said:

> I was not the smartest man in my class. I was mediocre. And I am willing to bet that most of you that are leading today, you were not the best in your class. You were mediocre. But what happened to the top of the class? It's gone, it's dead, it's in jail, it's on drugs, it's destroyed! We just got through. We were more submissive. We submitted to our teachers. And we let them bend us and mold us. And the more it looked like we accepted the bending and the molding, they applauded us, they patted us on the back, they gave us a star on the forehead, they gave us a passing grade, so you can come and be the *first* Negro to this, or the *first* Negro to do that,....

Mr. Farrakhan indicated that in some sense the "best and brightest" of African-American males are those who fill the prisons or are dead, because they are the ones who meet the oppressive system head on, rather than submit to as the cost of being "successful." This puts a new light on "unredeemability" as the "unredeemable" won advancement for their people. This message by Louis Farrakhan is exactly the kind of "dangerous memory" that needs to be resurfaced as a means of transfiguring the ascribed identities of blackness.

Critical Pedagogy in Africanist Critical Pedagogy

Let me illustrate this theme with another example of a young student teacher wishing to teach a lesson on racial discrimination. After viewing the film *Eye of the Storm* about Ms. Eliot's "experiment" with her fifth grade class, this young woman engaged her fifth graders in a discussion about similarities and differences among people, showing excerpts from the film when she debriefed the exercise.

The understanding this student teacher was working toward was that "we should look beyond our differences" and she concluded with the statement "so being black or white really doesn't matter," upon which the three African-American boys looked at each other. One of them blurted out in an angry, challenging tone: "Yeah? Well what about Rodney King?" The young teacher's face flushed red, as she was at a loss for words. She finally said: "Well, there is an exception to every rule," to which the three boys responded with derisive laughter and moments later were up from their seats and wandering around the room. From that afternoon forward all three African-American boys became "behavior problems" in that classroom.

What might the teacher in the preceding case have done differently to insert the epistemic of *credible protest?* The question "What about Rodney King?" uttered by the African-American student might have been taken as legitimate opposition and credible protest to a lesson that contradicted the sensibilities of the African-American children. The epistemic from an Africanist critical pedagogy would have directed her to the realization that learners have the right and obligation to question ideas that negate what they know and believe and understand as black people in America.

With this epistemic the teacher might have learned to interpret the student's question as a part of a discourse of inquiry rather than as a mere challenge to authority or an expression of mischief. The teacher may have also, on this account, responded to the student in an effort to make the instructional ideas "meet" the student's sensibilities and acknowledged "credible protest" as pedagogy. The protest in critical pedagogy is only credible when the teacher acts in the interests of promoting education that helps children clearly and critically interpret their social reality with what they learn.

Critical Consciousness in Africanist Critical Pedagogy

There are several dispositions or values important to an Africanist critical pedagogy that I draw from Freire. According to Freire (17), the critical pedagogy should promote the *value of self-generativity and self-agency*. Children need to learn that they "are the creators of culture, and that all their work can be creative. And as those who have been completely marginalized are so radically transformed, they are no longer willing to be mere objects, responding to changes occurring around them; they are more likely to decide to take upon themselves the struggle to change the structures of society, which until now have served to oppress them" (p. 15).

On this account, the critical pedagogy must also promote the *value of humanization*, so that dehumanization can be exposed wherever it occurs, and learners can see connections and actually decide whether or not they want to be complicit in a dehumanizing social and political system without seeking to change it. Finally, the critical pedagogy must also promote the *value of exposing the internal contradiction* that is inevitable in the process of coming to critical consciousness. Recall DuBois' dual consciousness—the condition of what Freire called "divided, inauthentic beings." He writes: "Only as individuals discover themselves to be 'hosts' of the oppressor can they contribute to the midwifery of their liberating pedagogy. As long as they live in the duality in which *to be* is *to be like*, and *to be like* is to *be like the oppressor*, this contribution is impossible" (p. 30).

Conclusion

What kind of critical Africanist epistemology of schooling is called for? One that engenders a project of academic progress, development, and political agency for children and adults. One that operates from a developmental perspective and gives particular attention to moral judgment and civic action. Because the representations of race, gender, social class, and role in the social contexts of schooling deeply affect how children and adults think and act, a critical epistemology of schooling must make explicit what those representations are and how they may need to be pedagogically reconstructed in the school culture. It is an epistemology of schooling that pays careful attention to the social world of children while at the same time valuing deep critique and plain talk.

First, I examined what constitutes an Africanist critical pedagogy and literacy for the emancipatory education of African-American children in under-resourced urban public schools. Second, I advanced a theory of Africanist critical literacy by examining how a Freirian literacy framework might invest African-American children with an enduring sense of subjectivity and critical agency. Finally, I elaborated on five themes of an Africanist critical pedagogy. I close with the words of Paulo Freire:

> I think that a pedagogy will be much more critical and radical, the more investigative and less certain of 'certainties' it is. The more 'unquiet' a pedagogy, the more critical it will become.

REFERENCES

1. Freire, P., and D. Macedo, *Literacy: Reading the Word and the World* (New York: Bergin & Garvey, 1987).

2. West, C., *Race Matters* (Boston: Beacon Press, 1993).

3. Smith, J. A., ed., *Outstanding Black Sermons* (New York: Edwin Mellon, 1976).

4. Kotlewitcz, A., *There Are No Children Here* (New York: Doubleday, 1991).

5. Kozol, J., *Savage Inequalities* (New York: Crown, 1991).

6. Kozol, J., *Amazing Grace: The Lives of Children and the Consciousness of a Nation* (New York: Crown, 1995).

7. Walker, V. S., *Their Highest Potential: An African American School Community in the Segregated South* (Chapel Hill, N.C.: University of North Carolina Press, 1996).

8. Freire, P., *Pedagogy of the Oppressed* (New York: Continuum, 1970, 1993).

9. Woodson, C. G., *The Miseducation of the Negro* (Washington, D.C.: Africa World Press, 1933, 1990).

10. Anderson, J., *The Education of Blacks in the South 1800-1935* (Chapel Hill, N.C.: University of North Carolina Press, 1988), p. 1.

11. Bourdieu, P. and C. Passerson., *Reproduction in Education, Society, and Culture* (Beverly Hills, Calif.: Sage Publications, 1977).

12. Bowles, S., and H. Gintes., *Schooling in Capitalist America* (New York: Basic Books, 1976).

13. Bruner, J., *The Culture of Education* (Cambridge, Mass.: Harvard University Press, 1996).

14. Shore, B., *Culture in Mind: Cognition, Culture, and the Problem of Meaning* (New York: Oxford University Press, 1996).

15. Delpit, L., *Other Peoples' Children*.

16. Geertz, C., *Interpretation of Cultures* (New York: Basic Books, 1973).

17. Freire, P., *Pedagogy of the City* (New York: Continuum Publishing, 1993).

18. Hilliard, A. G., foreword in E. K. Addae (Erriel D. Roberson, ed.), *To Heal a People: Afrikan Scholars Defining a New Reality* (Columbia, Md.: Kujichagulia Press, 1996) pp. xxiii-xxvii.

19. Balibar, E., *Is There a "Neo Racism"?* In E. Balibar & I. Wallerstein, eds., *Race, Nation, Class: Ambiguous Identities*, Trans. by Chris Turner (New York: Verson Publishers, 1991), pp.15-18.

20. Willis, P., *Learning to Labor* (Aldershot: Gower, 1977).

21. Ani, M., (Dona Richards), *Yurugu: An African-Centered Critique of European Cultural Thought and Behavior* (Trenton, N.J.: African World Press, 1995).

22. Ture, K., and C. V. Hamilton, *Black Power: The Politics of Liberation* (New York: Vintage Books, 1967, 1992).

23. Ignatiev, N., *How the Irish Became White* (New York: Routledge, 1995).

24. Morrison, T., *Playing in the Dark: Whiteness and the Literary Imagination* (Cambridge, Mass: Harvard University Press, 1992).

25. Addae, E. K., (Erriel D. Roberson), *Reality Revolution: Return to the Way* (Columbia, Md.: Kujichagulia Press, 1996).

26. Gates, H. L., and C. West., *The Future of the Race* (New York: Knopf, 1996).

27. hooks, b., *Teaching to Transgress: Education as the Practice of Freedom* (New York: Routledge Press, 1994).

28. Darder, A., *Culture and Power in the Classroom: A Critical Foundation for Bicultural Education* (New York: Bergin & Garvey Press, 1992).

29. DuBois, W. E. B., *The Souls of Black Folk* (New York: Bantam Books, 1903, 1989).

30. Fordham, S., and J. Ogbu, "Black Students' School Success: Coping with the Burden of 'Acting White,'" *The Urban Review*, 18, no. 3, pp. 1-31, (1986.).

31. Roediger, D. R., *The Wages of Whiteness: Race and the Making of the American Working Class* (New York: Verso Press, 1991).

NOTES

1. The conception of ideology applied here is more inclusive than the neo-Marxist conception of a tacit system of symbols and ideas, emanating from the dominate culture and capitalist ruling interests, whose purpose is to obscure the agenda of domination. Rather, the meaning applied here is that of Clifford Geertz, who characterizes ideologies as "maps of problematic social reality and matrices for the creation of collective conscience" (16; p. 220). In this view, ideology is an aspect of culture, rather than the politic agency of the powerful. This does not mean, however, that the hegemonic influences of the culture of power on the consciousness of African Americans can be ignored.

2. See, for example, the work of Etienne Balibar (19) who theorizes on the emergence of "the new racism" based not so much on biological heredity or physiological features as it is on the "insurmountability of cultural differences."

CHAPTER FOUR

BREAKING DOWN THE DICHOTOMY BETWEEN LEARNING AND TEACHING MATHEMATICS

Marilyn Frankenstein

All during the 1970s people urged me to read Paulo Freire and I resisted. I rejected reading theory because my work in alternative high school education had established a dichotomy in my mind between activists and intellecuals. The activists spent long hours learning with the students and experimenting with teaching methods and curricula, with the goal of students' developing themselves as subjects (in the Freirean sense). The intellectuals spent long hours discussing and evaluating theories, and avoiding the daily life of teacher-student interaction. At the end of the 1970s when I started teaching at the College of Public and Community Service, I had more time to reflect on my work, and my activist intellectual colleagues inspired me to read critical education theory. It was the ideas of Paulo Freire that made me realize the value of combining theoretical reflection with concrete action.

In particular, Freire's philosophical discussions of teaching methodology made me realize the political possibilities of my "humanistic" teaching methods. For example, I first started having my high school math students teach problems at the board, rather than merely explaining their solution, because I wanted them to see what it felt like to ask a question and have no one answer; to stand in front of the room and try to spark discussions when everyone was either looking out the window or down at their desks. I thought that experience would encourage students to participate more actively when I was teaching. (And it did!) But after reflecting on Freire's concept of students and teachers as "critical coinvestigators" in the process of learning, I realized that having students teach also involved them in the kinds of learning situations that can be part of the process of developing new social relations in the struggle for human dignity. The experience of teaching can also lead to students' gaining increasing self-respect for their own intellectual work. When students begin to take their intellectual work seriously, they can begin to question many of the myths about learning and knowledge that they have been taught (e.g., that teachers have all the knowledge). Such questioning is an important part of the development of critical consciousness.

I now start my college criticalmathematical literacy classes by having students reflect on Paulo Freire's insistence that, "Our task is not to teach students to think—they can already think, but to exchange our ways of thinking with each other and look together for better ways of approaching the decodification of an object" (Freire, 1982). We discuss that this idea is so important because it implies a completely different set of assumptions about people, pedagogy, and knowledge creation. It presents a strong challenge to the linear conception of knowledge that most students have internalized: because people, for example, need to learn basic mathematics and writing, it does not follow that they cannot express very complex analyses of social, political, economic, ethical, and other issues. Further, many people with an excellent grasp of basic reading, writing, and mathematics skills need to learn much about the world, about philosophy, about psychology, and other areas in order to deepen their understandings of issues. I end my introductory classes by exploring the mathematical knowledge students already have and outlining how we will use that knowledge as a foundation for learning more mathematics.

This chapter focuses on the aspects of my criticalmathematical literacy curriculum that involve students as Freirian "critical coinvestigators" and that explores the dialectics between learning and teaching. When students teach, rather than explain, they learn more mathematics, but they also learn about teaching. When students comment on math education research, they learn more mathematics because they are challenged when they analyze why they did not previously learn mathematics, and they are empowered when they understand how to proceed to learn more mathematics. As humanistic, sociopolitically concerned educators, we often talk about what we learn from our students when we teach. Peggy McIntosh (1990) goes so far as to define "teaching" as the development of self through the development of others." Certainly when we teach we learn about learning. This chapter argues that learning develops through teaching and through reflecting on teaching and learning. So, students' mathematical understanding is deepened when they learn about mathematics teaching as they learn mathematics. Underlying this argument is Paulo Freire's concept that learning and teaching are part of the same process, are different moments in the cycle of gaining existing knowledge, re-creating that knowledge and producing new knowledge (Freire, 1982).

Criticalmathematical Literacy

At a math conference on problem-solving, the teacher illustrating Polya's (1957) ideas on problem-solving by identifying analogous problems, stated that in the problem, "if three people take ten hours to dig a hole, how many hours would it take ten people to dig that same size hole? It's obviously equivalent if people dig the hole or if machines dig the hole." From a criticalmathematics perspective, whether people or machines dig holes involves crucial issues of concern to our society, issues such as automation, unemployment, and quality of life. To learn mathematical problem-solving without engaging these issues is to become functionally, as opposed to critically, literate. Giroux's (1982) categorization of the instrumental ideology underlying so much of language literacy is helpful in understanding the nature of this kind of mathematics literacy. Instrumental ideology views knowledge as objective and external to the knower. Facts are neutral, stripped of the subjectivity of class, race, and gender perspectives. Functional mathematics curricula, based on this ideology, strip mathematics of its relationship to the learner and to our society, concentrating instead on mechanical proficiency and rote memorization. These instumental curricula are based on a fragmented view of mathematical knowledge, a view which omits how statistical knowledge is often used to obscure economic and social realities. At its worst, this view of mathematical knowledge can result in the kind of blind pursuit of "neutral" knowledge that produces, for example, nuclear weapons without awareness or questioning of the interests and choices that direct this science. As Marcuse (1964) argues:

> In this society, the rational rather than the irrational becomes the most effective vehicle of mystification.... For example, the scientific approach to the vexing problem of mutual annihilation—the mathematics and calculations of kill and over-kill, the measurement of spreading or not-quite-so-spreading fallout...—is mystifying to the extent to which it promotes (and even demands) behavior which accepts the insanity. It thus counteracts a truly rational behavior—namely, the refusal to go along, and the effort to do away with the conditions which produce the insanity. (pp. 189–190)

Criticalmathematical literacy, on the other hand, involves the ability to ask basic statistical questions in order to deepen one's appreciation of particular issues, and the ability to present data to change people's perceptions of those issues. A critical understanding of numerical data prompts one to question "taken-for-granted" assumptions about how a society is structured, enabling us to act from a more informed position on societal structures and processes (Frankenstein and Powell, 1989). For example, a criticalmathematical interrogation of housing subsidy data asks why aren't homeowner's tax deductions counted as housing subsidies?[1] For another example, a criticalmathematical analysis of declining block rates for various utility costs reveals how this structure transfers money from the poor to the rich.[2] The themes in my criticalmathematical literacy curriculum range from demystifying the structure of mathematics to using numerical data for demystifying the structure of society. Mathematics "anxiety" is analyzed in terms of misconceptions about learning mathematics (Frankenstein, 1984); understanding mathematics is presented as an important aspect of reading comprehension in most disciplines; and mathematical data are used to illuminate political, economic, and social issues.[3] This chapter argues that an important aspect of students' developing criticalmathematical literacy involves the integration of learning about mathematics and learning about mathematics education.

The Context for My Criticalmathematical Literacy Curriculum

My students at the College of Public and College Service (University of Massachusetts/Boston) are mainly working class, urban adults in their thirties, forties, fifties, and older, who have not been "tracked" for college; many of them were labeled as "failures" in secondary school; most have internalized negative self-images about their knowledge and ability in mathematics. Approximately 60 percent are women; 30 percent people of color. Most work full-time (or are looking for work), have families, and attend school full-time. Most work in various public and community service jobs; many have been involved organizing for social change. Students can work toward their degree using prior learning from work or community organizing, or new learning in classes, or new learning from community service (e.g., students lobbied the legislature and organized for welfare rights forming the Massachusetts Coalition for Basic Human Needs (CBHN); students, asked by the community, worked with faculty to serve as consultants for the Roxbury Technical Assistance Project to help that community participate in planning its own development).

The faculty are activists as well as intellectuals; approximately 50 percent are women, 30 percent people of color. Teachers have less institutional power over students than in most universities, because we don't give grades, and students can choose another faculty member to evaluate their work if they are dissatisfied with the first faculty evaluation. We cannot require attendance or any other work that is not clearly discussed in the competency statement which details the criteria and standards for demonstrating knowledge of the topic that students are studying.

Classroom Methods: Basic Math Learners Practicing Mathematics Teaching

Because, as Freire says, "a project's methods cannot be dichotomized from its content and objectives, as if methods were neutral and equally appropriate for liberation or domination," (1970, p. 44) a truly criticalmathematical literacy curriculum will involve students as active participants. Further, I think that Lave's (1988) research, which argues that mathematical knowledge and context cannot be considered separately, supports the development of a classroom context in which mathematics is learned through "teaching" experiences. If "activity-in-setting [is] seamlessly stretched across persons-acting" (p. 154) with no clear dichotomy between the "abstract" concept and its application, it seems to me that having students learn mathematics as they act in what are traditionally considered teachers' roles—questioning other students about how they would solve the math problem, evaluating their own work, creating math problems and quizzes—would result in a deeper understanding of the mathematics. This section discusses the four main ways in which this integration of learning and teaching occurs in my criticalmathematics literacy curriculum, and the reasons why I suggest that students' mathematical understanding is strengthened through their involvement in teaching.

Students Teaching.

I soon realized that having my students teach had many benefits in addition to encouraging them to participate when I was teaching.[4] The student teachers effectively involved even the very quiet students who were more motivated to participate to help a classmate. A feeling of solidarity developed in the class as students, learning from each other, came to a greater respect for one another. Equally important, the student-teachers learned more mathematics, because they had to be able to recognize many correct methods of solving the problems as well as the logic behind any incorrect responses, so they could teach starting from the class's understanding rather than just explaining their own understanding of the problem. So, through helping each other, students became more independent learners, because they could teach themselves more effectively.

Students quickly learned how to teach. First, a student would explain a problem at the board. I would discuss the differences between explaining and teaching, particularly that teachers ask questions so they can discover what their students understand about a problem, and so they can start instructing from that understanding. A good teacher does not reject any problem-solving attempts as incorrect, but asks students to justify their responses; in this way, the class group almost always corrects its mistakes, or the teacher learns a new way of approaching the problem. I stressed that a good teacher assumes the students are reasoning thoughtfully, even if she or he does not yet see the underlying logic that the students are using. The next step involved me teaching the problem the student had explained, interrupting my teaching to comment on why I was proceeding in particular ways. Finally, students began to teach individual problems, after which we would have a brief class discussion about the differences between explaining and teaching, and we would evaluate what worked well, including suggestions for improvement.

Students Learning in Groups.
By having students work together to learn mathematics, they both learn more mathematics, and they begin to break the patterns of social relationships which have often led to their internalizing society's incorrect belief that they have no math knowledge to share with others. Before we learn in groups, we discuss the rationale behind cooperative work and review the "teaching versus explaining" methods discussed in the preceding section. We also discuss two common misconceptions about group work: that one cannot contribute anything to the group unless she or he already knows how to solve the math problem; and that one is wasting time in a group if she or he already understands how to solve the problem.

To address the first misconception, we focus on out-of-school experiences we've all had where each individual in a group couldn't solve a particular problem, but where by bouncing ideas off each other, the entire group wound up solving the problem. I usually quote Myles Horton, founder of the Highlander Research and Education Center in Tennessee, who observed, while meeting with farmers who wanted to know how to do such things as testing their wells for typhoid:

To my amazement my inability to answer questions didn't bother them...
you don't have to know the answers! You raise the questions, sharpen the
questions, get people discussing them. We found in that group of moun-
tain people a lot of the answers were available if they pooled their knowledge. (Thrasher, 1982; p. 5)

We conclude that this works because different people understand
different aspects of the problem, and because as each individual
tries out a solution others improve upon the ideas. To deal with the
second misconception, we focus on how much one learns by teaching someone else. This reinforces what students are learning about
pedagogy when they are teaching problems at the board to the
entire class.

I also have students conduct short interviews asking others
about their experiences learning in groups. The results usually indicate that the positive feelings about group work are the opportunity to learn the different ways that others solve problems and the
chance to gain improved self-confidence and understanding
through helping others. On the other hand, many have had negative experiences with people who dominated the group, or with not
feeling comfortable contributing to the group. I have found it helpful to discuss the experience of educator David Reed, who worked
with a group that:

> challenged the notion of calling [some people] the "silent ones" and
> affirmed that their form of participation...was a result of the dynamics of
> the entire group, not just individual problems.... One conclusion...was that
> if the problems of some people not speaking-up were to be resolved it
> would be through a collective effort including those who were more
> aggressive and vocal. (Reed, 1981; p. 95)

Students Evaluating Their Own Learning.

There are a variety of useful ways in which students can control the
major part of the evaluation of their own learning. I argue that when
students realize that they already understand some mathematics,
and when they are able to pinpoint where they get stuck solving
problems, they are empowered and motivated to find out what they
need to learn in order to understand *more*. Teachers can prepare

answer keys that pose questions about potential errors and that ask the student to choose whether she or he got "the wrong answer, because I am confused about _____, but I understand _____," or "the correct answer but I am unsure of the method or the reasoning," or "the correct answer and I understand it well enough to teach it to others."

In the evaluation of learning, I stress it is important to realize that there is always some correct reasoning involved in any attempt to solve a problem. In order to illustrate this, I ask students to reflect on examples from "Ethomathematics," (Ascher and Ascher, 1986) such as a frequently repeated anecdote in math history books that tells of an exchange between an African sheep herder and what is variously described as an explorer, trader, or anthropologist. The anecdote is intended to show that the herder cannot comprehend the simple arithmetic fact that 2+2=4. It describes how the herder agrees to accept two sticks of tobacco for one sheep but becomes confused and upset when he is instead given four sticks of tobacco after a second sheep is selected. Through class discussion, we conclude that from the sheep herder's perspective, sheep are not standardized mathematical units. Students extend the realization that there is a logic to the sheep herder's reasoning to a growing respect of their own reasoning, and an increasing motivation to search for the logic in evaluating their own mathematical problem-solving. So when one of my students, Andrea Booker, got stuck figuring out how many telephones there were for each person in the world (using information from a news clipping that stated there were about 4 billion people and 423.1 million phones), she reflected:

$$\frac{4,000,000,000}{423,100,000} = 9 \text{ phones per person}$$

I think I divided the people by the phones. The answer does not sound right because if there are more people than phones then how can I get a number where the phones out-number the people.

$$\frac{423,100,000}{4,000,000,000} = .1057$$

I looked up the answer in the back and saw that the first way was the correct way. I got the people and the phones mixed up.

Answer: It should be 9 people to every one phone.

When another student, Gloria Cardona, got stuck trying to calculate how long it would take to spend $1 billion at the rate of $1000 per hour, she evaluated:

$$\frac{\$1,000,000,000}{1,000 \text{ hrs}} = \frac{\$1,000,000}{365}$$

My mistake was that when I divided 1,000,000,000 by 1000 and I came up with 1,000,000 I thought 1 million = $ instead of hours that is why I divided by 365. At this point I noticed I was not going to get a coherent answer because I didn't have the "right group." So... $1,000,000 had to be something else. I went back to read the problem again and realized (how *long*) that the answer had to do with time, so 1,000,000 = hours. Then I thought of the smallest unit of hours which is days:

1,000,000 divided by 24 (hrs in 1 day) = 41,666 days divided by 365 (days in 1 year) = 114 yrs.

The preceding examples of journal entries are focused on analyzing a particular problem that the student is solving. More extensive kinds of journal writing enable students to further self-evaluation through understanding and overcoming their math "anxiety," and through clarifying which learning techniques work best for them. Reflections from a variety of my students' journals illustrate how writing about one's learning process can relieve tension and help one discover how one learns best:

I can see now how important that is [to get everyone to participate in the class discussions...[for everyone to help each other].... The fact that another student can answer the question that one presents is an encouragement...to put forth a little more effort because if another student can understand enough to answer, then you can understand.

I think I know part of the reason math is difficult for me. I seem to do math in a disorganized manner.... While doing my homework I became conscious of the amount of scrap paper I used. The figures were all over the paper and at times I couldn't figure out what part of the problem I was working on and what I had figured out before.... I'm going to have to find a method of keeping things organized.

The concept, about the teacher (authoritarian) who has power because she or he possesses the answers, while the student doesn't, made a big impression on me. I feel that much of the retreating, which I did in school, was because I felt most teachers were very judgmental.... The concept of self-evaluation is a very freeing one.

Self-evaluation through journal writing can also help students discover solutions to problems through the process of thinking about them in writing. Mathematics educator Arthur B. Powell and José López, a student who worked with Powell in a participatory research project on using journal writing to learn mathematics, conclude that:

Writing because the writer and others can see it, allows one to explore relationships, make meanings, and manipulate thoughts; to extend, expand, or drop ideas; and to review, comment upon and monitor reflections.... The more learners are involved in choosing language the more they are engaged in constructing and reconstructing meaning, making sense of mathematics for themselves. (Powell and López, 1989; pp. 173–174)

Therefore, even if students don't initially know how to solve a problem, the process of writing can help them decide what directions to explore.

Students Creating Their Own Mathematics Problems.

Students gain greater control over mathematics problem-solving when, in addition to evaluating their own work, they can create their own problems. When students can understand what questions it makes sense to ask from given numerical information, and can identify the various decisions that are involved in creating different kinds of problems, they can more easily solve problems others create. Further, criticalmathematical literacy involves both interpreting and critically analyzing other people's use of numbers in arguments. To do the latter you need practice in determining what kinds of questions can be asked and answered from the available numerical data, and what kinds of situations can be clarified through numerical data.

Freire's concept of problem-posing education emphasizes that problems with their neat, pared-down data and clear-cut solutions give a false picture of how mathematics can help us "read the world." Real life is "messy," with many problems intersecting and interacting. Real life poses problems whose solutions require dialogue and collective action. Traditional problem-solving curricula isolate and simplify particular aspects of reality in order to give students practice in mathematical techniques. Freirian problem-posing is intended to reveal the interconnections and complexities of real-life situations where "often, problems are not solved, only a better understanding of their nature may be possible" (Connolly, 1981; p. 73).

I teach problem posing gradually, since most students' prior schooling has very effectively taught them that the teacher is the source of all problems (in both senses of the phrase!). We begin with reading articles in which the key arguments supporting the main idea are mathematical. There are usually very few numbers in the article, but I ask students to generate lists of what mathematical understandings and what further statistical data would be needed to fully understand the article. For instance, an editorial on "NATO's real numbers" (*Boston Globe*, Feb. 1, 1989) argues that in the case of NATO versus Warsaw Pact military strength, breaking down the statistical data into greater detail, "both casting the net more broadly and teasing out some relevant sub-categories," gives a different, more accurate picture, a picture which contradicts NATO's "dogma for decades that the Soviet Union and its allies enjoy a vast advantage in non-nuclear forces." For another example, an article on "The Useful Myth of U.S. Dependence on Strategic Minerals" (*In These Times*, 9/7–13/88) discusses a report by a Zimbabwean economist who uses U.S. Bureau of Mines Statistics to show that U.S. claims about mineral dependence on South Africa are "blatantly ludicrous."

Next, I have students create math problems from articles that suggest some obvious questions. For example, the following article "No Raise for the Weary" (*In These Times*, 9/14–2/88):

> Consumer advocate Ralph Nader sent a Labor Day note to Congress reminding the lawmakers that people working for the minimum wage haven't gotten a raise in seven years. Nader also reminded them that they've given themselves about $28,000 in salary increases since 1981. At the current salary of $89,500 a year, a member of Congress makes about $43 an hour—if he or she works a 40-hour week for 50 weeks a year. Compare that to someone who makes the $3.35-an-hour minimum wage and works 40 hours a week for 50 weeks a year. That totals less than $7,000 a year, or well under the poverty level for a family of four.

clearly yields problems asking for verification of the salary calculations. One of my students, Mary Edwards, went further and asked "How many hours would a minimum wage employee need to work in order to earn the hourly salary of a member of congress?" Further development of problem-creating comes from having students consider what questions and mathematical operations they would use (and what other data they would research) to clarify given statistical data, such as the following chart from the U.S. Census Bureau (Statistical Abstracts of the United States, 1983, Nov. 709, p. 429):

Household Incomes (Current Dollars)

	1967	1976	1977	1978	1980	1981
white families	7,449	13,289	14,272	15,660	18,689	20,153
black families	4,325	7,902	8,422	9,411	10,764	11,309

Finally, I have students create their own reviews/tests. In this way they learn to grapple with mathematics pedagogy issues such as: what are the key concepts and topics to include on a review of a particular curriculum unit? What are clear, fair, and challenging questions to ask in order to evaluate understanding of those concepts and topics?

Curriculum Content: Basic Math Learners Reflecting on Theories about Mathematics Teaching

As the students are involved in practicing mathematics pedagogy by teaching, learning in groups, evaluating their own work, and creating their own math problems, I make explicit the rationale behind using those methods of having them learn math. I discuss my belief that cooperative learning and self-reflection are part of a larger process of developing new social relations toward a more just organization of society. As Elizabeth Cagan has argued:

> . . . collectivist education must be self-consciously oppositionist; it must take a clear stand against the mainstream of American ideology and institutions and ally itself with a more comprehensive movement for social change. Otherwise, not only will this effort fail, but it may be subtly transformed into a means of increasing conformity to existing social institutions and arrangements. (1978; p. 244)

I also discuss how having students teach at the same time they are learning is based on Paulo Freire's theory that liberatory education does not dichotomize the activity of teachers and students—a person is not "cognitive"—only learning—at one point and then she or he "knows it all," so at the next point she or he owns the knowledge which as a teacher she or he stuffs into the heads of students. Rather, each of us constantly reforms our knowledge based on our own and others reflections. According to Freire, students and teachers are "critical coinvestigators" in the process of learning-teaching. Only by creating and recreating the knowledge for themselves can students truly understand the structure of mathematics and how that knowledge is an important part of understanding and re-creating the world.

> Knowing, whatever its level, is not the act by which a subject transformed into an object docilely and passively accepts the contents others give or impose on him or her. Knowledge, on the contrary, necessitates the curious presence of subjects confronted with the world. It requires their transforming action on reality. It demands a constant searching. It implies invention and re-invention. It claims from each person a critical reflection on the very act of knowing. It must be a reflection which recognizes the knowing process, and in this recognition becomes aware of the "raison d'être" behind the knowing and conditioning to which that process is subject. (Freire, 1973, p. 101)

As I pondered Freire's insistence that knowing involves reflection on the very act of knowing, I began to expand the math pedagogy aspects of my criticalmathematical literacy curriculum beyond having students practice math teaching, to having them read and reflect on theories about mathematics education. This section presents examples illustrating the various types of readings that students analyze, and suggests how this learning about mathematics pedagogy assists them in learning mathematics.

Students Reflecting on Theories about Teaching.

Throughout the course I have students reflect on a variety of ideas about how to teach effectively. For example, as part of an early homework assignment, I ask students to summarize the main point and discuss why they agree or disagree with New Orleans jazz great Sidney Bechet's ideas about teaching:

> Being a teacher, that's an awful hard thing to learn. There's so many kinds of teachers, many of them saying the opposite from one another. A good teacher has got to be able to know what a person can be taught. Everyone has his own way of learning, but a teacher is most interested in teaching the normal way, the way the average person learns. And there's some people, they're lacking in knowing how to do things the average way. It don't make no sense to them. Or else other times, a teacher only knows how he's learned something...maybe how he's supposed to have learned it. That kind of teacher comes along and says: "here now; you hold your instrument this way. That's the way to play that thing." Well, you don't know how to play it that way. You know how to play it your own way, and he wants you to play it his way. Well, you take it...you hold it his way...you try to play it that way, but you can't. Nothing comes out. There's no music. That way he's wanting you to hold it just don't fit. So you turn it around...you pick it up and hold it like you want. Right there it's all changed. Right away you know what to do with it...you really got something now. You're playing maybe what he wants, or how he wants to hear you, only you're doing it your own way. And that's what counts...having a way that is your own... all the way to you from inside your own self...
>
> The way I see it, whatever way you do something best, that's the way to do it. There isn't but just that one way. Teachers, they mostly forget that. Some of those teachers I had, they was real musicianers, but they all of them tried to make me do their way. (Bechet, 1978; pp. 80–81)

Most of my adult students agree with Bechet, but there are always a few students who insist that learning mathematics is different from learning music. This usually leads to a discussion in which I argue that there are many correct methods and even, for mathematics problems in real contexts, often many correct answers. I start with this excerpt to encourage students to think about how they best learn, so they can make concrete suggestions for change if the course is not meeting their needs. Also, their analysis of the similarities and differences in studying mathematics compared to other kinds of knowledge is an effective way of correcting many misconceptions students have about the nature of mathematical knowledge.

I also have students read some very specific pedagogical advice, such as the following selection from a mathematics teacher preparation textbook (Weissglass, 1979):

Asking Questions

Another advantage of a small group is that the students can assume a greater responsibility for the rate of presentation of new information. How fast and how well you learn depend largely on you. I think you will often be delighted and surprised and feel more confidence in yourself. However, sometimes you may feel frustrated or confused. This is also part of learning. The frustration and confusion can be reduced by the small groups themselves as they try to ensure that new ideas are presented in context and at the proper rate.

One of the best ways to do this is by asking questions and by encouraging others to do the same.

Here are some suggestions for encouraging question-asking in your group:

Do not criticize the questions of others nor hesitate to ask questions yourself for fear of criticism. Set an example for those in your group in this respect.

Encourage questions by being friendly and cheerful and by expressing thanks and appreciation to those who ask questions.

If someone is obviously confused, encourage that person to ask a question or ask a question yourself to try to clear things up.

Use a series of simple questions to bring out an explanation rather than simply telling someone the answer.

Remember that the *process* of learning is even more important than the *facts* learned.

Show respect for your group and keep morale up by being on time and prepared. Being prepared means knowing what questions you want to ask, it does not mean knowing all the answers.

Approach the group each day with aims of helping everyone else learn, asking interesting questions, and making the experience an enjoyable one.

If your group encounters difficulties in freely asking questions, it is helpful to pair off and examine the causes of this problem and then report to the full group. You might each try to remember when you were able to ask questions freely and why it was that you stopped.

I usually assign this reading after the students have had two or three experiences working in small groups, so they have an opportunity to see which of Weissglass' ideas they are already using and which they might want to incorporate. Students are asked to write about and/or discuss which of Weissglass's points makes the most sense to them and why. They are also asked to write about one question they have, suggested by his ideas, whether that be an aspect of what he says with which they disagree or something that he says that generated more ideas for them to explore. Often our discussion leads to the topic of asking questions in class, why many find that so hard, and why I urge students to do this so that they can have some control over their learning.

Students Reflecting on Theories about Mathematics Teaching.

By reading articles about teaching mathematics, students gain insights that help with their own learning of mathematics. For example, after reading "The Dangers of Drill" (Lerman, 1988) which focuses on how repetitive practice "can rob students of the confidence they need to function as people who can do mathematics independently," one of my students, Carmen Arocho, wrote that:

> I can also add in some cases, because the teacher has been so in control and does not allow the use of any other methods it has driven the inquisitive student to boredom and some eventually to become so discouraged that they drop out of the course or school.

Another student, Lisa Simonetti, speculated that the reason she has feared math

> could be due from a teacher who taught one method of math and expected his students to learn his style as if there were no other, which in turn reflected upon my performance, I could not perform independently, I relied on my teacher correcting my math according to his style. I felt doomed to never learning math. Perhaps if I got a few words of encouragement now and again I would have tried more earnestly. [Now because] my learning is encouraged, I try harder....

And Gail Greene, another student, commenting also on Karen Shaw's mathematical art (which appears on the title page to Part II

of my text) summed up the article by saying "less drill is more learning."

By reading math researchers' analyses of other students' difficulties with mathematics, my students begin to develop strategies for dealing with their own problems in learning mathematics. For example, students read excerpts from "Mathematics in the Streets and in Schools," (Carreher, Carreher, & Schliemann, 1985) a research study conducted in Brazil that found "performance on mathematical problems embedded in real-life contexts was superior to that on school-type word problems and context-free computational problems involving the same numbers and operations." The researchers' analysis concludes that:

> In the informal test, children rely upon mental calculations which are closely linked to the quantities that are being dealt with…. In the formal test, where paper and pencil were used…the children try to follow, without success, school-prescribed routines. Mistakes often occur as a result of confusing [the algorithms]. Moreover, there is no evidence, once the numbers are written down, that the children try to relate the obtained results to the problem at hand in order to assess the adequacy of their answers.

> The results [of this study] support the thesis…that thinking sustained by daily human sense can be—in the same subject—at a higher level than thinking out of context. (p. 27)

My students then reevaluate their own math problem-solving, making connections between their real-life knowledge and their performance on homework and tests. We discuss how they often hand in answers they would know are wrong simply because they do not check to see if their answers made sense. Becoming aware of the seeming disjunction between their work in school and their use of math in their lives helps move students toward reconnecting their knowledge in those two arenas.

Finally, by reading excerpts from studies such as "The Development of Addition in the Contexts of Culture, Social Class, and Race," (Ginsberg, 1982) students develop more self-confidence in their abilities to learn mathematics. The study concludes that:

> in the vast majority of cases, children of different social classes and races demonstrated similar basic competence on the various [mathematical]

tasks and used similar strategies for solving them...These results suggest that although culture clearly influences aspects of cognition (e.g., linguistic style), other cognitive systems develop in a uniform and robust fashion, despite variation in environment or culture. Children in different social classes, both black and white, develop similar cognitive abilities. The research suggests...that educators must take seriously the notion that upon entrance to school virtually all children possess many intellectual strengths on which education can build...without the benefits of schooling, young children already understand basic notions of mathematics...If we fail to educate poor children, then it does not help to blame the victim by proposing poor children are cognitively deficient or genetically inferior. We need instead to consider things like motivational factors linked to expectations of limited economic opportunities, inadequate educational practices, and bias on the part of teachers.... (pp. 207–209)

Students Reflecting on Political Issues in Mathematics Teaching.

During most of the curriculum students learn how mathematics is an important part of understanding economic, political, and social issues. They reflect on the methodologies that help them learn best, and they reflect on what studies in the psychology of learning mathematics have to tell them about their own math learning. Another aspect of the curriculum involves students reading excerpts from articles focusing on sociopolitical concerns in mathematics education. They are asked to grapple with issues such as what structures of our society have resulted in their mathematical disempowerment, and who might benefit from their avoidance of mathematics. They also explore the distorted historiography of mathematics and the nature of mathematical knowledge. For example, I ask students to comment on the last section of my article on math "anxiety" (Frankenstein, 1984):

A Final Note on the Label "Math Anxiety"

I have always felt uncomfortable calling people "math anxious": The effect of such a label is contradictory. On the one hand, students are initially relieved that their feelings about mathematics are so common that educators "have a name for them." On the other hand, the label can focus the problem inward, "blaming the victims" and encouraging solutions

directed solely at them (Apple, 1979; p. 135). The label can direct attention away from the broader social context of how these misconceptions
about learning come to be so universally believed, and what purpose
society's having large numbers of math "anxious" women, for example,
might serve.... The political, economic, and social structure of our society
naturally produces math "anxiety"....having students explore these underlying causes is the most epistemologically sound way of turning their
inward "anxiety" into an outward constructive anger that will move them
toward true mathematics accomplishment. (p. 177)

Students gain an appreciation for the intellectual contributions of
all peoples through reading excerpts like the following (Frankentein
and Powell, 1994), which analyzes why the contributions of
European males have dominated the story of the development of
mathematical knowledge. For those who have been omitted from
this story, "unfreezing" this information is a key factor in their struggle against the mathematical underdevelopment caused by racism,
sexism, and imperialism (Gerdes, 1985).

Freire (1970, 1973) insists that in our struggle toward human liberation the
"culture of silence" represents a major obstacle to be overcome. Through
its mechanisms the oppressed participate in their own domination by
internalizing the views of oppressors and by not speaking or otherwise
acting against those oppressive views. A significant reason why oppressed
people, such as many women and people of color, are "mathematically
silent" is because of the widespread myths presented in Western "his-sto-
ries" of mathematics. The prevailing Eurocentric, and malecentric, myth,
expressed in the writings of many Western mathematicians such as Kline,
(1953) is that

[mathematics] finally secured a firm grip on life in the highly congenial
soil of Greece and waxed strongly for a short period... With the decline
of Greek civilization, the plant remained dormant for a thousand years...
[until it] was transported to Europe and once more embedded in fertile
soil. (pp. 9–10)

We gain further insight into why such myths were created and perpetuat-
ed, which deny a community and culture its history, when we examine
how racism and sexism have impacted on academic research. For example, European scholars arbitrarily, yet purposefully, changed the date of
the origination of the Egyptian calendar from 4241 BC to 2773 BC, claim-

ing that "such precise mathematical and astronomical work cannot be seriously ascribed to a people slowly emerging from neolithic conditions." (Struik, 1967, cited in Lumpkin, p. 100)[5] For another example, the name of a key researcher in the theory of the elasticity of metals—the research that made possible such remarkable engineering feats as the Eiffel Tower—was not listed among the 72 scientists whose names are inscribed on that structure. They are all men, and the contribution of Sophie Germain remains unrecognized (Mozans, cited in Osen, 1974, p. 42). This is just a small piece of a much larger historical picture that obliterated knowledge that, despite sexism, women did contribute to the mathematical sciences.

Instead, if we understand the creation and development of mathematics as inextricably linked to the material development of society, we can undistort and uncover its hidden history. In ancient agricultural societies the need for recording numerical information that demarcated the times to plant gave rise to the development of calendars such as that found on the Ishango bone, approximately 25,000 years old, discovered at a fishing site on Lake Edwards in Zaire (Marshak, 1991). And, since African women, for the most part, were the first farmers, they were most probably the first people involved in the struggle to observe and understand nature, and, therefore, to contribute to the development of mathematics (Anderson, 1990; p. 354). Then, as societies evolved, the more complex mathematical calculations that were needed to keep track of trade and commerce gave rise to the development of place-value notation by Babylonians (circa 2000 BC) (Joseph, 1987; p. 27). And this continues to the present day when, for example, military needs and funding drive the development of artificial intelligence. (Weizenbaum, 1985)

Students' reflections about the distorted historiography of the development of mathematical knowledge lead to discussions about the nonneutral nature of knowledge. Freire (1970) has argued that knowledge does not exist apart from how and why it is used, and in whose interest. By the end of the term, many students realize that all knowledge is created from particular perspectives developed in particular social contexts. In our current world, these perspectives and contexts are shaped by racism, sexism, and other alienating institutional structures. A goal of the criticalmathematical literacy curriculum is for students to understand this nonneutrality, and also to understand that information about the world can be learned from critically interrogating numerical data.

Conclusion

Initially, my students feel that learning basic math is hard enough; confusing it with lots of reading and writing, with having to evaluate their own work and create their own problems, and with practicing and reflecting on theories about mathematics pedagogy, makes learning the math so much harder. Students have internalized the dominant educational view of what mathematics is—manipulating meaningless symbols according to rote, memorized rules. And many students have internalized the dominant society's view that, "the intellectual activity of those without power is always characterized as nonintellectual" (Freire and Macedo, 1987; p. 122). My students often don't realize that they already know much about math—the "academic math" decimal point, for example, is the same as the point used to write dollars and cents. And, my students are often reluctant to realize that, in spite of many gaps in their knowledge of math, they already think logically about math. I spend time urging students to take their intellectual work in math seriously. One of the homework assignments toward the beginning of the term asks students to reflect on the meaning of the following excerpts from a text used in São Tome and Principe after these African countries won their freedom from the Portuguese.

The Act of Studying: I

It had rained all night. There were enormous pools of water in the lowest parts of the land. In certain places, the earth was so soaked that it had turned into mud. At times, one's feet slid on it. At times, rather than sliding, one's feet became stuck in the mud up to the ankles. It was difficult to walk. Pedro and Antonio were transporting baskets full of cocoa beans in a truck to the place where they were to be dried. At a certain point the truck could not cross a mudhole in front of them. They stopped. They got out of the truck. They crossed two meters of mud, protected by their high-legged boots. They felt the thickness of the mud. They thought about it. They discussed how to resolve the problem. Then, with the help of some rocks and dry tree branches, they established the minimal consistency in the dirt for the wheels of the truck to pass over it without getting stuck.

Pedro and Antonio studied. They tried to understand the problem they had to resolve and, immediately, they found an answer. One does not only study in school.

Pedro and Antonio studied while they worked. To study is to assume a serious and curious attitude in the face of a problem.

The Act of Studying: II

This curious and serious attitude in the search to understand things and facts characterizes the act of studying. It doesn't matter that study is done at the time and in the place of our work, as in the case of Pedro and Antonio, which we just saw. It doesn't matter that study is done in another place and another time like the study that we did in the Culture Circle. Study always demands a serious and curious attitude in the search to understand the things and facts we observe.

A text to be read is a text to be studied. A text to be studied is a text to be interpreted. We cannot interpret a text if we read it without paying attention, without curiosity; if we stop reading at the first difficulty. What would have become of the crop of cocoa beans on that farm if Pedro and Antonio had stopped carrying on the work because of a mudhole?

If a text is difficult, you insist on understanding it. You work with it as Pedro and Antonio did in relation to the problem of the mudhole.

To study demands discipline, to study is not easy, because to study is to create and re-create and not to repeat what others say.

To study is a revolutionary duty! (Freire and Macedo, 1987, pp. 76–77)

By the end of the term, most students have learned a lot of math and have revised their concept of what mathematics is. Research interviews need to be done to explore the particular effects on mathematics learning that result from the aspects of this curriculum that develop student, "meta-perception" of their needs (Moellwald, 1990).

However, the following comments from anonymous student evaluations show some indication that breaking down the dichotomy between teaching and learning mathematics contributes to students' mathematical knowledge. But most comments focus on how the connection of mathematics to the real world was the most important aspect of that learning.

> The one big thing I learned: math is not relegated to the classroom but is truly connected with everyday life and the outside world. Learning math truly helps one deal with life better.

> I've learned to open my mind to new ideas; I've learned that there are several ways to the same end; I've learned to listen to "all" sides; I've learned to give it a try, even when I'm not sure; I've learned to look deeper at the numbers; I've learned to look behind those numbers.

> I learned that every math problem and number represents something, that it is not so beneficial to know how to get an answer, but rather how to set it up. How to analyze articles more closely.

> I feel like my brain is waking up and it's starting to think again. I've been given the opportunity to try to figure things out for myself.

> I was able to understand [math] more because you make us ask our own questions, make up our own ideas and you always say there is more than one answer and more than one way to arrive at it.

> In the past I had thought of math as merely a conglomerate of memories, formulas, philosophies,etc. Now I perceive math as a way of communication.

> I particularly liked the readings and math problems relative to what is happening in the country today. It made the course a living math course.

N O T E S

1. In 1981 alone, these deductions amounted to more than had been spent by the federal government on all housing assistance for low-income families since 1937 (*Dollars and Sense*, 1983).

2. In 1972, "residents of Detroits inner city paid 66% more per unit of electricity than did wealthy residents of nearby Bloomfield Hills." At that time, about "$10,000,000 every year left the city of Detroit to support the quantity discounts of suburban resident" (Morgan, 1980).

3. The theory and practice of this curriculum are discussed in depth in Frankenstein (1987) and in my text, *Relearning Mathematics* (1989).

4. I used this technique more regularly with high school classes that meet daily. In my current situation, where classes meet only twice a week, the reality of time unfortunately limits my application.

5. Lumpkin goes on to report that new discoveries caused Struik to reconsider. In a personal communication to her: "As to mathematics, the Stonehenge discussions have made it necessary to rethink our ideas of what neolithic people knew. Cillings (1972) has shown the ancient Egyptians could work with their fractions in a most sophisticated way."

REFERENCES

Apple, M., *Ideology and Curriculum* (London: Routledge & Kegan Paul, 1979).

Anderson, S.E., "Worldmath Curriculum: Fighting Eurocentrism in Mathematics," *Journal of Negro Education*, vol. 59, no. 3: pp. 348-359, (1990).

Ascher, M. and R. Ascher, "Ethnomathematics," *History of Science,* xxiv: 125-144 (1986).

Bechet, S. *Treat It Gentle,* (New York: Da Capo Press, 1978).

Bernal, M., *Black Athena: The Afro-Asiatic Roots of Classical Civilization*, vol. 1 (London: Free Association Books, 1987).

Cagan, E., "Individualism, Collectivism, and Radical Educational Reform," *Harvard Educational Review,* vol. 48, no. 2: pp. 229-266, (1978).

Carraher, T., & D. Carraher, & A. Schliemann "Mathematics in the Streets and in Schools," *British Journal of Developmental Psychology*, vol. 3: 21-29 (1985).

Connolly, R., "Freire, Praxis, and Education," in R. Mackie, ed., *Literacy and Revolution: The Pedagogy of Paulo Friere* (New York: Continuum, 1981), pp. 70-81.

"Reagan Condemns Public Housing," *Dollars & Sense* April: pp. 12-14 (1983).

Frankenstein, M., "Overcoming Math Anxiety by Learning About Learning," *Mathematics and Computer Education,* vol. 18, no. 3: 169-180 (1984).

Frankenstein, M., "Critical Mathematics Education: An Application of Paulo Freire's Epistemology," in I. Shor, ed., *Freire for the Classroom: A Sourcebook for Liberatory Teaching* (Portsmouth, NH: Boynton/Cook, 1987) pp. 180–210.

Frankenstein, M., *Relearning Mathematics: A Different Third R—Radical Maths* (London: Free Association Books, 1989).

Frankenstein, M., and A .B. Powell, "Empowering Non-Traditional College Students: On Social Ideology and Mathematics Education," *Science & Nature* no. 9/10: 100-112 (1989).

Frankenstein, M., and A .B. Powell, "Toward Liberatory Mathematics: Paulo Friere's Epistemology and Ethnomathematics," in P. McLaren and C. Lankshear, eds., *Politics of Liberation: Paths from Friere* (New York: Routledge, 1994), pp. 74-99." (1994).

Freire, P., *Pedagogy of the Oppressed* (New York: Seabury, 1970).

Freire, P., *Education for Critical Consciousness* (New York: Seabury, 1973).

Freire, P., "Education for Critical Consciousness," unpublished Boston College course notes taken by Frankenstein, M., July 5-15, 1982.

Freire, P., and D. Macedo, *Literacy: Reading the Word and the World* (South Hadley, Mass.: Bergen & Garvey, 1987).

Gerdes, P., "Conditions and Strategies for Emancipatory Mathematics Education in Undeveloped Countries," *For the Learning of Mathematics,* vol. 5, no. 1: 15-20 (1985).

Gillings, R. J., *Mathematics in the Time of the Pharaohs* (Cambridge, Mass.: MIT Press 1972; Dover reprint, 1982).

Ginsberg, H., "The Development of Addition in the Context of Culture, Social Class and Race," in T. P. Carpenter, J. M. Moser, and T. A. Romberg, eds., *Addition and Subtraction: A Cognitive Perspective* (Hillsdale, NJ: Erlbaum, 1982) pp. 191–220.

Giroux, H., "Literacy, Ideology, and the Politics of Schooling," *Humanities in Society,* September: 335-361, 1982.

Joseph, G.G., "Foundations of Eurocentrism in Mathematics," *Race & Class,* vol. 28, no. 3: 13-28 (1987).

Kline, M., *Mathematics in Western Culture* (New York: Oxford University Press, 1953).

Lave, J., *Cognition in Practice* (Cambridge, England: Cambridge University Press, 1988)

Lerman, S., "The Dangers of Drill" *The Mathematics Teacher* (1988), pp. 412–413.

Lumpkin, B., "Africa in the Mainstream of Mathematics History," 100-109, in I. Van Sertima, ed. *Blacks in Science: Ancient and Modern* (New Brunswick, NJ: Transaction Books, 1983).

Marcuse, H., *One-Dimentional Man* (Boston: Beacon Press, 1964).

Marshack, A., *The Roots of Civilization,* rev. ed., (Mount Kisco, NY: Moyer Bell, 1991).

McIntosh, P., "Interactive Phases of Personal and Pedagogical Change," talk at Rutgers University/Newark, Nov. 14, 1990.

Moellwald, F., letter to author (1990).

Morgan, R. E., *The Rate Watcher's Guide* (Washington, DC: Environmental Action Foundation, 1980).

Osen, L., *Women in Mathematics* (Cambridge, Mass.: MIT Press, 1974).

Polya, G., *How to Solve It* (New York: Doubleday, 1957).

Powell, A. B., and J. A. López, "Writing as a Vehicle to Learn Mathematics: A Case Study," 157-177 in P. Connolly, and T. Vilardi, eds., *The Role of Writing in Learning Mathematics and Science* (New York: Teachers College Press, 1989).

Reed, D., *Education for Building a People's Movement* (Boston: South End Press, 1981).

Thrasher, S., "Fifty Years with Highlander" Southern Changes.

Weissglass, J., *Exploring Elementary Mathematics* (San Francisco: W. H. Freeman, 1979).

Weizenbaum, J., "Computers in Uniform: A Good Fit?" *Science for the People*, vol.17, nos. 1 and 2, pp. 26–29 (1985).

CHAPTER FIVE

A LETTER TO PAULO

Michelle Fine

September, 1996
Paulo Freire
San Paulo, Brazil

Dear Paulo: I write eager, but struggling, trying to imagine how we can best communicate, in writing, when so much of you (and even a bit of me) is about our hands, our pauses, twinkles in eyes, smiles, grimaces, translations across dialects, and leaps from passion to words. I hope we can talk across the borders of language, geography, and paper, and still retain that which makes you magic; that which makes me smile. Do you think we can fax and FedEx delight and outrage? I'll try to start us in this conversation, speaking to my worrisome thoughts on critical consciousness gone awry in the 1990s.

I write, like all of us, multiply positioned. As mother of Caleb, a newborn, trusting, smiling; Sam, a delighted, inquiring nine-year-old, filled with wonder, fledgling politics, and still unscathed trust; and Demetrius, a 19-year-old adolescent still peeling the emotional shackles of foster care off his body and mind, revealing a gorgeous, smart young man who has seen too much, growing into love. I write, too, as a researcher with urban adolescents who have been long deadened by social and school structures and practices, and yet remain alive with the possibilities of dropping out, fleeing, and voicing critique. Ultimately most reproduce their poverties through often courageous acts of resistance. And I write as educational theorist and activist seesawing between a deep desire for what could be, and an equally deep despair, for what is.

I read Myles Horton revealing much the same to you, and the end of his life, in *We Make the Road by Walking*.[1] He was searching for what he saw as "pockets" of radical possibility. I want us to shift metaphors and imagine, instead, that we are searching for connected raindrops of radical consciousness, sprinkled globally. If we can imagine that, I want you to help me invent pedagogical strategies, organizing tactics, that inspire a refreshing, collective shower. That is, I ask you, Paulo, for no less than a rain dance.

Your work has enabled so many of us to imagine "what could be:" democratic classrooms, engaging pedagogies, schools as sites of provoking *conscientização*. Puddles of possibilities ripple across the U.S., and the world, indebted to you for intellectual vision and for political commitments. Schools, neighborhoods of adults and children, community-based organizations breathe your legacy.

And yet...in daily praxis, within most schools, especially those educating the most impoverished students, we confront the next generation of theoretical and political Freirian contradictions: the gaping space between "what is" and "what could be." These spaces are filled with oppressive structures and relations of what presumes to be a "public" education. These bureaucracies are committed, at once, to stealing dignity and to disciplining the bodies and minds of students, teachers, and parents. There are few bad guys—but deeply perverse politics, well-suited institutions, and people doing their jobs.

In my work, I collect narratives of young children and teens growing old while young, in poverty, sacrificed bodily, intellectually, emotionally, and spiritually for global capitalism, emboldened sexism, and modern racism. Five-year-olds in some neighborhoods know better than I their chances of their surviving gunshots outside their windows.

In these communities, critical consciousness nevertheless flourishes. But it has been dispersed, institutionally exported, and contorted. Witness the loathing and fragmented urban diaspora of adolescent passion and outrage. We hear it in humor, drugs, and rap; in depression, desire, and crushed spirits; in painful violence and in the sweet making of innocent babies filled with hope, and likely to find little. Inside this diaspora lay the buried mana of critical consciousness. Bubbling in individuals, exiled from institutions, often ripping the insides of communities. One might hopefully say, it awaits creative "sense making"; that is, critical consciousness work.

In *Education for Critical Consciousness* you invite readers into your hope—"the more accurately men grasp true causality, the more critical their understanding of reality will be." You continue, "once man perceives a challenge, understands it, and recognizes the possibilities of response, he acts. The nature of that action corresponds to the nature of his understanding. Critical understanding leads to critical action."[2]

I excuse you "the man," assuming you know and share my concerns for the symbols and meanings of language and exclusions. But more fundamentally, we are now surrounded by a series of ironies related to the critical insights you assume will provoke action. Indeed, in the United States, fantasies and mythologies of merit, mobility, and justice have been deservedly debunked, and replaced by cynicism and critical thoughts, proliferating among children, adolescents, and young adults. But these thoughts, rich in analysis and critique, are detouring into flight, outrage, and Othering of equally oppressed, though differently raced, classed, or gendered Others. It is this dispersion and the perversion of critical consciousness that I'm worried about these days. Critique may lead to action, or to individualism, despair, self-blame, or racist violence. Let me try to explain.

On Dispersion. To capture the notion of critical dispersion, I introduce some data, collected almost a decade ago, indicating that urban students who embodied and voiced the most dramatic forms of critical consciousness were the most likely to drop out of high school. In the early 1980s, in a small study of low-income urban students, I found urban dropouts to be among the most sophisticated adolescent narrators of critique, possibility, and focused outrage. Depleted by institutions that had deadened their spirits and flattened their passions, they simply left.[3] Suspect of the relation of schooling and the economy, schooling and their cultures, schooling and their spirits, some retreated, some "acted out," most questioned in silence. Almost all exiled prior to graduation.

At 17, seeking transformation and embodying resistance, they were riveting. Four years later, by age 21, they were defeated. Bathing in despair, their critique of economic and social arrangements had boomeranged, converted into regrets and self-blame. They were, by young adulthood, self-impaled on the knife of social reproduction that had been camouflaged as resistance. As unskilled and undereducated young adults, they couldn't mobilize, for self or collective. The strength of their earlier social critique had collapsed. They were now young adults—surrounded by debts, obligations, children, and regrets.

Like these students-cum-dropouts, across the United States, and in urban schools in particular, I hear public school teachers who also carry critique, resist oppressive pedagogies and curricula, and try to transform their workplace bureaucracies. Over time, I've learned that they too are those most likely to flee public schools early in their careers, or at least close their doors because their schools were suffocating them intellectually and spiritually. Bureaucratic structures force a silencing of possibility and an exiling of critique. Teachers' spirits are broken not so much by students, but by the oppressive conditions of their labor that privilege bureaucratic rationality over community; fragmentation over connection; substitutability over relationality.

Bureaucracy has no room for critical consciousness, from children or adults. Its tacit job is to surround and contain critique, and so the voicing of critical consciousness provokes institutional exporting of children's and adults' bodies and spirits. Silencing is not simply a feature of this institutional life—it is the defining feature.

So, now, back to consciousness and action, but with a focus on us. Haven't we accumulated enough evidence of the "public" genocide of voice and critical consciousness in schools to move *us* into action? Haven't *we* learned enough to force *us* to press relentlessly for a democratic public sphere and to speak out against bureaucratic "efficiency" smothering public life? Haven't *we* witnessed for too long the dispersion and destruction of critical consciousness turned against self and Other?

On perversion. There is another twist in which I worry critical consciousness, these days, is going substantially awry. You may be unwilling to concede it sufficiently critical, but bear with me. This is "critical consciousness" perverted through Othering, exclusion and race hatred expressed most recently by poor, working-class and middle-class whites.[4] Indeed, in many public school communities that are predominantly low income, African American, and Latino, we see what Cornel West has called "the crushing of spirits."[5] Sometimes, expression of individualized outrage. But from white working-class communities we can hear a different kind of liveliness. A "critical" energy brews a felt, critical consciousness, which is performed often through Othering, that is racial/ethnic assault. White identity formation is being organized oppositionally, sustained as a binary conflict, sautéed in hatred.

Indeed, as you say, understanding leads to action. This time it's segregation, racism, and violence; State sponsored and community narrated violence toward immigrants, Affirmative Action, teen mothers, women on welfare. *We* may claim their consciousness is insufficiently critical, or misdirected. But they wouldn't. Critique surfaces from economic dislocation, loss of community, xenophobic and racist fears of invasion, and violence. Their critical consciousness, unlike dropouts and fleeing teachers, surfaces collectively and loud. Little self-blame, few regrets, get in the way of these actions.

We might argue that these white folks, like the Irish who refused to allow lesbians and gays to march in the St. Patrick's Day parade, suffer from class oppression dislocated/projected onto a raced or sexualized Other. Even if that were the case,[6] do we have the pedagogies that incite, for those so near the "bottom" and still looking "down" for the "origin" of social problems, a *systemic* analysis of power? How do we assure that critical consciousness does not drift downward, or outward, into victim blaming? How can we reveal the dialectics of capital, race, gender, and the State that prompt despair and exit rather than voice and organizing, that deflect pain and outrage away from the State and elites, and onto the bodies of Others? And how can we stir this talk in public, not just in radical pockets or safe havens?

As I re-read you, I resonate to your notion of a "militant democracy." You advocate "a democracy which does not fear the people, which suppresses privilege, which can plan without becoming rigid, which defends itself without hate, which is nourished by a critical spirit rather than irrationality." (*Pedagogy of the Oppressed*, p. 58). But I worry that class privilege has been so thoroughly laminated around and embodied by people and institutions, that even compelling collective critique drips back onto "the people" or deflects spontaneously onto anointed Others. Pockets of radical possibilities, at best, create safe spaces (ghettos?) for analysis. Meanwhile, broad-based institutional violence persists, skillfully accommodating (or annihilating) pockets of radical resistance.

Hegemony and oppression tear with many rips, leaving tattered communities, adults, and children. Yet, as I have tried to argue, hegemony is not total. Crumbs of critical consciousness sprinkle throughout adolescents' intellectual, cultural, and emotional lives, embroidered with gender, race, class, politics, biographies, languages, geographies, sexualities.... When I'm engaged in an adolescent's interview, or reading her writings, reviewing his photographs, or listening to their music, I hear how keenly they know that something is terribly wrong. Adolescents know they can't trust the institutions they are supposed to trust, nor can they hope to make these institutions better. While shadows and legacies of feminist, civil rights, and other liberations movements lace commentary narrated by adolescents, they need our help converting self-blame to social analysis; individual access to institutional transformation; personal pain to collective outrage. Listen to a poem written by a young African American teen, Tanzania Roach, about schooling, educators, and social researchers—about us:

Don't Hurt Me Anymore

Don't follow me
like a rapist stalks his prey
Don't quiet the words I have to say
like a rapist covers the mouth of his victim
to hold back what she must say
Don't rip savagely apart my dreams
as a rapist rips the clothes off his victim
don't throw me down when I try to get up
like a rapist throws his victim down
when she tries to escape
Don't beat me when I struggle to learn and survive
Don't pin my thoughts down
like a rapist pins the arms of his victim
on the cold concrete
Don't heave your hateful thoughts down on me
like a rapist thrusts his body into his screaming victim
don't force me to say what you want
like a rapist forces his victim
to perform debasing sexual acts
Don't leave me crying without a shred of confidence to go on
without a shred of dignity to continue living
Don't make me second guess myself
when I know I have the right to speak
You've left me with the hate I never asked for
Rapist. Racist. They look almost the same.
Rapist. Racist. They are the same.

Our responsibility, as theorists, activists, teachers, and worriers is to listen to Tanzania; to wedge open these plural critical consciousnesses; educate against the dispersion of social critique and the retreat to self-blame; resist the projection of "something's wrong" onto raced or sexualized Others. And, if that's not enough, we need to link these diffuse puddles of radical possibility—Horton's pockets—into what Chantal Mouffe calls "chains of equivalence."

Bear with me a moment longer—can you imagine any of this happening within the bureaucratic institutions of hierarchy, power, and containment that currently constitute public schools?

You were Brazil's Commissioner of Education, and so I lay at your feet questions you have fed me over the years. I have taken seriously your vision, and have traveled with you between theory, politics, research, and praxis. Now I ask you to take seriously the fruits of your intellectual and political commitments.

Paulo, on late nights, in the rain, when I'm depressed about urban schooling and yet thrilled by the questions of children and adolescents, when the possibilities of rippling social movements are, at once, seemingly endless and impossible to envision, you've gotten me through. Now I relish our chatting in texts, across pages and geography. I look forward to having you inside my mind again, blending your words with mine, struggling together through the grandchildren questions of Freirian theory and praxis.

My fondest thoughts and thanks,

Michelle Fine, Professor
CUNY/Graduate Center

REFERENCES

1. Freire, Paulo, and Myles Horton, edited by Brenda Bell, John Gaventa, and John Peters, *We Make the Road by Walking: Conversations on Education and Social Change* (Philadelphia: Temple University Press, 1990).

2. Freire, Paulo, *Education for Critical Consciousness* (New York: Seabury, 1973), p. 44.

3. Fine, Michelle, *Framing Dropouts* (Albany, NY: State University of New York Press, 1990).

4. See Lois Weis, *Working Class Without Work* (Albany, NY: State University of New York Press, 1991); and Powell, Weis and Wong, eds., *Off-White: Essays on Race, Power, and Culture* (New York: Routledge, 1996).

5. See, for example, Cornel West, *Keeping Faith: Philosophy and Race in America* (New York: Routledge, 1993).

6. I don't quite believe that it is, because elite whites may feel the same but don't have to say it, because their working-class brothers and sisters will do the dirty narrative work for them.

CHAPTER SIX

FREIRIAN PEDAGOGY
The Challenge of Postmodernism and the Politics of Race

Peter McLaren

I suggest those who have not read Amilcar Cabral's works on the struggle in Guinea Bissau take up the task of reviewing them. I am much impressed by his works, as well as those of Che Guevara. Furthermore, both shared a mutual respect for the other. It was in Guinea Bissau where the two met for the first time. They kept silence, observing one another. I would call it a revolutionary love with clasped hands (even though Amilcar was short and Guevara was an extraordinary specimen of a man). They both shared a love based on the revolution. And what was most interesting of all, they did many similar things—like being eminent pedagogues, great educators of the revolution.

> Paulo Freire
> *Paulo Freire on Higher Education*

It is a shame—since our North American cousins have unspeakable interests in this regards—that we continue to live in Latin America without knowing each other.

> Paulo Freire
> *Paulo Freire on Higher Education*

I myself was a university professor for a long time, long before the coup in Brasil. But the professor I have become is not the professor I was. It couldn't be! It would be horrible! Even exile played an important part in my reeducation. It taught me that radicalization is a fundamental course and enabled me to go through different experiences as a university professor in different parts of the world: in Latin America, in the United States, in Canada, in Europe, in Africa, and in Asia.

> Paulo Freire
> *Paulo Freire on Higher Education*

I remember in 1968 young people rebelled all around the world without
coordinating themselves. Students in Mexico in 1968 were not telephon-
ing young people in Harvard, or Columbia, or Prague, or Brazil.
Nevertheless they carried out more or less the same movement. It was
impressive. I also remember that communication between world universities was non-existent, and it was unbelievably easy for dominant classes to repress world-wide movements.

Paulo Freire
Paulo Freire on Higher Education

Educators and cultural workers in the United States live in
the twilight of a crisis of democracy. The democratic aspiration of
U.S. schooling and social, cultural, and institutional practices in general have been carried forth to an unheralded present moment in
what retrospectively appears to have been an act of bad faith. The
consequences of such an act for future generations are only faintly
visible and are bathed in an ethos eerily reminiscent of earlier swin-
dles of hope. The "democratizing" imperatives of private enterprise,
wage labor, free trade, and other fundamental axes for the new capitalist world system ushered in by the third industrial revolution of
computer technology have shrouded individuals in a web of
promotional logic patterned by the conquering dynamism of
Eurocentrism. Colonization has gone transnational and corporatist.
(Miyoshi; 1993). As Jacques Attali (1991; p. 120) warns, "From
Santiago to Beijing, from Johannesburg to Moscow, all economic
systems will worship at the altar of the market. People will sacrifice
for the gods of profit." We live in an age in which desires,
formerly-tilted inward, are now constructed on the surface of bodies like pathologically narcissistic tattoos that reflect lost hope and
empty dreams—forfeited identifications turned into grotesqueries,
unable to escape the circuit of deceit and despair constructed out of
capitalist relations and rationalizations.

Capitalism carries the seeds of its own vulnerability and frailty
even though its cunning appears inexhaustible and its mechanisms
of production and exchange irreproachable and unchallenged. Its
vulnerability is, ironically, the most steadfast and dangerous pre-

condition for its further development. So long as it has bourgeois universal reason and the epistemic privilege of science as its spokesperson and Eurocentrism as its cultural anchor, and whiteness as its foundation of cultural calculability, its very constitution as a discourse of power within an increasingly homogeneous "world culture" needs to be challenged by popular movements of renewal within a polycentric cultural milieu.

Against the backdrop of the global underclass and the struggle for democracy exists the work of Paulo Freire, one of the great revolutionaries of our generation. It is important to make clear that Freire's work cannot be articulated outside the diverse and conflicting registers of indigenist cultural, intellectual, and ideological production in the Third World. The "Third World" is a term that I use most advisedly after Benita Parry and Franz Fanon to mean a "self-chosen phrase to designate a force independent of both capitalism and actually existing socialism, while remaining committed to socialist goals" (Parry, 1993; p. 130). As such, it offers a starting point for a critique of imperialism and "retains its radical edge for interrogating the Western chronicle."

Of course, one of the powerful implications surrounding the distinction between First and Third Worlds involves the politics of underdevelopment. Andrew Ross (1989) describes the classic model of underdevelopment as one that benefits the small, indigenous elites of Western developed nations. Foreign markets such as those in Latin America provide a consumption outlet for the developed nations of the First World for absorbing the effects of a crisis of overproduction in the core economy. According to Ross, the peripheral economy (Latin America) underproduces for its domestic population. He reports that "The economic surplus which results from peripheral consumption of core products is appropriated either by core companies or by the domestic elites; it is not invested in the domestic economy of the peripheral nation" (1989; p. 129). Of course, what happens as a result is that the domestic economies of Latin America and foreign capital certainly do encourage peripheral economies to develop, but such development—if you can call it that —is almost always uneven and consequently such contact forces the peripheral economy to undevelop its own domestic spheres.

When there is economic dependency, cultural dependency often follows in its wake. However, the capitalist culture industry is not simply superstructural but constitutive in that the masses—in both First and Third Worlds—do not simply consume culture passively as mindless dupes. There is often resistance at the level of symbolic meaning that prevents the culture industry from serving simply as a vehicle of repressive homogenization of meaning (Martin-Barbero, 1992; McLaren, 1992). According to Ross (1989), the elites of the peripheral nations are the first to acquire access to Westernized popular culture but because of the limited access of the indigenous population to the media, the media generally serve to encourage affluent groups to adopt the consumer values of the most developed countries. The elites basically serve in a supervisory capacity when it comes to the cultural consumption of the indigenous peasantry. However, the continuing ties of the peasantry to their own ethnic cultures does help them become less dependent on Western information. Foreign mass-produced culture is often interpreted and resisted at the level of popular culture and we must remember that First World cultural values can also be affected by its contact with the cultures of less developed countries. And, further, not everything about contact with Western culture is to be shunned, although the emergence of a new, transnational class appears to have all the ideological trappings of the older Western bourgeoisie. My own contact with Brasilian feminists has revealed to me that oppositional feminist critique in the United States can be successfully appropriated by Brasilian women in their struggle against the structures of patriarchal oppression, structures that can permit men to kill their wives if they suspect them of infidelity on the grounds that their "male honor" has been violated.

The image of Freire that is evoked against this recurring narrative of the decline and deceit of Western democracy and the cultural hegemony of developed nations is a distant voice in a crowd, a disturbing interloper among the privileged and powerful—one who bravely announces that the emperor has no clothes. Ethically and politically Freire remains haunted by the ghosts of history's victims and possessed by the spirits that populate the broken dreams of utopian thinkers and millennarian dreamers—a man whose capacities for nurturing affinities between disparate social, cultural, and political groups and for forging a trajectory towards moral, social, and political liberation exceed the disasters that currently befall this world.

Freire's internationally celebrated praxis began in the late 1940s and continued unabated until 1964, when he was arrested in Brazil as a result of a literacy program he designed and implemented in 1962. He was imprisoned by the military government for seventy days, and exiled for his work in the national literacy campaign, of which he had served as director. Freire's sixteen years of exile were tumultuous and productive times: a five-year stay in Chile as a UNESCO consultant with the Chilean Agrarian Reform Corporation, specifically the Reform Training and Research Institute; an appointment in 1969 to Harvard University's Center for Studies in Development and Social Change; a move to Geneva, Switzerland in 1970 as consultant to the Office of Education of the World Council of Churches, where he developed literacy programs for Tanzania and Guinea-Bissau that focused on the re-Africanization of those countries; the development of literacy programs in some postrevolutionary former Portuguese colonies such as Angola and Mozambique; assisting the governments of Peru and Nicaragua with their literacy campaigns; the establishment of the Institute of Cultural Action in Geneva in 1971; a brief return to Chile after Salvador Allende was assassinated in 1973; provoking General Pinochet to declare Freire a subversive; and his eventual return to Brazil in 1980 to teach at the Pontificia Universidade Catolica de São Paulo and the Universidade de São Paulo and the Universidade de Campinas. These events were accompanied by numerous works, most notably *Pedagogy of the Oppressed*, *Cultural Action for Freedom*, and *Pedagogy in Process: Letters to Guinea-Bissau*. Little did Freire realize that on November 15, 1988, the Partido dos Trabalhadores (Workers Party or PT) would win the municipal elections in São Paulo and he would be appointed Secretary of

Education of the city of São Paulo by Mayor Luiza Erundina de Sousa.

Relentlessly destabilizing as *sui generis* and autochthonous mercenary pedagogy—that is spontaneous pedagogy wantonly designed to stimulate the curiosity of students, yet imposed in such a bourgeois manner so as to "save" those who live in situations of domestication only when they are reinitiated into the conditions of their own oppression—Freire's praxis of solidarity, that is, his critical pedagogy, speaks to a new way of being and becoming human. This "way of being and becoming" constitutes a quest for the historical self-realization of the oppressed by the oppressed themselves through the formation of collective agents of insurgency. Against the treason of modern reason, Freire aligns the role of the educator with that of the organic intellectual. It should come as no surprise, then, that against perspectives generated in the metropolitan epicenters of education designed to serve and protect the status quo, Freire's work has, even today, been selected for a special disapprobation by the lettered bourgeoise and epigones of apolitical pedagogy as a literature to be roundly condemned, travestied, traduced, and relegated to the margins of the education debate. That Freire's work has been placed under prohibition, having been judged to be politically inflammatory and subversive and an inadmissible feature of academic criticism is understandable given the current historical conjunction. But it is not inevitable.

It is not the purpose of this essay to address the often egregious misrepresentations of Freire's work by mainstream educators, nor to simply situate Freire unproblematically within the context of First World efforts to ground liberation struggles in pedagogical practices. Instead it is merely to elaborate on one of the central themes of Freire's work, which is the role of the educator as an active agent of social change.

Critical Pedagogy versus The Academy

While their political strategies vary considerably, critical educators of various stripes (many of whom have been directly influenced by

Freire's work) generally hold certain presuppositions in common that can be summarized as follows: pedagogies constitute a form of social and cultural criticism; all knowledge is fundamentally mediated by linguistic relations that inescapably are socially and historically constituted; individuals are synechochically related to the wider society through traditions of mediation (family, friends, religion, formal schooling, popular culture, etc.); social facts can never be isolated from the domain of values or removed from forms of ideological production as inscription; the relationship between concept and object and signifier and signified is neither inherently stable nor transcendentally fixed and is often mediated by circuits of capitalist production, consumption, and social relations; language is central to the formation of subjectivity (conscious and unconscious awareness); certain groups in any society are unnecessarily and often unjustly privileged over others, and while the reasons for this privileging may vary widely, the oppression that characterizes contemporary societies is most forcefully secured when subordinates accept their social status as natural, necessary, inevitable or bequeathed to them as an exercise of historical chance: oppression has many faces and focusing on only one at the expense of others (e.g., class oppression versus racism) often elides or occults the interconnection among them; power and oppression cannot be understood simply in terms of an irrefutable calculus of meaning linked to cause and effect conditions and this means that an unforeseen world of social relations awaits us; domination and oppression are implicated in the radical contingency of social development and our responses to it; and mainstream research practices are generally and unwittingly implicated in the reproduction of systems of class, race, and gender oppression (Kincheloe and McLaren, 1994). Some criticalists, myself included, follow Niklas Luhmann, in arguing that "Reality is what one does not perceive when one perceives it" (1990, p. 68). In other words, knowing anything presupposes a paradoxical understanding; cognition depends upon a necessary blind spot, a collusion with self-reference. Hence the importance of multiple observers in dialogue as part of any critical inquiry.

Freire's work certainly reflects this list of assumptions to different degrees and while his corpus of writing does not easily fall under the rubric of poststructuralism, his emphasis on the relationship among language, experience, power and identity certainly gives weight to certain poststructuralist assumptions. For instance, Freire's work stresses that language practices among individuals and groups do more than reflect reality, they effectively organize our social universe and reinforce what is considered to be the limits of the possible while constructing at the same time the faultlines of the practical. To a large extent, the sign systems and semiotic codes that we use are always already populated by prior interpretations since they have been necessarily conditioned by the material, historical, and social formations that help to give rise to them. They endorse and enforce particular social arrangements since they are situated in historically conditioned social practices in which the desires and motivations of certain groups have been culturally and ideologically inscribed, not to mention overdetermined. All sign systems are fundamentally arbitrary but certain systems have been accorded a privileged distinction over others, in ways that bear the imprint of race, class, and gender struggles (Gee, 1993). Sign systems not only are culture-bound and conventional but also are distributed socially, historically, and geopolitically (Berlin, 1993). For U.S. educators, this implicates our language use in Euro-American social practices that have been forged in the crucible of patriarchy and white supremacy (Giroux, 1993).

Knowledge does not, according to the view sketched above, possess any inherent meaningfulness in and of itself but depends on the context in which such knowledge is produced and the purpose to which such knowledge is put. If there is no preontological basis for meaning that is extralinguistically verifiable, no philosophical calculus that can assist us in making choices—then we can come to see language as a form of power that apprentices us to particular ways of seeing and engaging the self and others and this, in turn, has particular social consequences and political effects (McLaren and Leonard, 1993). Few educators have helped us to judge the political effects of language practices as much as Paulo Freire. And few educators have been as misused and misunderstood. Clearly, Freire does not see individuals and groups to be agentless beings invariably trapped in and immobilized by language effects. Rather, human beings are *politically accountable* for their language practices and as such, agency is considered immanent (McLaren and Lankshear, in press). Freire's position reflects Gramsci's notion that the structural intentionality of human beings needs to be critically interrogated through a form of *conscientization* or *conscientização* (this Portuguese word is defined by Freire as a deep or critical reading of common sense reality).

The Educational Institution as (a) Moral Agent

When the surgical pick of Egas Moniz was poised to perform the first medical lobotomy (a procedure which, it may be recalled, won him the Nobel Prize and which led reactionary advocates to consider lobotomies for individuals subversive of good citizenship practices) it was inconceivable at that time to think that such an act of cerebral terrorism could be achieved at a cultural level more effectively and much less painfully through the powerful articulations of new and ever more insidious forms of capitalist hegemony. The emancipatory role of university and public intellectuals has been greatly diminished by this process, as well as the function of the organic intellectual. In fact, emancipatory praxis has been largely orphaned in our institutions of education as educators are either unable or refuse to name the political location of their own pedagogical praxis. Part of the problem is that postmodern traditions of mediation have become simulacra whose ideological dimensions cannot easily be identified with or organically linked to the most oppressive effects of capitalist social relations and material practices. The redoubled seduction of new information technologies not only rearticulates a submission to multinational financial strategies, but creates possibilities for a resignification of, resistance to, and popular participation in, the politics of everyday life. The fact that relationships between the specific and the general have become blurred by these new electronic forces of mediation has both increased a reorganization and liberation of difference and also posed a danger of further cultural fragmentation and dissolution, limiting the struggle for strategic convergences among sites of intellectual production, the formation of new moral economies, and the expansion of new social movements. This disaggregation of public spheres and the massification of *mestizaje* identities makes it difficult to establish the solidarities necessary for developing liberating idioms of social transformation (Martin-Barbero, 1992; McLaren, 1992). It is to a deeper understanding of the relationship between the role of hegemony in the formation of public intellectuals and the function of the university itself in the context of wider social and political formations that Freire's work needs to be engaged. Part of this engagement necessitates an engagement with postmodernist criticisms.

Freire's work has not explicitly addressed current political debates surrounding the pedagogy and politics of postmodernism. What can be loosely described as postmodern social theory has been influential in, among other things, offering criticisms of material and economic causality and the Cartesian notion of subjectivity by placing an emphasis on reading social reality as a text, on language as a model of representation that helps "construct" social reality, on power as both a condition and an effect of discourse, on world-construction as an interplay of signifying relations and on unmasking Enlightenment conceptions of truth as the aesthetic effectiveness of the rhetoric of reading and writing practices.

Recently Sande Cohen has, from a postmodern perspective, offered a forceful challenge to the timid and frequently duplicitous role that university intellectuals have assumed in relation to the sociality of capital and the "catastrophe of socialized expectations." Following the persistent contentions of Baudrillard, Nietzsche, and others, Cohen maintains that objectivity can no longer hide or deny its subjectively based interests—a situation that has serious implications for the role of the intellectual in contemporary North American society. He writes:

> For intellectuals it is suggested that our texts and objects now fail to connect with everything but *our own simulacra, image, power, formation of*

exchange. In doubting and negating everything, in affirming and conse-
crating everything, intellectuals remain prisoners of the futile role of the
subject-in-consciousness and enforce the pretense that our efforts *translate* and *represent* for the truth of others, the reality of the world. (author's
italics, 1993; p. 154)

For Cohen, as for Freire, the dilemma of the intellectual lies in the
failure to forcefully challenge the perils of capitalism. In response to
this dilemma, Cohen mounts an articulate and vigorous attack on
the U.S. professoriate. University discourse and practices are condemned as mobilizing the academicization and domestication of
meaning through a modernist process of historicization—a process
that, in effect, amounts to creating various self-serving theologies of
the social that enable professors to speculate on the future in order
to justify their social function as intellectuals. Resulting from this
process are acute forms of antiskepticism leading in many instances
to a debilitating cynicism. According to Cohen, universities and their
academic gentry operate as a discursive assemblage directed at creating a regime of truth, a process that fails to undertake the important task of "inventing systems independent of the system of capital" (p. 3). In this instance, academic criticism is crippled by its
inability to break from conventional categories such as "resem-
blance." Critical languages forged in the theoretical ovens of the
academy simply and regrettably pursue their own hegemony
through the production of pretense and the desire for power.
Further, in the face of the cultural logic of late capitalism, "the category of the intellectual is disengaged from any possible antimod-
ernist argument" (p. 68). This situation recenters "high status"
knowledge within the liberal tradition of therapeutic discourse.
According to Cohen, "Universities cannot speak to their own participation in the destruction of events without undoing their 'need' and
control structures" (p. 114).

Even Habermas's now popular appeal for a rational means of
resolving differences and restoring democratic social life in the ideal
speech situation is described as "psychologically based moral economy" (p. 67) in which "intellectuals are empowered so long as they
stay in the precut grooves of providing resocialization with con-

cepts, theory, sophistication, the seductions, one might say, of bureaucratic integration" (p. 70). With this dilemma in mind, Cohen asserts:

> Why isn't capitalism—which makes mincemeat of real argumentation by its homogenization of signifiers, accomplished, for example, by the media's ordinary excessive displacement of analysis or the marginalization of unfamiliar cultural and social voices—rendered more critically?...Why is the economic mode so accepted in the first place as an unalterable form of social relation? Why is criticism so often an opposition that acts under the identity of a "loyal opposition"? (p. 70)

In order to escape the inevitability under capitalism of a modernist historicist recoding of knowledge, Cohen astutely adopts Lyotard's notion of "dispossession." Dispossession is recruited in this context in terms of "the dispossession of historicizing, narrating, reducing, demanding" (p. 72). More specifically, it refers to a form of "uncontrolled presentation (which is not reducible to presence)" (p. 73). It also points to the suspension of identification—including negative identification. Cohen also conscripts into the service of a critique of capitalism Hannah Arendt's concept of "active critique" of ends and goals "that never identif[ies] with time valuations which are, unavoidably, always already atrophied" (p. 113). We are advised here to "strangify," a term he employs in tandem with an unyielding commitment to resubjectification—to making subjectivity different outside the acts of negation and opposition through the creation of insubordinate signifiers that loosen and "neutralize...the Platonic control on the power to select" (p. 118). To strangify is to engage in a nonreduction of meaning that terrorizes all forms of equational logic, positive and negative (p. 119).

Cohen's project of strangification—a type of postmodern extension of Freire's term of conscientization—is directed at destabilizing and decentering the monumentalization of the already known and the militarization of existing sign systems established by the academic gentry and mandarins of high status knowledge whose participation is aimed at the legitimization of their own power. Along with smashing through the Western arcs of destiny—those supposedly unassailable narratives of individual freedom arching toward

Disneyland, Aztecland, Inca-Blinka, San Banadov, or Gangsterland
—strangification unsettles foundational myths that anchor meaning
in a sedentary web of contradictory appearances and precode the
world in such a way that entrance to the world of "success" depends
on the imprimatur of one's cultural capital and the potential for
earning power.

A number of questions are raised by Cohen's analysis for those
who are developing Freirian based pedagogical work. These questions include, among others:

❧ Of what importance does "postmodern theory" and "resistance postmodernism" have for the Brasilian sociopolitical context?

❧ The recent thesis on "the death of the subject" advanced by many post-
structuralists (the individual is constituted by discourse or is simply a position in language, systems of signification, chains of signs) has called into
question the feasibility of historical agency of political praxis. How can
we think of agency outside of a transhistorical and prediscursive "I" and
yet not fall into the cynical trap that suggests that individuals are simply
the pawns of the interpretive communities in which they find themselves?
If the subject has been aestheticized and reduced to simply a "desiring
machine," how are we to address the concepts of morality and ethics and
multidimensional forms of agency?

❧ How are we to react to those who proclaim the "death of History" thesis that decries the metanarratives of the Enlightenment as misguided
beliefs in the power of rational reflection? If we are to reject "grand theories" that essentialize others and speak for their needs from a perspective that refuses to critically interrogate their own ideological constitutive-
ness, then are we simply left with a micropolitics of local struggles? In
other words, is it possible to build global alliances in the postmodern era
that do not produce the same forms of technocratic capitalism that are
part of the problem?

❧ If master narratives are colonizing practices that repress differences and
the recognition of multiple subjectivities, if all of our observations are produced by contingent observers, if the social is always virtual, partial, and
perspectival, and if it is virtually impossible to represent the real outside
the constraints of regimes of representation, how should we begin to
rethink and practice liberation?

❦ While postmodern theorists have developed new understandings of desire as a means of criticizing the disabling effects of instrumental reason, how can we address pragmatically, the project of human freedom?

Postmodern critiques of educational institutions such as those advanced by Cohen can be helpful to Freirian educators in placing social and educational critique within a wider contemporary problematic.

The Nocturnal Academy and TKE Politics of Difference

Western intellectuals need to further understand that while affirming the experiences of subaltern groups is exceedingly important within a praxis of liberation, it is a highly questionable practice to render the "other" as transparent by inviting the other to speak for herself. Freire and other critics make this point very clear. As Gaurav Desai (following Gayatri Spivak, Lata Mani, and Partha Chattergee) notes, the position of permitting the other to speak for herself is uncomfortably "complicitious with a Western epistemological tradition that takes the conditions of the possibility of subaltern counterinvention for granted without engaging in a critique of the effects of global capitalism on such counterinvention" (1993; 137). Since the oppressed speak for themselves within a particular sign structure, the language of critique adopted by the insurgent intellectual needs to be able to analyze the embeddedness of such a sign system in the larger episteme of colonialism and White supremacist, capitalist patriarchy. Insurgent intellectuals must apply the same critique to their own assumptions about the other as they do to the other's self-understanding. In fact, critical educators need to counterinvent a discourse that transcends existing epistemes (Desai, 1993).

> Jim Merod (1987) poses the challenge of the Intellectual as follows: The critic's task is not only to question truth in its present guises. It is to find ways of putting fragments of knowledge, partial views, and separate disciplines in contact with questions about the use of expert labor so that the world we live in can be seen for what it is. (1987:188)

The problem, as Merod sees it, is that there exists within the North

American academy no political base for alliances among radical social theorists and the oppressed. He writes:

> The belief among liberal humanists that they have no "liberation strategy" to direct their steps is a vivid reminder of the humanities' class origin. Yet intellectuals always have something to fight for more important than their own professional position. North American intellectuals need to move beyond theory, tactics, and great dignified moral sentiments to support, in the most concrete ways possible, people harmed or endangered by the guiltless counterrevolutionary violence of state power.... The major intellectual task today is to build a political community where ideas can be argued and sent into the...world of news and information as a force with a collective voice, a voice that names cultural distortions and the unused possibilities of human intelligence. (1987:191)

One important task of the critical educator is to translate cultural difference. This is certainly the challenge for Freirian educators. The act of translation is, in Bhabha's (1990) terms, "a borderline moment" (p. 314). As Walter Benjamin pointed out, all cultural languages are to a certain extent foreign to themselves and from the perspective of otherness it is possible to interrogate the contextual specificity of cultural systems (Bhabha, 1990). It is in this sense, then, that "it becomes possible to inscribe the specific locality of cultural systems—their incommensurable differences—and through that apprehension of difference, to perform the act of cultural translation" (ibid., 314).

All forms of cultural meaning are open to translation because all cultural meanings resist totalization and complete closure. In other words, cultural meanings are hybrid and cannot be contained within any discourse of authenticity or race, class, gender, essences. Bhabha describes the subject of cultural difference as follows:

> The subject of cultural difference is neither pluralistic nor relativistic. The frontiers of cultural differences are always belated or secondary in the sense that their hybridity is never simply a question of the admixture of pre-given identities or essences. Hybridity is the perplexity of the living as it interrupts the representation of the fullness of life; it is an instance of iteration, in the minority discourse, of the time of the arbitrary sign—'the minus in the origin'—through which all forms of cultural meaning are open to translation because their enunciation resists totalization. (1987:191)

The subaltern voices of minority cultures constitute "those people who speak the encrypted discourse of the melancholic and the migrant" (ibid., 315). The transfer of their meaning can never be total. The "desolate silences of the wandering people" (ibid., 316) illustrate the incommensurability of translation which confronts the discourse of White supremacist and capitalist patriarchy with its own alterity.

As translators, critical educators must assume a transformative role by "dialogizing the other" rather than trying to "represent the other" (Hitchcock, 1993). The site of translation is always an arena of struggle. The translation of other cultures must resist the authoritative representation of the other through a decentering process that challenges dialogues that have become institutionalized through the semantic authority of state power. Neither the practice of signification nor translation occurs in an ideological void, and for this reason educators need to interrogate the sign systems that are used to produce readings of experience. As Joan Scott notes, "experience is a subject's history. Language is the site of history's enactment" (1992;34). It is Freire's particular strength that he has developed a critical vernacular that can help to translate both the Other's experience and his own experience of the other in such a way that ideological representations can be challenged. The challenge here is to rethink authorative representations of the other in a critical language that does not simply reauthorize the imperatives of "First World" translation practices. To do otherwise would open translation to a form of cultural imperialism. Experiences never speak for themselves, even those of the oppressed. Freire is careful to make sure his language of translation provides the oppressed with tools to analyze their own experiences while at the same time recognizing that the translation process itself is never immune from inscription in ideological relations of power and privilege.

While Freire's dialogue does not centrally address the politics of race, his message can nonetheless be elaborated through an engagement with the work of Black insurgent intellectuals. Cornel West blames what he perceives as a decline in Black literate intellectual activity on the "relatively greater Black integration into postindustrial capitalist America with its bureaucratized, elite universities, dull middlebrow colleges, and decaying high schools, which have little concern for and confidence in Black students as potential intellectuals" (1991; p. 137). He is highly critical of "aspects of the exclusionary and repressive effects of White academic institutions and humanistic scholarship" (p. 137) and, in particular, "the rampant xenophobia of bourgeois humanism predominant in the whole academy" (p.142). West sketches out four models for Black intellectual activity as a means of enabling critical forms of Black literate activity in the United States. The bourgeois humanist model is premised on Black intellectuals possessing sufficient legitimacy and placement within the "hierarchial ranking and the deep-seated racism shot through bourgeois humanistic scholarship" (p. 138). Such legitimation and placement must, however, "result in Black control over a portion of, or significant participation within, the larger White infrastructures for intellectual activity" (p. 140).

The Marxist revolutionary model, according to West, is "the least xenophobic White intellectual subculture available to Black intellectuals" (p. 140). However, West is also highly critical of the constraints Marxist discourse places on the creative life of Black intellectuals in terms of constructing a project of possibility and hope, including an analytical apparatus to engage short-term public policies. According to West:

> the Marxist model yields Black-intellectual self-satisfaction which often inhibits growth; also highlights social structural constraints with little practical direction regarding conjunctural opportunities. This self-satisfaction results in either dogmatic submission to and upward mobility with sectarian party or pre-party formations, or marginal placement in the bourgeois academy equipped with cantankerous Marxist rhetoric and sometimes insightful analysis utterly divorced from the integral dynamics, concrete realities, and progressive possibilities of the Black community. The preoccupation with social structural constraints tends to produce either preposterous chiliastic projections or paralyzing, pessimistic pronouncements. (p. 141)

It is important to point out amid all of this criticism that West does recognize the enabling aspects of the Marxist revolutionary model in its promotion of critical consciousness and its criticisms of dominant research programs within the bourgeois academy.

The Foucaultian postmodern skeptic model invoked by West investigates the relationship among knowledge, power, discourse, politics, cognition, and social control. It offers a fundamental rethinking of the role of the intellectual within the contemporary postmodern condition. Foucault's "political economy of truth" is viewed by West as a critique of both bourgeois humanist and Marxist approaches through the role of Foucault's specific Intellectual. The specific intellectual, according to West:

> shuns the labels of scientificity, civility, and prophecy, and instead delves into the specificity of the political, economic, and cultural matrices within which regimes of truth are produced, distributed, circulated, and consumed. No longer should intellectuals deceive themselves by believing— as do humanist and Marxist intellectuals—that they are struggling "on behalf" of the truth; rather the problem is the struggle over the very status of truth and the vast institutional mechanism which account for this status. (p. 142)

West summarizes the Foucaultian model as an encouragement of "an intense and incessant interrogation of power-laden discourses" (p. 143). But the Foucaultian model is not a call to revolution. Rather, it's an invitation to revolt against the repressive effects of contemporary regimes of truth.

Selectively appropriating from these three models, West goes on to propose his own "insurgency model" which posits the Black intellectual as a critical, organic catalyst for social justice. His insurgency model for Black intellectual life recovers the emphasis on human will and heroic effort from the bourgeois model, highlights the emphasis on structural constraints, class formations, and radical democratic values from the Marxist model, and recuperates the worldly skepticism evidenced in the Foucaultian model's destabilization of regimes of truth. However, unlike the bourgeois model, the insurgency model privileges collective intellectual work and communal resistance and struggle. Contrary to the Marxist model, the insurgency model does not privilege the industrial working class as the chosen agent of history but rather attacks a variety of forms of social hierarchy and subordination, both vertical and horizontal. Further, the insurgency model places much more emphasis on social conflict and struggle than does the Foucaultian model. While Freire's critique of domesticating forms of pedagogy gives a specifically Latin American context for the development of the insurgent intellectual, West's own typology extends some central Freirian themes in order to deepen its engagement with issues of race.

bell hooks describes an intellectual as "somebody who trades in ideas by transgressing discursive frontiers...who trades in ideas in their vital bearing on a wider political culture." (p. 152). However, hooks argues that White supremacist capitalist patriarchy has denied Black women, especially, "the opportunity to pursue a life of the mind." This is a problem that is also firmly entrenched in the racist White university system that involves "persecution by professors, peers, and professional colleagues" (p. 157). hooks rightly notes that "any discussion of intellectual work that does not underscore the conditions that make such work possible misrepresents the concrete circumstances that allow for intellectual production" (p. 158). She further elaborates:

> Within a White supremacist capitalist, patriarchal social context like this culture, no Black woman can become an intellectual without decolonizing her mind. Individual Black women may become successful academics without undergoing this process and, indeed, maintaining a colonized mind may enable them to excel in the academy but it does not enhance the intellectual process. The insurgency model that Cornel West advocates, appropriately identifies both the process Black females must engage to become intellectuals and the critical standpoints we must assume to sustain and nurture that choice. (p. 160)

I have employed criticisms of the academy by West, hooks, and Cohen because concerns dealing with postmodern social conditions and theory and those of race and gender help to widen Freire's criticisms by situating his insights more fully within the context and concerns of North American liberation struggles, specifically as they address struggles of the poor, of women, and people of color. Of course, there is room to broaden the context even further in relation to the struggles of indigenous peoples, of gays and lesbians, and other cultural workers within and outside of university settings. Freirian-based educators need to raise more questions related to race and gender so that these issues are given a more central focus in the struggle for social transformation. These questions include:

- In what ways have pedagogical practices been colonized by racialized discourses?

- What is the relationship between racial differentiation and sub-ordination and dominant discourses about race and ethnicity? How are these relationships reproduced by White supremacist discursive regimes and communicative practices?

- While the struggle for racial and gender equality is deemed worthwhile, those who struggle on behalf of this worthy goal are often labeled as deviant when they step outside of the legitimating norms of what is considered to be the "common culture." How are race and gender inequality reproduced within liberal humanist discourses?

- If there is no necessary racial teleology within the educational practices of most U.S. schools, how does the reproduction of racist discourses occur in most school sites?

- How does the hypervisibility of White cultures actually hide their obviousness in relations of domination and oppression?

- How does race constitute a boundary constraint on what is considered normal and appropriate behavior?

- In what ways are the conditions within the dominant culture for being treated justly and humanely predicted on utilitarian forms of rationality and the values inscribed and legitimated by bourgeois, working class, and elite forms of White culture? How do these forms of rationality work within the episteme of a larger discourse of colonialism?

- How can criticalists develop a cultural politics that is able to phenomenologize ideology critique and critical analyses at the level of lived experience so as to avoid a leftist elitism? How can a public vernacular develop around critical studies that is inclusive and life-world-sensitive?

Despite these absent discourses, Freire's work remains vitally important in the current debates over the role of universities, public schools, and educational sites of all kinds throughout North America. Freire warns educators that the activity of reading the word in relation to the social world has been regrettably pragmatic rather than principled. In other words, schooling (in relation to both universities and public schools) revolves around the necessity of differentially reproducing a citizenry distinguished by class, race, and gender injustices. The challenges of educators in both First and Third World contexts is to transform these reproductive processes. But I need to nuance this idea. Freirian pedagogy is set firmly against what Kristin Ross calls "the integral 'pedagogicizing' of society" by which she refers to the "general infantilization" of individuals or, groups through the discourses and social practices of "the nineteenth-century European myth of progress" (1993:669).

Ross conceives of critical pedagogy through what she refers to as the "antidisciplinary practice" of cultural studies. Drawing upon revisionist theories of allegory of Walter Benjamin, Paul de Man, and others, Ross moves away from the essentialist conceptions of cultural identity informed by a symbolic (mimetic and synechdochical) model of experience and representation in which one part timelessly and ahistorically reflects the whole. According to this model, the plight of, say, White women in New York City reflects the plight of Black women in the southern United States. Rather than viewing this relationship as an unmediated one in which the plight of Black women constitutes an authentic reflection of the plight of White women, Ross prefers to see this and similar relationships as allegorical rather than mimetic.

According to Ross:

Allegory preserves the differences of each historically situated and embedded experience, all the while drawing a relationship between those experiences. In other words, one experience is read in terms of another but not necessarily in terms of establishing identity, not obliterating the qualities particular to each. (1993:672)

Since it is impossible to represent every cultural group in the curriculum, the task of critical pedagogy, in Ross's terms, is to construct cultural identity allegorically—for each group to see his or her cultural narrative in a broader and comparative relation to others and within a larger narrative of social transformation.

For students to recognize the historical and cultural specificity of their own lived experiences allegorically—in allegorical relations to other narratives—is especially urgent. As Ross puts it:

> At a time of growing global homogenization the non-West is conceived in two, equally reductive ways: [in which] one whereby differences are reified and one whereby differences are lost. In the first, the non-West is assigned the role of the repository for some more genuine or organic lived experience; minority culture and non-Western cultures in the West are increasingly made to provide something like an authenticity rush for blasé or jaded Westerners, and this is too heavy a burden for anyone to bear. In the second, non-Western experiences are recoded and judged according to how closely they converge on the same: a single public culture or global average, that is, how far each has progressed toward a putative goal of modernization. (1993:673)

An emancipatory curriculum cannot present First and Third World cultures in the context of binary oppositions as relations of domination and resistance, since this move usually permits the First World perspective to prevail as the privileged point of normative civilizations (Ross, 1993). While Freire's work calls attention to the danger of a reductive dichotomization of First and Third World cultures, his interpreters often attempt simply to transplant Freire's perspective into First World contexts as a fortuitous equivalence or natural counterpart to subaltern resistance without recoding Freire's arguments sufficiently in terms of First World contexts. This leads to an unwitting embrace of pedagogy as a Western "civilizing" practice. Freirian criticalists working in the West need to be wary of the process through which liberal democracy represses the contingency of its own selectivity. Democracy is negatively prejudiced by the choice of its definitional terms, its articulation of freedom. United States democracy, in particular, is undergirded by an opportunist celebration of pluralism that disavows its own purging of oppositional views and refuses to confront its hierarchies of privilege.

As a teacher, Freire has provided the pedagogical conditions necessary to understand that Enlightenment humanism and its specifically Eurocentric (and EuroAmerican) "voice of reason" has not always been insightful or even reasonable in exercising its transcontinental thinking in the service of truth and justice. Freire's work helps us to further confront this issue as well as many others of concern to educators and cultural workers.

The perspectives of Freire can help deepen the debate over the role of the university in contemporary North American culture and, by extension, can also help to situate the struggle of Latin American educators within the concerns of postmodern and insurgent criticisms of the academy as exemplified by the perspectives of West, hooks, and Cohen.

In a world of global capitalism we need global alliances through cultural and political contact in the form of critical dialogue. Samir Amin (1989) notes that we collectively face a problem that "resides in the objective necessity for a reform of the world system; failing this, the only way out is through the worst barbarity, the genocide of entire peoples or a worldwide conflagration" (p. 114).

In attempting to develop a project premised on the construction of an emancipatory cultural imaginary that is directed at transforming the conditions that create the victims of capitalist expansion, educators need to go beyond simply severing their arterial connections to the forces of production and consumption that defraud them through the massification and commodification of their subjectivities. Rather, they need to create new alliances through a politics of difference. Otherwise, they face the prospect of becoming extensions of multinational corporations within the larger apparatus of capitalist expansion in the service of unequal accumulation and further underdevelopment in the peripheral and semiperipheral countries of Latin America. In short, what is needed is a politics of radical hope. Hope needs to be conjugated with some aspect of the carnal, tangible world of historical and material relations in order to be made a referent point for a critically transformative praxis.

We are reminded by Freire and his colleagues not to engage in controversies about difference but rather to be encouraged to dialogue about difference. It is in this sense that the university is invited to become truly plural and dialogical, a place where students are not only required to read texts but to understand contexts. A place where educators are required to learn to talk about student experiences and then form this talk into a philosophy of learning and a praxis of transformation. Clearly, we need to work within an ontological and intersubjective articulation of strategic pluralism within what has come to be known as "a politics of location." That is, we need to work from—and feminist theory has been at the forefront here—our diverse subjective positions, from the context of our partial, contingent, and situated knowledges.

I have recently witnessed in Brasil an experiment using Freire's work in conjunction with contributions by critical educators in Europe and the United States at Escola de 1 E 2, Graus José Cesar de Mesquita. The project is currently supported by the Sindicato dos Metalugicos de Porto Alegre and Nize Maria Campos Pellanda, who serves as Consultora Pedagogica. Here, the curriculum has been forged out of dialogues among teachers, researchers and scholars from many different countries in both First and Third Worlds. While there exists a great deal of political opposition to this school for workers (a public school and high school consisting of 1,000 students who live in an industrial zone in Porto Alegre) from both reactionary and neo-liberal educators, administrators, and politicians, the experiment itself is a testament to the Freirian vision of transcultural alliances and geo-political realignment.

Critical pedagogy argues that pedagogical sites, whether they are universities, public schools, museums, art galleries, or other spaces, must have a vision that is not content with adapting individuals to a world of conditions that promote such conditions. This means more than simply reconfiguring or collectively refashioning subjectivities outside of the compulsive ethics and consumerist ethos of flexible specialization or the homogenizing calculus of capitalist expansion. Enjoined on all of us working from a criticalist perspective is the creation of new forms of sociality, new idioms of transgression, and new instances of popular mobilization that can connect the institutional memory of the academy to the tendential forces of historical struggle and the dreams of liberation that one day might be possible to guide them. This is a mission that is not simply Freirian but immanently human.

Peter McLaren
Santa Maria
Rio Grande do Sul, Brasil

This paper is a revised version of Peter McLaren, (foreword) *Paulo Freire on Higher Education*, edited by Miguel Escobar, Alfredo Fernandez, and Gilberto Guevara (Albany, New York: State University of New York Press, 1994). An expanded version will appear in *Cultural Critique*.

REFERENCES

Amin, Samir, *Eurocentrism*. (New York: Monthly Review Press, 1989).

Attali, Jocques, *Millennium* (New York: Random House, Inc., 1991).

Berlin, Jim, "Literacy, pedagogy, and english studies: Postmodern connections," in Colin Lankshear and Peter McLaren, eds., *Critical Literacy: Politics, Praxis, and the Postmodern* (Albany, N. Y.: SUNY Press,1993), pp. 247-270.

Bhabha, Homi K., *Nation and Narration* (London and New York: Routledge, 1990).

Cohen, Sande, *Academia and the Luster of Capital* (Minneapolis, Minnesota: University of Minnesota Press, 1993).

Desai, Gaurau, "The invention of invention." *Cultural Critique* 24, 1993, pp. 119-142.

Gee, Jim, "Postmodernism and literacies." in Colin Lankshear and Peter McLaren, eds., *Critical Literacy: Politics, Praxis, and the Postmodern*. (Albany, N. Y.: SUNY Press, 1993), pp. 271-296.

Giroux, Henry. *Border Crossings* (New York: Routledge, 1993).

hooks, bell, and Cornel West, *Breaking Bread: Insurgent Black Intellectual Life*. (Boston, Mass.: South End Press, 1991).

Hitchcock, Peter, *Dialogies of the oppressed* (Minneapolis: University of Minnesota Press, 1993).

Kincheloe, Joe, and Peter McLaren, "Rethinking critical theory and qualitative research." in Norm K. Denzin and Yvonna S. Lincoln, eds. *Handbook of Qualitative Research*. (Newbury Park, CA: Sage Publications, 1994), pp. 138-157.

Martin-Barbero, Jesus, *Communication, Culture and Hegemony: From Media to Mediation*. (London: Sage Publications, 1992).

Merod, Jim, *The Political Responsibility of the Critic*. (Ithaca and London: Cornell University Press, 1987).

McLaren, Peter, and Peter Leonard, eds., *Paulo Freire: A Critical Encounter*. (London and New York: Routledge, 1993).

McLaren, Peter, and Colin Lankshear, eds., *Politics of Liberation: Paths from Freire*. (London and New York: Routledge, in press).

McLaren, Peter, "Collisions with otherness: Multiculturalism, the politics of difference, and the enthographer as nomad." *The American Journal of Semiotics,* vol. 9, nos. 2-3, pp. 121-148 (1992).

Miyoshi, Masao, "A Borderless World? From Colonialism to Transnationalism and the Decline of the Nation-State," *Critical Inquiry,* 19, pp. 726-751 (1993).

Parry, Benita, "A critique mishandled." *Social Text,* 35, pp. 121-133 (1993).

Ross, Andrew, *No Respect: Intellectuals and Popular Culture.* (New York and London: Routledge, 1989).

Ross, Kristin, "The World Literature and Cultural Studies Program," *Critical Inquiry,* 19, pp. 666-676 (1993).

Scott, Joan W., "Experience." in Judith Butler and Joan W. Scott, eds. *Feminists Theorize the Political.* (New York and London: Routledge, 1992), pp. 22-40.

Torres, Caries Alberto, (1993). *Democratic Socialism, Social Movements and Educational Policy in Brazil: The Work of Paulo Freire as Secretary of Education in the Municipality of São Paulo.* Manuscript in progress.

I KNOW WHY THIS DOESN'T FEEL EMPOWERING
A Critical *Race* Analysis of Critical Pedagogy

Gloria Ladson-Billings

Seen as a welcome change from positivist paradigms that dominated our notions of education, critical theory/pedagogy provided a way to understand and critique the ways that education reproduces current social inequalities.[1] So enamored were they by the bold challenge of critical theorists' and pedagogues, to the established order, many marginalized scholars failed to look carefully at the ways in which critical theory/pedagogy (as it was being advocated and written about) contributed to that marginalization.

In 1989, Ellsworth[2] raised the question, "Why doesn't this feel empowering?" to uncover and analyze the ways that critical pedagogy creates and perpetuates "repressive myths." According to Ellsworth, symbolic "others" continue to be marginalized by the very discourse that purports to support and represent them.

This chapter attempts to address one problematic and enduring aspect of critical theory/pedagogy—its failure to address adequately the question of race. The essay begins with a discussion of how discourse about race is denied and muted in analysis of educational and social inequality. Next, the essay contrasts critical race theory and critical theory, and concludes with a discussion of how critical race theory might serve as a rubric for what the author terms "culturally relevant pedagogy."[3,4]

The dilemma of Making *Race* an Understandable Category

Race—W. E. B. DuBois suggested that it was the major problem of the 20th century.[5] Swedish sociologist Gunnar Myrdal called it the "American dilemma."[6] U.S. social critic Studs Terkel called it an "American obsession."[7] Scholar Cornel West argues that we have not yet "learned to talk" of it.[8] I want to argue that we struggle with issues of race because, as Lee says, "race has a unique status in United States history and society."[9] That is, the category of race, despite being a part of the common lexicon, fails to provide us with a useful understanding of human diversity and variability.

Unlike gender, which is biologically determined and socially mediated, and class, which is represented by wealth and status in a given society, race is a slippery category created for one purpose—to rank and dominate. But all three, race, class, and gender have social significance. They are real, in a biological or economic sense, however, the import or difference they make in how we live our lives and understand others is socially constructed. According to Lee:

> One can agree on relatively objective criteria for measuring class (for example, using combinations of education, income, and occupational data) but race eludes such objectivity. As social constructions and ideology, race can therefore be meaningfully studied to gain insight into the construction of social meanings in a society. (p.90)

Scientists have long ago abandoned race as a classification tool. The lumping of human beings into three categories based on skin color, facial features, and hair texture failed to provide meaningful labels for understanding the myriad of ways in which human genetics crosses these arbitrary physical boundaries or how human beings group and regroup themselves.[10] Why were even the darkest-skinned people of the Indian subcontinent once labeled "Caucasoid?" What does "one drop of Black blood" mean? Are Jews a race?

Race is such a nebulous construct that in this country, the government fails to define it. Citizens filling out their census report are asked to select a racial category. This self-reporting is not challenged in the general census. Thus, according to the U.S. government, we are what we say we are. But the state's willingness to accept our self-definitions does not mean that others will accept them. It also does not mean that the state is uninterested in racial categorization. By merely posing the question (and arbitrarily devising the categories), the state is supporting a particular ideology that is grounded in racial categorization. Although we "say who we are" (within the state's categorical designations), the social order responds with its own prescriptive rules that tell us who we are.

While we may argue that race is used as a descriptor, to distinguish between and among people, we also have come to accept the notion of race as a category that serves the purpose of distinguishing those who are "not White" without an adequate analysis of what it means to be "White" in the society. Thus, a central focus of discussion about race must be on the "construction of whiteness."[11]

A historical reflection on race and ethnicity in the early United States indicates that language, culture, and national origin were ways that various peoples identified themselves and others.[12] Thus, this emerging nation comprised Europeans who defined themselves as "English," "Irish," "Scotch Irish," "Germans," "French," and so forth. The historical class hierarchies were reproduced with the conscription of "indentured servants"—people who worked (and were worked) in order to pay off a debt or pay for their passage to this new land. There were both White and Black indentured servants. However, the increasing need for laborers coupled with a growing racism rendered the indentured servants of African descent vulnerable to the category of slave.

Eventually, there would be a need to determine who was eligible for slavery and who (by virtue of birth and lineage) was not. The "not eligible for slavery" group was composed exclusively of peoples of European descent. They reconstituted themselves from separate national groupings into one "racial" grouping. Now, rather than Scots, Irish, English, Germans, and French, they were White. With this whiteness came privilege.[13] Rather than the class rankings that existed in Europe, particularly England, race could be used to rank the peoples of the "New World." Instead of manors and feudal lords, the plantation system of the American South served to replicate the social ranking so common in Europe. Thus, those without white skin were placed at the bottom of the social hierarchy.

So fixed and rigid were these racial categories that immigrants and "strangers" could arrive on these shores and eventually move into their "appropriate" place in the social hierarchy. The closer a group could approximate the "markers" of whiteness (skin color, hair texture, facial features) the higher up the social ladder they could climb. This climbing meant leaping over the positions of African Americans, Native Americans, and Latinos who were less able to dispose of their non white physical and cultural markers.

In present-day schooling in the United States, race and class often are linked. The proportion of African Americans who are poor is much higher than that of Whites. However, even when class is "held constant," African-American students continue to perform at lower levels than their white classmates. Thus, being "middle class" does not shield African-American students from discriminatory and racist individual and institutional behaviors. Neither, does critical theory, as it is presented, provide an explanation.

Critical Race Theory versus Critical Theory

Critical theory, while diverse and multifaceted, does hold some concepts and ideas in common. These ideas include the premise that "men and women are essentially unfree and inhabit a world rife with contradictions and asymmetries of power and privilege," as McLaren puts it. Critical theorists recognize the dialectical nature of social problems—that they are both individually and socially located and created. Thus, according to McLaren critical theory helps "focus simultaneously on both sides of a social contradiction."[14]

Gibson argues that some of the principles of critical theory include: (1) a realization that facts are socially constructed, (2) a commitment to emancipation, (3) a revision of Marxist theory that suggests that certain elements of the superstructure operate autonomously and are not merely a result of economic determinism, (4) the significance of culture, (5) the centrality of ideology, and (6) the power of language.[1]

While critical theory may be explicit about unequal power relations vis-a-vis class and culture, it tends to be mute in relation to race (as well as gender, as explained by Ellsworth).[2] Thus, scholars of color in a variety of fields have begun to challenge the "universal" applicability of critical theory to their specific social, political, educational, and economic concerns.

In response to the "silenced voice of race," some legal scholars have proposed a critical race theory. Matsuda suggests that critical race legal theory is "the work of progressive legal scholars who are attempting to develop a jurisprudence that accounts for the role of racism in American law and that moves toward the elimination of racism as a part of a larger goal of eliminating forms of subordination."[15]

Further, Delgado suggests that, critical race theory is characterized by: (1) an insistence on "naming one's own reality"; (2) the use of critical social science research; (3) doubts about the foundation of moderate/incremental civil rights law; (4) the belief that knowledge is power; (5) the debunking of myths used by powerful groups to support racial oppression; (6) criticism of liberal legalism; and (7) an interest in structural determinism.[16]

The overarching theme of critical race theory deals with what Bell (1980) terms the "interest convergence principle":

> The interest of Blacks in achieving racial equality will be accommodated only when it converges with the interests of whites; however, the fourteenth amendment, standing alone, will not authorize a judicial remedy providing effective racial equality for Blacks where the remedy sought threatens the superior societal status of middle- and upper-class whites.[17]

The application of critical race theory to education[18] means that critiques of education can no longer be "race neutral" or "colorblind." Critical race theory recognizes that African-American students, regardless of their economic standing and/or gender, suffer the pernicious effects of a racist society. Said another way, issues of class and gender represent "additive" means of oppression for African Americans. The growing African-American middle class is still subject to, and likely to encounter, racism.[19,20] African-American women are still subject to, and likely to encounter, racism.[21]

Thus, a critical race perspective always foregrounds race as an explanatory tool for the persistence of inequality. The power of racial coding allows even the poorest White in the society to define the most credentialed, wealthy African American to be referred to as "nigger." For African Americans, their understanding of inequity is filtered through the lens of race and racism.

An example of how early children learn the "rules of racial standing"[22] is illustrated in a vignette described by Madeline Cartwright.[23] According to Cartwright, who was a teacher in this school, there was only one White child in the entire school. This White boy broke every school rule with impunity, while African American youngsters were suspended for the slightest infractions. Not only did the White youngster break the rules, he bragged about it and indicated that his white skin provided him with status and protection. Finally, the youngster's behavior got so out of hand that the assistant principal sent for his parents. A Black woman appeared and was told by the assistant principal that one of the boy's parents would have to come. The woman asserted, "I am his mother!" From that moment on, the boy was treated with the same lack of regard as the (other) African-American children. His white protective coating had been exposed. The quirks of genetics had produced a white skin that the rules of the social structure responded to in a privileging manner. Once the child's "lineage" indicated that he was "socially Black," his life in school began to resemble that of the other children.

Culturally Relevant Teaching as a Critical Race Pedagogy

Since 1989 I have been engaged in research to examine the pedagogical expertise of those teachers who are successful teachers of African-American students. There is no reason to use space here to delineate the host of indices that represent academic and school failure for African-American students. Suffice it to say that African-American students lag behind their White counterparts on every standard measure of school achievement.[24] However, I was convinced that there were some teachers who were capable of assisting African-American students to be academically successful.

Work on pedagogy by Shulman[25] suggests that an important aspect of the knowledge base for teaching is the "wisdom of practice." More specifically, this wisdom of practice includes "the maxims that guide (or provide reflective rationalization for) the practices of able teachers" (p.11). But missing from this dialogue on the wisdom of practice are issues of race and ethnicity. This means that although Shulman provides us with interesting new ways to think about pedagogy, his (and others') thinking dismisses the salience of race in a racialized society. Real-life classrooms of teachers and students are racially constructed. My interests lie in investigating those classrooms where teachers' wisdom of practice proves effective for African-American students.

The first dilemma that needed to be solved in conducting this research was in defining success. Several researchers have indicated that academic success for students of color often correlates with "cultural failure."[26] Twenty years ago, Dickeman argued that, "[It] should come as no surprise...that recent research on the Black family reveals that those Black youths who reject their parents have greater chances of future success."[27] This belief that, to be successful, African-American students must reject "blackness" ran counter to what African-American parents wanted for their children when they talked of success.

In an attempt to locate teachers whom *parents* believed were successful teachers of African-American students, I asked the parents to define what they meant by success. Space constraints do not permit a full discussion of what parents said; however, one parent's comment seemed to sum up the general sentiment. "I want him to be able to hold his own in the classroom without forgetting his own at home." This wonderful use of language captured the essence of the tension that exists between academic and cultural success for African-Americans. The parents wanted the best for their children, but not at the expense of a loss of community and cultural affiliation.

By combining the parents' recommendations with those of the school principals I was able to locate eight teachers who were willing to participate in a study of effective pedagogical practice for African-American students. This study involved intensive classroom observations over a two-and-a-half-year period. Space prohibits my explanation of methodological issues regarding the study but other writings do attend to this aspect of my work.[28],[29]

My discussion here is concerned with ways in which the teachers who participated in the study made attention to race a way to help students achieve both academic and cultural excellence. Through the use of two classroom vignettes (there are many more), I want to show how the teachers eschewed a "color blind" or "race neutral" approach in order to make race problematic and open to critique.

The Beautiful Blond Princess

Students in Julia Devereaux's fourth-grade classroom knew that they would spend lots of time reading. Ms. Devereaux, an African-American teacher, insisted that all the students had to be at least fourth-grade readers so that they would enter fifth grade prepared. One day, the students were finishing a story based on a Greek myth in which the daughter of a king had gotten herself into trouble. "What's another name for a king's daughter?" asked Ms. Devereaux. "A princess," chimed several of the students. "What characteristics does the princess in this story have? How might we describe her?" Ms. Devereaux's questions were aimed at eliciting personality traits of the character, but several students misunderstood her and began suggesting physical traits despite the fact that the story contained no illustrations, and little attention was paid to physical characteristics in the text. One student said, "She is beautiful with long, blond hair." "Do you agree with that?" Ms. Devereaux asked the class. "Yeah," shouted several children. "Why do you think that the princess has long, blond hair?" Devereaux queried. "Cause all the princesses we ever seen got long, blond hair," remarked one girl. "Oh, then I couldn't be a princess, since I've got short, black hair. Is that right?" Some of the children seemed a little confused as to how to respond, but the girl who spoke of only seeing princesses with long blond hair held firm. "What if I share a story about a princess without long blond hair?" asked Ms. Devereaux. "What would you think?"

Ms. Devereaux began reading John Steptoe's *Mufaro's Beautiful Daughters*,[30] an African tale based on the stories collected by the people of Zimbabwe in the late 1800s. In the tale, Nyasha, the kind and generous daughter of Mufaro, is selected to wed the king.

After reading the book Ms. Devereaux leads a discussion with the class about how they had come to believe that only long haired, blond (White) women could be seen as princesses. They talk about ways in which everything around them devalues Blacks and elevates Whites. The students share examples of how news media portrayals construct Blacks as criminals, homeless, and/or on welfare. Ms. Devereaux reminds the students that they have many instances in their daily lives that contradict those images. She asks the students to begin enumerating them as she lists them on the board. The lesson that began as a reading lesson with a Greek myth as text has become one that explicitly challenges notions about racial superiority.

Roughing It

Ann Lewis, an Italian-American teacher who has lived her entire life in the working class and low-income community in which she teaches, believes in confronting racism head on. Each year, Ann takes her classroom of African-American and Latino/a students on a week-long camping experience that helps strengthen their sense of team or family feeling. The funds for the camping experience come out of a county-wide program that is designed to both build students' understanding and appreciation of the environment and allow them to interact with students of different races, ethnicities, and cultural and economic backgrounds. Ms. Lewis' sixth-grade class is excited to be going to camp, but she is aware of the potential for conflict when her African-American and Latino/a students come together with students from other school districts.

"What if someone calls you a name at camp?" Ms. Lewis asks. "What will you do?" "I'll bust they chops," yells Jerry, a chunky African-American boy. "And then they'll send you home and talk about how poorly the Black kids from _____ [name of school district] acted." "Well, what kind of name are you talking about?" asks one of the girls. "I mean, if someone just says 'Hey, ugly,' I might just call them a name back and go on about my business." "What if it's a really bad name?" asks Ms. Lewis. "Like what, like what, " the students ask, eager to see if Ms. Lewis will say something "shocking." "Well, when I was a little girl, people used to say terrible things about Italians and if I heard any of those words, I just flew into a rage. I got into a lot of fights because of that." "But what did they call you, Miz Lewis?" the students asked. "Oh, names like 'Dago,' 'Guinea,'" Ms. Lewis responded. The names seemed not to register to the students. They did not understand them as racial slurs. Ms. Lewis pointed out that they were the equivalent of saying "nigger." Right away, the students indicated their discomfort and anger with that term, "Nobody better not call me no nigger," replied Larry. "Me neither, " came a chorus of other students. Ms. Lewis had hit a nerve. "But what if they do? What can you do to respond without getting thrown out of the camp and ruining the program for our whole school?" The students began brainstorming strategies for diffusing such a situation and still getting "justice." They treated the discussion as a hypothetical situation. However, during the camp-out week, a high-school-aged junior counselor made several racial slurs and epithets to a group of Ms. Lewis' African-American boys. Because of his size and age the boys initially felt hurt and powerless. Finally, some of the boys remembered the classroom discussion and began to write down what was said to them and when. They reported what happened to Ms. Lewis, who was in a different cabin with some of the female students. She proceeded to investigate and reported these incidents to the camp directors. The young man was expelled from the camp program and suspended from his home school. The way in which they handled themselves in the midst of a "racial crisis" was one of the most discussed aspects of the camp-out when the students returned home.

Despite the differing contexts, each teacher just described has made a conscious decision to make race problematic. Clearly, Julia Devereaux could have dismissed the students' perceptions about princesses needing to have "long blond hair" with a simple statement that they were incorrect. Instead, she opted to challenge their thinking about where their notions came from, how they were formed, and what ways they could rethink not only "princesses" but also standards of beauty.

In Ann Lewis's case, she could have focused her energy on preparing the students for the camp-out and left them with some platitudes about "good behavior" and how they were to act. She chose, however, to confront them with examples of the kinds of mean-spirited and provocative things that people say about race in a racialized society. Her reminding the students of the real-life struggles they must confront because of their race helped them to create strategies that worked to their advantage and in the favor of justice.

These teachers refused to employ a "race neutral" or "color-blind" approach to teaching. Both exhibited aspects of critical pedagogy, believing with Giroux and Simon:

> [that] pedagogy refers to a deliberate attempt to influence how and what knowledge and identities are produced within and among particular sets of social relations…As both a political and a practical activity, it attempts to influence the occurrence and qualities of experiences. When one practices pedagogy, one acts with the intent of creating experiences that will organize and disorganize a variety of understandings of our natural and social world in particular ways…[31]

These teachers augment these notions of pedagogy by insisting that race, its conceptions and constructions, remains a site of struggle for themselves and their students. Not only are they informed by these constructions of race, but they are empowered by it. Any effort at critical pedagogy in the context of a racialized society without significant attention being paid to race will never be empowering.

Epilogue

Space constrains a full and adequate treatment of the multiple ways in which we must struggle with our understandings of race. However, what I have attempted to do in this chapter is say aloud what Nobel Laureate Toni Morrison[32] calls "unspeakable things unspoken" in challenging those of us who call ourselves critical theorists/pedagogues. How might we enter into meaningful dialogue around the issue of race? In what ways might our understandings of critical theory and pedagogy be informed by our understandings of race? What are the potentials for struggling together around issues of race that ultimately will empower us to teach and learn in ways that are empowering, not alienating? What can we learn from those teachers who already have made race problematic and who work in ways that support students' greater understanding of the role race plays in our society?

These are but a few of the questions the notion of a critical race theoretical perspective provokes. In this chapter we begin to peel but one layer off the "flesh of an onion." We need many more opportunities to engage in meaningful dialogue concerning race. Until we agree to wrestle with it and its pernicious and pervasive effects, we will continue to disenfranchise and alienate students who reside outside of the circles of influence. They will never know what it means to experience education as an empowering force.

REFERENCES

1. Gibson, R., *Critical Theory and Education* (London: Hodder and Stoughton, 1986).

2. Ellsworth, E., "Why Doesn't this Feel Empowering? Working Through the Repressive Myths of Critical Pedagogy," *Harvard Educational Review*, vol. 59, pp. 297-324 (1989).

3. Ladson-Billings, G., "Liberatory Consequences of Literacy: A Case of Culturally Relevant Instruction for African American Students," *The Journal of Negro Education*, vol. 61, pp. 378-391 (1992).

4. Ladson-Billings, G., "Reading Between the Lines and Beyond the Pages: A Culturally Relevant Approach to Literacy Teaching," *Theory into Practice*, vol. 31, pp. 312-320, (1992).

5. DuBois, W. E. B., *The Souls of Black Folks* (New York: Penguin Books, 1903, 1969).

6. Myrdal, G., *An American Dilemma: the Negro Problem and Modern Democracy*, 2 vols. (New York: Harper and Brothers, 1944).

7. Terkel, S. *Race: How Whites and Blacks Think and Feel About the American Obsession* (New York: New Press, 1992).

8. West, C., "Learning to Talk of Race," *New York Times Magazine*, August 2, 1992, pp. 24-26.

9. Lee, E., "Racial Classifications in the U.S. Census: 1890-1990," *Ethnic and Racial Studies*, vol. 16, pp. 75-94 (1993).

10. Cavalli-Sforza, L. L., "Genes, Peoples and Languages," *Scientific American*, pp. 104-110 (November, 1991).

11. Marable, M., "The Impact of Columbus on African-Americans," paper presented at the Conference on Preparing Alternative Responses to the Columbus Quincentennial, University of Wisconsin, Madison, October 1, 1991.

12. Takaki, R., *A Different Mirror: A Multicultural History of the United States* (New York: Little, Brown, 1993).

13. McIntosh, P., "White Privilege and Male Privilege: A Personal Account of Coming to See Correspondences Through Work in Women's Studies," *Working Paper* No. 189 (Wellesley, Mass.: Center on Research on Women, 1988).

14. McLaren, P., *Life in Schools* (White Plains, NY: Longman, 1989), p. 166.

15. Matsuda, M., "Voices of America: Accent, Antidiscrimination Law, and

a Jurisprudence for the Last Reconstruction," *Yale Law Journal*, Vol. 100, pp. 1329-1467 (1991).

16. Delgado, R., "When a Story Is Just a Story: Does Voice Really Matter?" *Virginia Law Review*, vol. 76, pp. 95-111 (1990).

17. Bell, D., "Brown and the Interest-Convergence Dilemma," in D. Bell, ed., *New Perspectives on School Desegregation* (New York: Teachers College Press, 1980), pp. 90-107.

18. Ladson-Billings and Tate, 1993.

19. Cary, L., *Black Ice* (New York: Knopf, 1991).

20. Dent, D., "The New Black Suburbs," *New York Times Magazine*, June 14, 1992, pp. 18-25.

21. Collins, P. H., *Black Feminist Thought: Knowledge, Consciousness, and the Politics of Empowerment* (New York: Routledge, 1991).

22. Bell, D., *Faces at the Bottom of the Well: The Permanence of Racism* (New York: Basic Books, 1992), p. 95.

23. Cartwright, M., *For the Children* (New York: Doubleday, 1993).

24. Irving, J., *Black School Failure*.

25. Schulman, L., "Knowledge and Teaching: Foundations of the New Reform," *Harvard Educational Review*, vol. 57, pp. 1-22 (1987).

26. Fordham, S., and J. Ogbu, "Black Students' School Success: Coping with the Burden of 'Acting White'," *The Urban Review*, vol. 18, pp. 176-206 (1986).

27. Dickeman, M., "Teaching Cultural Pluralism," in J. Banks, ed., *Teaching Ethnic Studies* (43rd Yearbook, National Council for the Social Studies: Washington, D.C.: NCCS, 1973).

28. Ladson-Billings, G., "Like Lightning in a Bottle: Attempting to Capture the Pedagogical Excellence of Successful Teachers of Black Students," *The International Journal of Qualitative Studies in Education*, vol. 3, pp. 335-344 (1990).

29. Ladson-Billings, G., "Culturally Relevant Teaching: The Key to Making Multicultural Education Work," in C. Grant, ed., *Research in Multicultural Education* (Washington, D.C.: Falmer Press, 1991), pp. 106-121.

30. Steptoe, J., *Mufaro's Beautiful Daughters* (New York: Lothrop, Lee, and Shepard, 1987).

31. Giroux, H., and R. Simon, "Popular Cultural and Critical Pedagogy: Everyday Life as a Basis for Curriculum Knowledge," in H. Giroux and P. McLaren, *Critical Pedagogy, The State and Cultural Struggle* (Albany,

NY: State University of New York Press, 1989), pp. 236-252.

32. Morrison, T., "Unspeakable Things Unspoken: the Afro-American Presence in American Literature," *Michigan Quarterly Review*, vol. 28, pp. 1-38 (1989).

CHAPTER EIGHT

LIMITING THE ACADEMICS OF POSSIBILITIES
A Self-Reflective Exercise in Freirian Politics

Anita Sheth and George Dei

"It is possible that some may question my right to discuss revolutionary cultural action, a subject of which I have no concrete experience. However, the fact that I have not personally participated in revolutionary action does not negate the possibility of my reflection on this theme."

Paulo Freire, *Pedagogy of the Oppressed*, p. 24

While being mindful of Paulo Freire's desire to "trust in the oppressed and their ability to reason," (p. 53) we explore the practice of representing the Other or to use Deleuze's phrasing, "the indignity of speaking for others." In so doing, we answer the questions: who are the "oppressed" in Freire's work and what is the constitutive role of his own discourse on the reflections in the academy on the "theme" of oppression? The voyeuristic, antiessentialist stance taken by Freire in conceptualizing "the oppressed" will be examined in light of the critical arguments emerging from nonwhite, nonheterosexual peoples of the Anglo-Euro-North American academy. How does Freire's work speak to us, one as teacher, one as student, both as nonwhite, one heterosexual male, one nonheterosexual female? Can our desire to "name the world" dialogically be possible without an embodied, expressed recognition of our limitations? Put differently, can we engage in a politics of possibilities without concurrently acknowledging the need for a politics of limitations? Do situatedness and experience matter in "denunciation/annunciation"? If so, why is there a conspicuous absence of critical material from "the oppressor" group, in naming their every-day/every-night practices of domination? If Freire is correct in stating that "dialogue cannot occur between those who want to name the world and those who do not wish this naming" (p. 76), then how is it that in the Anglo-Euro-American academy Freirians at "the center" are forever found naming the people at "the margin," against our will? Has the desire for a liberatory education unwittingly produced more jobs in the academy for "the oppressor," even while changing ever so slightly the gender, sex, race, class scape of the bodies that people it? Does this then make us rethink the voyeuristic, antiessentialist debate in *Pedagogy of the Oppressed* with renewed vigor? Can we afford not to in these alleged "postmodern" times?

Before we move on to situate ourselves and put forth our bid for a politics of limitations to read against a politics of possibilities, in what immediately follows we analyze the practices of "desire," "voyeurism," "antiessentialism," and "othering," as made available in Freire's articulation of a liberatory pedagogy. The question that guides this part of our deliberation is: what did Freire have to "do" in order to posit his theory of pedagogy of the oppressed? In other words, what were the mechanics involved that made it possible for him to occupy the position of "speaking on behalf of others"? The point of this exercise, as will become clear, is not to "put Freire on trial" or to single him out in our critique of the enormous privilege that he appropriates for himself and/or is appropriated by others on his behalf. Clearly, the academic traditions in virtually all parts of the world have indulged in the daily practices of oppression and exclusion of some people. Conceptual categorizations and methodological applications that have historically absented, stereotyped, and marginalized enormous sectors of humanity still operate in the minds, hearts, and spirits of people present in the academy who now continually struggle for liberation. This is how deep the hateful ideologies of colonialism, imperialism, capitalism, classism, racism, sexism, heterosexism, and ableism run. Allowing this would mean, of course, that we, who are not from the dominant white, hetero-patriarchal group, have internalized oppressive practices and act them out daily, even while fighting hard against the perpetrators and their culture. In drawing attention to Freire in this manner then, we have no intention of "pointing the finger at him" for not doing more than repetitiously denouncing and exposing the intricate and corruptive logic of bourgeois ideology. On the contrary, our purpose in engaging in this project, other than having an opportunity to publish, is to show how we, in our differently located positions in academia, are also caught in and constitute a complex system of enunciation and action where self-reflection or self-awareness, though paramount as Freire himself argues, are so difficult to live by.

Giving Freire His Body Back

"The truth of reason is not necessarily a lived truth."

Trinh Minh-ha, *Framer Framed*

How dare we, from our differently marginalized locations, give back to Freire his body, and what does it mean for us to speak this way? We dare because we want to disallow Freire's desire to transcend his body in history. When we speak this way, what we experience is shame and anxiety that years of oppression have produced. But at one and the same time we experience political doubt in that by "giving Freire his body back" we might be still serving the Master. As most of our readers will tacitly acknowledge, there has sprung up a huge industry around Freire and Freirian products in that sector of the academic markets that constantly yearns for liberatory change. Traces of Freirian engagement are to be found in many disciplines, including history, literature, political science, sociology, economics, mass communications, education, and in newer ones such as women studies, cultural studies, multiculturalism, and antiracist pedagogy. His work has also spoken to people far beyond the academy. His contribution to the world of radical ideas and politics remains unquestionable, even though the mass phenomenalization of the Freirian agent evokes disquieting suspicion in the people that Freire absents (e.g. women, nonwhites, nonheterosexuals, disabled).

Suffice it to say that the near cultism that has developed around Freire has less to do with Freire himself than with the social relations of the Anglo-Euro-American academy. The very oppressive practices of intellectualism, with all their disembodied cultural interventions and public displays, exhausts the time, energy, and silence necessary for knowing the subject through the Other's sensuous gaze and articulation. As Freire (1988) notes of "the oppressor" who has joined "the oppressed":

> Theirs is a fundamental role and has been so throughout the history of this struggle. It happens, however, that as they cease to be exploiters or indifferent spectators or simply the heirs of exploitation and move to the side of the exploited, they almost always bring with them the marks of their origin: Their prejudices and their deformations, which include a lack of confidence in the people's ability to think, to want, and to know.... Our converts...truly desire to transform the unjust order, but because of their background they believe that they must be the executors of transformation. They talk about the people, but they do not trust them and trusting the people is the indispensable precondition for revolutionary change.... Those who authentically commit themselves to the people must re-examine themselves constantly." (46-7)

"Reexamination" is an interesting concept and practice in the academy. Without doubt when it has sensuously occurred it has evolved largely from the bottom up. In classroom after classroom in postgraduate studies, particularly in areas of progressive pedagogy, you will find some students repeatedly engaged in challenging the teacher's reflections on "the theme of oppression." In every sense, it is often those students who are nonwhite, nonheterosexual, working-class women who have truly pushed the pedagogues, who are often white, heterosexual middle-class able-bodied men, to acknowledge the limitations of their embodied privilege. Hundreds of hours of debate by student after student such as those mentioned might produce an opening, a reflective possibility in the teacher who is vulnerable or guilty enough to learn. This is, however, hard to detect because so often the learning that goes on in the teacher is not relayed back to these students. Instead, it is accidentally found by them in articles or chapters written by their teachers at a much later time and in a different reading context. This too is frequently indirect because the teachers who recount a "reexamining" often fail to list the names of the students they have learned from. The indication of a date, year, and title of a course in the writing or the collective reference of students in a particular classroom, in the acknowledgment section of the publication, never quite provides the empowerment that these students deserve. The need for non-classificatory identification of students who teach their teachers has little to do with personal affirmation of the ego. Rather, it has to do with mapping the intricate network of the painful labor-intensive dynamics of the "pedagogy from the oppressed" (Xerri, 1993) in progressive teacher reexamination. What else could the pleasure be, rare as this is, in some students when they see their name in print or their words referenced in a publication put out by their reflecting pedagogue?

But this kind of sensuous reexamination of "the oppressor" who has "joined the oppressed" is objectionably infrequent. The heavy teaching schedules, funding submissions, and reading materials leave even the Freirian pedagogues with virtually no time to self-reflect in a collective mirror, as it were. Moreover, feminist and non-white faculty members who take daily risks, particularly the non-tenured staff, have even less time to fully reexamine the white heterosexual, middle-class privilege as it manifests itself in departmental meetings, the faculty association, and administrative policies and decisionmaking. In most cases, faculty of a particular department hardly ever socialize together, let alone are found in each other's offices, dialogically debating the politics of race, gender, sex, class, and ability of the academy. Of course, there are exceptions but, as with all exceptions, they are not the rule; neither are the exceptions continually the exceptions, thus never forming a group of exceptions within a department. Constraints of work, time, and the individualist setting of the academy isolate faculty, thus making reexamination, if one could purposefully misuse this Freirian term here, only possible through the reading of others' printed texts. That is to say, reexamination occurs, if at all, nondialogically, is mediated through abstractions and secondhand account telling, and is propelled by the desire, despite its emancipatory intent, to publish, not perish, or to put it differently, a desire to explain the world, not to concretely embody or change it.

However, collaborative writing is becoming more and more popular in the academy. Collaboration could minimally expand the possibility of dialogic reexamination, even though the choice of collaborative publishing is also isolative and restrictive as it is currently situated and rewarded. Generally, collaboration occurs between like and like, as in one white, heterosexual, middle-class, able-bodied male academic with another of the same selection. Furthermore, when collaboration occurs across locations in the noninterview or respondent-to-respondent writing format, it is impossible to trace the different sites of ruling that mediated the differently situated writers in negotiating the end product, thus losing any possible collaborative learning or reexamination that might have operated between the members in dialogically naming the world. In every sense we are differently guilty, and willfully so, of this very process. Because our collaboration also has locked within it an acceptance of the "master-slave" dynamic, even while we both desperately desire a different relationship with the world. Our unequal power ordinates crush our will to set up a dialogic communion, imaginary and fictive as this is in prevailing social relations of the academy. To name our differences, then, does not in itself name "the oppressor" among or within us; neither does it provide a concrete and overt description of the complex power exchanges that operated between us in collaboratively authoring this text. So inadequate is the process of naming that the very act of identifying the categories of race, sex, gender, class, and so forth becomes a way of obfuscating self-reflection, awareness, or reexamination. Naming the body in discourse then loses its politicizing mobility if it is not done on the grounds of concrete materiality. To name in this way does not speak of "the self in the act of meeting the world" (Dworkin in Taylor, 1991; p. 63), nor does it recognize the self as being deeply inserted into the social order (Taylor, 1991; p. 63). As bell hooks (1990) points out in thinking about the benefits of being an oppressor in the academy, "naming yourself as privileged is not to name yourself as oppressive or dominating..." (p. 75).

Of course, Freire understood the deception associated with the word in education. He warned against verbalism and against the exclusive few who feel that the right to name the word lies with them alone. However, Freire does not follow through on his conceptualization. Nowhere do we find him reflecting on the skin of his body; at no time does he stop his enunciation and make concrete his own existence in terms of "the oppressed" and "the oppressor." Had he imaged himself in history, he might have disclosed his contribution to and constitution of the space in the intellectual climate out of which the pedagogue acts. To say this is not to deny or doubt Freire's steadfast opposition to oppressive ideology. It is, however, to indicate the missing yet necessary data of theoretical formulations on oppression. If every story of victimization was dialogically met with at least one story of perpetration, we might not have to spend so much time reflecting on "the theme of oppression," nor would we have to conceptualize and reconceptualize how oppression occurs. Furthermore, "the oppressed" would not have to constantly depict the acts of violence from "the oppressor" localized on their bodies. If "the oppressor" forfeited his privilege and felt his body and lived with and within it, he would fully recognize "its social and economic structuring" (Taylor, 1991; p.61). In so doing, he might begin to refuse the narrative impulse of hetero-patriarchal, and colonialist sense-making that has become and is him. The desire of his imagination would be disallowed through the skin of his body, as it were.

The following excerpt from an interchange between a student, Kelly Estrada, and a teacher, Peter McLaren, illustrates again the reason for the impossibility associated with white male pedagogic self-reflection:

KE: This sociocultural "skewing" toward a White, majority population operates at many levels within the educational hierarchy, from teaching to research about teaching and schooling. Many of the most visible and vocal critical educators are

White males. Critical pedagogical discourse derives in part from an academic tradition created and shaped by Western European and Anglo-American thinkers. While we cannot deny that this work has contributed substantially to a praxis for interrogating the dominant world view, the most vehement criticism of critical pedagogy is that it really is all about White males speaking for everybody else.

PMcL: As a White male whose early years were working class and whose adolescence and years as a young adult were middle class, I need to consider my own positionality as an intellectual and social agent, to interrogate my own location in terms of the privilege it affords me. But I reserve the right to be part of a collective struggle for liberation. In taking part in such a struggle, however, all of us must be wary of speaking for others. Speaking to others and in solidarity with others does not exempt me from taking into account my own situatedness within the bourgeois academy. As difficult as it is, I do believe that intellectuals can and should make a difference through an active engagement in counter-hegemonic struggles of resistance to racism, sexism, homophobia, and capitalist exploitation in its many insidious formations.

A politics of insurgency and transformation needs sincere commitment through a decolonization of our dominant ideologies but also through concrete praxis in our daily lives as educators, as parents, as siblings, as lovers. Of course, we will make mistakes along the way, as well as discover inconsistencies and contradictions in our thinking and behaviour. (1993, p. 30)

Self-reflection or reexamination of "the oppressor" who has joined "the oppressed" must translate into concrete practice. All the awareness of one's location in terms of privilege will not produce change if it is limited by and based on a narrative of colonialism. McLaren "reserves the right [his right] to be part of a collective struggle for liberation," even though he understands the importance of

seeing himself as more than "just an ensemble of mentalistic observations or a cluster of organized perception;...[or] just inner thought
or thought connected to some transcendental source—[I am a]...his-
toricized, bounded subject" (1993; p. 29). As he points out, I am "a
white male whose early years were working class and whose adolescence and years as a young adult were middle class...." But what
does this look like in terms of being oppressive and dominating in
the academy? Why doesn't he move on to describe examples of his
oppressive practices as educator before denouncing oppression or
transcending into articulating his vision of liberation? Surely, epistemological engagements of liberation, transcendence, and so forth
do not fully disrupt the ontological traces of the self by the mere act
of articulation and/or enunciation.

When marginalized students ask white pedagogues not to speak
on their behalf or to expect them, when they (the students) speak,
to speak from a location of victimization, they are pointing to the
still unrealized privilege embedded in and driving the same master
to enter the classroom, only this time with talk about and against
oppression. White middle-class male heterosexual, critical pedagogues must remember that their bodies in classrooms become,
within an environment of transformation, grand symbols of privilege
and oppressiveness. Despite expanding the reading lists and course
topics to include material by bell hooks, Gayatri Chakravorty
Spivak, Audre Lourde, June Jordan, Trinh-Minh-ha, Himani Bannerji,
Patricia Hill Collins, to name a few, their bodies become the text,
the concrete material against which students of color, nonheterosexual, working class, and women in particular, read and learn to
refuse their albeit seductive, yet oppressive, power. It is painfully
obvious that students cannot and will not accept on good faith
alone that the pedagogue in their sensuous midst is not their
oppressor. Think back to all the disappointments, disapprovals, and
disturbances voiced by students in the classroom; think also about
the insidious overt or tacit attacks by privileged students toward the
teacher who is ostensibly not male, not white, not heterosexual, not
middle class—all of these portray time and time again that what we
need is not yet another rendering of the Freirian analyses or some

such reworked formulation against oppression. What we need is for each of us to get into our historicized bodies and practice daily acts of decolonization. And this could begin with people at the center of the academic circle; the possible move away could make much-needed room for thinking about conceptual and methodological ways of collapsing the split-off categories of race, sex, class, gender, ability, and nationalism. Feminists have revolutionized the working of the category "man." Imagine what we could do if we inseparably linked the identifiers "women and color and lesbian, or white and male and heterosexual and middle class." To start, people at the center must get embodied, while the rest must constantly refuse the temptation to abandon the way of knowing with and through our bodies.

The Moment Prior to Our Writing

The point of displaying excerpts from the transcriptions of our taped conversation is to implicitly expose the assumptions, desires, angers, frustrations, and expectations that we each brought to the other, in an attempt to dialogically collaborate on a common project:

George Dei (GD):

> Okay, I want to take up two things that you mentioned, this whole idea of privileging and also how we, maybe, mediate our existence within the academy. Let's start with the whole issue of me as a pedagogue…. The way I present my views in the classroom, for example, by way of instruction or by way of interaction with the students, could be construed or could be seen as a way of maybe maintaining my privilege?…

Anita Sheth (AS):

> Yes, but I would prefer if we start with asking ourselves why we engaged in this project from our differentially located positions. What is driving us, what motivates us, you as teacher, me as student, to sit together like this…

GD: Sure, the whole issue of academic credentialization is relevant here. But also there is the political project. The current legitimate call for the school system and the academy to recognize the contributions and achievement of peoples of color and their societies to academic scholarship and world civilization, coupled with the heightened sense of racial, ethnic, and cultural pride of minority peoples in Euro-American society, presents other challenges to the nonwhite pedagogue. There is some sense that the community has invested in the minority scholar for him or her to give something back by way of either developing a critical voice that articulates the vision of what it is to be a minority scholar and also to help "uplift" the community. As a minority scholar I cannot afford not to be concerned with the larger educational context in which I teach....

AS: But as a student, I am growing weary of the articulations. There is a major dissonance between what you and other pedagogues say and write and how you all are in practice. I am not saying all the teachers are the same, that would be ridiculous at best and politically ignorant at worst. But I wonder constantly about this dislocation, I wonder about what it means to be a faculty member in terms of power relations, I wonder why faculty do not do more than name this privilege. I seem to find the pedagogue constantly talking on behalf of students, talking as if they understand the daily plight of students. Perhaps this is partially because all faculty have been students, so they remember the "times"; they can recall what student life was about. In a sense, how could one forget what one knows? But here's the problem. While you spend time telling me, you are not spending the time thinking of yourself concretely as a faculty member, who earns "X" number of dollars, who has "X" presentations to do in places never visited before, who has real power as a producer and disseminator of knowledge, who has a benefits package that is almost unmatched, who has tenure, and therefore can and does express controversial opinions with virtually no risk. I am aware that white, heterosexual, middle-class faculty members are the supreme powerholders, but we, in being part of the academy one way or another, are forced from within our different locations to play this oppressive educational game. I do not want to belittle the hardships associated with some faculty members; I do see that you are all exhausted all of the time. The more marginalized you are, the more intolerable it is, but I also wonder in the name of what, why do you live and work like this?

GD: As a pedagogue, I see my political project to build a contour around a political difference for antiracist, antisexist, anticlassist and antihomophobic work. I would like to be part of a community of scholars—by that I mean, teachers, researchers, students, administrators working in the academy, and with the wider society, for a radical transformation of the structures within which learning, teaching, and administration of education take place. This project entails a transformation of the power structures and positional inequalities within the school system to give junior faculty, students, and the public a voice in the running of the schools. It also entails working to redesign schooling to include learning and other pedagogical styles not typical of ideas and thoughts of the dominant groups who define the institutional practices of society, and who have served to oppress nonmainstream groups in society. But, for a nonwhite, junior faculty, a political project to transform the institution in which we work can be compromised when the pedagogue is oppressed by institutional demands and structures that privilege academic credentializations of "scholarly" writing and publishing over all other endeavours. This is where my disappointment comes in as a pedagogue. There are certain things that I want to see done by way of radical transformation, but I am aware of the political risk of talking, from a location of real experience of what is happening in the mainstream, patriarchal academy, as a nonwhite, junior pedagogue. To a large extent, mainstream, tenured white faculty do not have to worry about these risks.

AS: I understand this...I empathize and work hard as a student to fight against this in meeting upon meeting without a salary, without money. Actually, if you consider the fact that I pay tuition fees and don't spend my time concentrating on finishing my doctoral thesis, you see how students are indirectly paying money to sit on committees instead of receiving money either in the form of salaries or honoraria. However, my point is that you cannot put yourself "on the same side" as students. I grant you that all students are not the same; we have differences among us, too. But the question becomes, why haven't we organized education as a union? Why haven't you been self-reflective or acknowledged that perhaps you, or I for that matter, didn't try hard enough, that maybe there is some complacency here, that maybe, just maybe, there is no political vision, that sociology needs oppression to be the sociology as it is practiced here. Critical pedagogy can be wonderfully seductive in its appeal to marginalized voices, but there is a real danger, a real pain, a real betrayal when it is not practiced.

GD: Let me put my response in a form of a question. Do you think we can have a forum for education that would overthrow the status quo?

AS: If you don't believe this, then why do you bring into your classroom all the seductive texts that gesture toward this stand? I mean, can you imagine how many articles and books handed out to students contain debate about education, change, and revolution? If you don't believe this, why do you conduct your classroom as if this were possible? I am angry, I am sorry, but I think back to all the stories I have heard of students spending hours on the phone, or in the bars, or in lounges arguing with one another about making a difference in fundamentally changing education, which also means you as the pedagogue, and me as the student, not just some abstract notion of the academy. Don't you see that some students do believe, or else why would they spend hours sitting on committees to end racism, sexism, homophobia, etc., in the academy? Are we being innocent, idealistic, reactionary, what? I mean, we must also think of this in terms of student suicides, dropouts....

GD: You have misheard my question. I am not disagreeing with the issues you have raised, I am wondering about your construction of education as a site for radical change, and your construction of faculty as members standing commonly and equally against oppression. Also, I want to address the issue of speaking from our individual locations and try to understand that critically as bourgeois ideology. Do you see the contradictions between the emphasis of talking from individual locations, and trying to individualize?

AS: I am not talking about individualizing location. I am saying, if you, who are located differently, are going to speak on my behalf, you are rendering me absent, you cannot speak for me. Emotively I want to hold the position that if each of us absolutely policed ourselves in this, if we each acknowledged our limitations, then each of us would be forced to look at ourselves, you as a faculty member would be forced to submit to the fact that you are a member of a group, and that group you belong to has a culture. It is only then that you can talk with me or I with you. Furthermore, you would see the importance of not analyzing the "problem of dropouts," or racism, or whatever is "out there," but in here as well. Why can't all faculty twin their research of the "out there" with the "in here" in the academy? I am not making a claim for the individually interested self. I hope you can hear me say that I want to disallow the tourism, the voyeuristic publishing pleasure and reward that comes with looking yonder in explaining the other.

GD: But isn't there a limitation in being preoccupied with location, isn't there a real danger of falling into bourgeois ideology...?

AS: What do you mean "falling into it?" We are already in it. I think we have to acknowledge this every time we put pen to paper. If I don't do it, you don't do it, and the other person doesn't do it, then we are operating in bourgeois ideology; we in the academy, and they in the CocaCola industry. It's our business to talk against oppression, just as it's their business to produce Coke cans. Our greed for knowledge is their greed for money.

GD: Now are you saying that just because a faculty member has a paid job, or anyone for that matter, we cannot talk about being oppressed? I hear what you are saying, you are raising important issues, but can you clarify this for me?

AS: I cannot answer this...I don't know if I can tell you what I really think....

GD: Why is this, what are you resisting, what are you afraid of...?

AS: ...that I am angry...

GD: What are you angry at?

AS: This is exactly the problem I see with Freire saying that because he did not concretely take part in revolutionary action this does not disqualify him from reflecting on the theme (can you believe he used this word?) of oppression. And of course he did not only reflect, he also commented—yes. This thinking is dangerous; it is also quite a standard white male academic practice. If pushed to all its limits, it could make possible the oppressor speaking for the oppressed. It's voyeuristic at best and I am sure I will be charged with essentialism here. In response to this charge however, I would ask, before the so-called "identity politics" debate, couldn't the white, male, middle-class, heterosexual, academic, who exploded utterances on behalf of the rest of us, be said to be operating from within an antiessentialist frame. But this is an aside, and I know it does not answer your question...But maybe it does, indirectly.

GD: Yes, I think you have answered me indirectly.

Refusing the Master's Tools

The task of speaking the truth is an infinite labour; to respect it in its complexity is an obligation that no power can afford to shortchange, unless it would impose the silence of slavery.

M. Foucault, *Foucault Live*, p. 308

To resituate Foucault's question of the insane subject, we ask how can one tell the truth of our perpetrations in the classroom and belong at the same time to the identifiable "marginalized group," and at what cost, when those of the "perpetrator group" fail to give voice to their unspeakable acts of violence even while theoretically opposing oppression? By asking this we do not wish to invoke queries of multiple subjectivities or rethematize the internalizations of oppression by "the oppressed" or unsettle the now obvious erroneous split between "the oppressor" and "the oppressed." Our purpose is to drag our bodies into our very own printed articulations. This is a difficult task, because we are also well trained in the academic habit of decapitating to enunciate. The act of refusing to transcend our bodies, then, is not an act performed at the confessional; neither is it a passive-aggressive move to shore up the cowardice/hypocrisy implicit in the silencing of the repressed by the centrally situated "progressive" pedagogue. On the contrary, our telling is aimed at "interrogat[ing] the painful ironies of being implicated in the forms of power that (we) explicitly oppose" (Butler, 1992; P. 84), through another's sensuous gaze and expression. While Freire did not account for the realities of living in bodies that are not white, male, heterosexual, he did extend a reading for the duality experienced in being at one and the same time "the oppressed" and the "host" of "the oppressor." He notes, "... *to be is to be like, and to be like is to be like the oppressor...*" (p. 33).

GD: Tammy Smith, a white Canadian female graduate student in my class on "The Sociology of Race and Ethnic Relations" pointed out that during various times in class discussions she felt that she was being silenced. While she did not directly accuse me of silencing her, the implication I made as a black male teacher of her statement to the effect that the class overdiscussed race at the price of gender was exactly this. At the time, my response was that I regarded her intervention as unfair since at no point had I or any other student prevented her or anyone from bringing up legitimate concerns of the issues raised. I seriously believed that the class had adequately explored the interlocking systems of oppression and was certain that no student was being silenced by any other or me for that matter. At the end of the class, Tammy handed me the notes she kept of the course. In her notes, I read her description of class events as she experienced these events in her body. Although she repeatedly questioned her race privilege over me while taking the risk to voice out her concern, at no time did I in the class or immediately thereafter consider my gender and status/job privilege over her. In fact, my reaction to her statement about gender was leveled to dismiss what she raised as an unacceptable dynamic. After all, it is not unfamiliar for non-white faculty to experience white students practising everyday racism in the classrooms.

GD: Reflecting back on that moment now, I must submit that this was really the first time that I acknowledged to myself my gender, job/status privilege in the classroom beyond the peripheral admittance of it as manifested in my course material, presentations, and discussion with students. Ironically, it is only when I understood Tammy, through my experience of being marginalized as a black male faculty member (the only one here) did I concretely grasp the sexist violence that I am capable of extending. I am now more than ever aware that in my current position (and while debating and struggling against race oppression), I might be marginalizing women and other students oppressed by reason of their class and sexuality. However, equally relevant to my self-reflection was her diary. Had she not handed it to me or written at length about her contradiction in being white and female, I do not think I would have had the occasion to "dialogically" learn.

AS: In December of 1992, a Women of Colour Caucus meeting was set up to organize, among other things, a memorial service for Audre Lorde. Kelly McDowell, a student of Black African-American and white Quebec background, months later in a private conversation indicated to me that I was brutal and abusive in the way I talked to the women of color in that December meeting. I was shocked and extremely disturbed by her accounting of the events. I tried to justify my actions on political grounds, even before I could fully grasp what was being conveyed to me. The following was my justification:

AS: Here were "these" women talking about reading poetry, eating lunches together, and celebrating our new space, while upstairs on that same afternoon the administrators were discussing budget cuts. Earlier that day, I had attended a three-hour-long emergency council meeting on ways the institute planned to reduce its budget. None of these students were present; I was the only person of color in the room. Among the suggestions made was a freeze on new initiatives that the institute had committed itself to. This directly meant that the lobbying efforts by people of color in the past for antiracist education, the hiring of nonwhite faculty, and funding research projects on and by nonwhite people would be adversely affected. After attending this institute meeting and an hour into the Women of Colour Caucus meeting, I entered with the sole purpose of mobilizing the women here to take action. Not at all mindful or respectful of what was already in process, I became angry at listening to discussion of lunches and celebrations. I self-righteously judged this situation as once again indicative of the profound lack of understanding of the institute by its students and the times we faced as nonwhite people, particularly women, in academia. I did not feel like eating or celebrating; basically I was sickened at what I had just heard in the institute council meeting!

AS: Most of the students present at the caucus meeting, as I assessed them with prejudice of ageism, were new and some extremely young. The organizer, whom I knew was also young but not new, had never attended any institute meetings. Also I understood that she was being paid a minimal amount of money in the form of an assistantship to set up a Women of Colour group as suggested by the predominantly white Centre for Women Studies to whom she was responsible. Furthermore, I had heard that this center offered us, women of color, Cdn$500 to pay for the memorial service for Audre Lorde, and that the organizer accepted this on our behalf without asking questions as to why we were nominated to organize this service, especially when we as a group had never been recognized. I may well have projected the meeting held upstairs about budget cuts onto this group. Anyhow, these were my thoughts, and I must admit that while they did affect the way I conducted myself, they do not fully explain the preconceived notions I had of the women seated in a semicircle, with the organizer at the point of view.

AS: My anger with the organizer manifested itself indirectly in the way I contributed to the discussion. In fact, my presence and talk stopped the discussion from taking place and did not acknowledge the other women present. So preoccupied was I with the institute's cutbacks and my anger at the organizer that I failed to realize that the women who came to the Women of Colour Caucus meeting were here to find a safe place. Instead, I went back-and-forth disruptively with the organizer, whom I knew did not have any knowledge of the recent moves taken by the administrators; I referenced minutes from meetings that I knew she was not aware of, I talked about policies and past history—locking myself in a power game; misdirecting anger at racism as if it were only a concern to me and not to all present. I was angered at the fact that I, as a woman of color, made it my business to lobby the decisionmakers to deliver on the institute's antiracist mandate not without risks, and that the organizer had not bothered to show up at these meetings. Unlike her, I am not Canadian I thought; no one was paying me money to go to meetings. Of course I never did address any of this directly at the meeting.

AS: Kelly's comment that I was practicing everything that I talked about opposing, reoccurred to me in thinking through the power imbalances between me, a post-resident, Ph.D. student, the organizer, a Ph.D. student in residence, and Kelly, a first year M.A student. Ironically, the only way this back-and-forth between the organizer and me ended was when Kelly, who at the December meeting did not know either of us, intervened and acknowledged both our positions. In feeling the effects of racism at the institute that day, had I then to be oppressive to the very people who had not caused it, particularly the organizer who spent many hours in bringing us together? Of course not. I talked to Kelly (perhaps at her) as our relationship developed outside the academic setting, as I had talked to others long before, about doing things differently, about listening across borders, about a pedagogy that did not make the Other "feel less than," no matter who the Other is, about building community, about feminist antiracist, antihomophobic collective participation. Yet, in this first historic meeting I could not deliver. In this reflective moment and with the help of Kelly's initial questioning, I now ask, has my desire for doing things differently been simply a desire for articulating a space in which the historically silenced self now reinvents itself as noisily enunciative? And if so, does not "difference" then become a way for me to reinscribe my middle-class privilege, which is needless to say repeatedly rewarded in the white, heteropatriarchal, middle-class talkativeness of the academy? After the Caucus agreed to write a letter registering our concerns about the impending budget cuts that would negatively impact on the antiracist educational efforts already in place, I left and never did attend another Women of Colour meeting. Incidentally, Kelly was one of the two members who wrote this letter on our behalf. Unfortunately, as things turned out, we never did hold a memorial service for Audre Lorde, although I am told that we still have the Cdn.$500 to organize it.

"Those of us who stand outside the circle...know that *survival is not an academic skill*...It is learning how to take our differences and make them strengths. *For the master's tool will never dismantle the master's house*. They may allow us temporarily to beat him at his own game, but they will never enable us to bring about genuine change. And this fact is only threatening to those women who still define the master's house as their only source of power." (Audre Lorde, 1984; p.112)

While the practices of naming our oppressive acts, as marginalized people, work to disclose the shifting positionalities of our identities as constructed upon us and as constructing out of us, they also work to preempt critique by either the historically transfixed or fictively transitory Other. In the act of offering you (e.g., who are white/transitory Other) my stories of domination, I am rendered tolerable by virtue of your guilt or punishable by virtue of your prejudice. However, the same stories offered to you (e.g., who are not white/transfixed Other), renders me suspect by virtue of your knowing or inclusive by virtue of your solidarity. In the case of tolerance, I revictimize myself for I call upon the guilty among you to legitimate my acts of violence. In the case of punishment, I make myself simple-mindedly heroic, for I want to deny that you still have a hold on me. In the case of suspicion, you remind me that the "master's games" will be punishable if played in the "servant's house." In the case of inclusion, you tolerate me for you hope that my presence will also mean your presence.

Since the occasions to punish in the academy far outnumber the occasions to tolerate, we, who are marginalized while enunciatively struggling against oppression, choose to revictimize ourselves as a way of holding on to the positions minimally allotted to us. Accordingly, we too erroneously force a disassociation of radical politics from the ground on which they were first envisioned. In so doing, we reconstitute the practices of lifting words out of the bodies that produce them, dressing them up, and appropriately immersing them into the various academic discourses that claim transformation, inclusivity, liberation, truth, and union. As any insider knows, the more unintelligible your words appear to be in the knowledge-based discourses, the more power they seem to have.

Robin Tolmach Lakoff (1990), in "The Grooves of Academe," provides an explicit and uncompromising account of the talking powers of universities, implicating all its members from tenured faculty right down to undergraduates. She writes:

> But the university alone trades only in language, discourse, communication. The university's only acts are speech acts, in Austin's sense. Truth and knowledge are linguistic entities, existing only through and in language. Only for the university is language an end in itself. Therefore (one might argue) the members of university ought to be especially skillful communicators, since that is all they have to offer and this is solely how they achieve their effects.
>
> Well but…
>
> …Our power, our authority is intertwined with our ability to maintain secrets even as we seem to dispense them. We write and speak, but we do not communicate. This is our art." (p. 146)

The Politics of Limitations as Situated in the Self Reflective

Our desire to return Freire his body in the act of reading *Pedagogy of the Oppressed* back to him, impossible as this may be, produces in us a passionate refusal to maintain secrets. Yet our collaborative writing is full of haunting silences. Academia as a licensed site for the search for knowledge has imprisoned freedom, and in so doing, has paradoxically built into its arresting structures the willfully unattainable demand to communicate. Why else do we often find the same few centrally located, "progressive" pedagogues in talking about the importance of not "speaking *to* or *at* others but *with* others dialogically" and so on, use so much paper to produce singularly authored multiple monologues on this very thought? If one were to follow through on this evocatively brilliant suggestion, then readers would not have to put up much longer with reading the works of the same few authors, regardless of the alerted and therefore expected differences in titles of courses taken. Writers, on the other hand, would become not only more environmentally conscious but also realize that a thought worth expressing is the one that has withstood the test of self-practice. After all, it is in practice alone that we find the powerful effects of communication. However, given that that is not what happens in academia, the disappearance of the artwork around the appearance of communication necessitates, then, that the self-reflective actively enter the length and breath of our bodies and refuse to leave, particularly at the moments of the self-desiring to break into repetitious, voyeuristic enunciations. The truth shall not set us free because the truth is always the truth of the Other, and not of oneself in the act of meeting the Other.

As we have noted, we too are guilty of this, and in having now repeated it, deceptively co-opted the critique once again. But the intervention is made here to flag the beckoning call for "limitations." Freire talks about self-reflection and does not practice it. Of course, to practise it on the page is to render it to textual imprisonment which invokes a further limitation of "the possible" through the dominant medium of academia. Academia in turn poses its own limits on who says what to whom and how. However, this is not a vicious circle of realizing the impossible, but a temptation to return to our bodies and notice the frustrations, tiredness, denials, and secrets out of which we differently create our works of liberation, transformation, revolution, emancipation, and dreams. Learning to make each work a lived moment of communicative embodiment in

academia entails understanding the power that is possible in knowing one's own limitations. For to limit would mean to limit to the
body, and to limit to the body would mean only speaking through
the body as opposed to out of it. If Freire did practice self-reflectiv-
ity, he would have known that telling "the oppressed" that it is only
in freeing themselves that they free "the oppressor" positions him in
a place that we hear him wanting to reject. Just as we, in telling you
our acts of violence could be read as wanting to rid ourselves of the
guilt in having to carry these acts around noiselessly, especially after
insisting on the importance of embodiment.

Postscript

GD: I have reflected over some of the things we have talked
about in this chapter. I have been attentive to some of the
concerns you have narrated as you critique your own place
and location in the academy. There is another thing I find
very interesting working in the academy and though you
alluded to it somewhat, I think we have not directly spoken
about it. This has to do with what I perceive as the chase of
knowledge and the ownership of ideas. As a pedagogue I
am guilty about how I negotiate the search for knowledge
and recognition. But I also find students here to have uncritically bought some of the trappings of the pursuit of knowledge and recognition in the academy. Why do I get the
sense that within this institution, and you know what I
mean, there is, to borrow your own words the other day, "a
price tag dangling out of the mouth of students." What I
mean by this is we have a situation here, where you hear
some students complaining about professors stealing their
ideas to publish them first, that the student was the first to
use this phrase or to work in this area and so forth, and that
a professor goes to a conference and never acknowledges
the ideas he or she has "stolen" from students in a classroom
presentation or what have you. Anita, tell me, because you
also hear this all the time, tell me why this is so and how

does one account for this claim to ownership of ideas? Aren't we all using each other's ideas? If as a pedagogue I am "guilty" of the charge of not acknowledging students' ideas, why should students in the classes I teach also not be guilty of using other students' and the professors' ideas. I am not simply talking about the "guilt." You and I know that students also write term papers and publish papers without acknowledging that they developed some thoughts through interactions with a particular professor, student(s), and people who do not have the privilege of studying here but nevertheless generate critiques in the alternative films they produce, the music they sing, the poetry they write. They acknowledge what is in print, not the spoken words with a teacher or a fellow student over a cup of tea, coffee, lunch, or bottle of beer in the pub. Aren't students talking on the backs of other people all the time, or is it only professors who do that? Aren't professors and students both guilty of this?

AS: Yes, I did use the "price tag" visual the other day. As you know I have constantly questioned this for a few years now, arguing on both sides of the issue with my student colleagues. In every sense this is not a unique question. This is really the old question of power dressed up in this new postmodern context of shared faculty/student writing and/or presenting. If we engage this question of "whose idea was it first" within the broader context of pedagogy, publishing, and who gets to speak, a number of things come to light. At the forefront for me, anyway, is the experience that critical pedagogy is not simply content anymore, it is practice; it is a political tool, a questioning strategy by which to disrupt the older power and silencing relations that exist within formal educative sites. White feminists constantly question some white men in academia about employing ideas lifted from their writings without reference or trace. Feminists of color constantly question some white feminists and men of color for appropriating our work. White and nonwhite lesbians and gays question all heterosexuals for borrowing and reworking ideas generated in particular marginalized contexts to fit mainstream notions, and on and on it goes. This is not to be reductive about the power relations that continue to exist. Rather it is to acknowledge that with power differentials still operating, you must expect these critiques, perhaps even generate some on your own, as you are doing.

GD: I know what you mean and I have complained about some of these issues when, as a student myself, I want to move beyond the "power differential" here. Please don't tell me as pedagogues that what we are paid for, that is to teach and to present ideas and occasion dialogue with students. Remember, we are all learners...we are all students...we are all pedagogues, and we have the potential in the academy to speak on the backs of other people. I mean there are those people who do not have the privilege of being in the academy or who do not have the space and time to write and even to speak the way we are able to. What is the source of our knowledge? Is it only in lived experience, textbooks, and so forth. Are there other sources that can be located in our everyday conversations with people, with our families, or friends? And do we always acknowledge these sources? I guess what I am getting at is my concern with the claim of ownership of ideas, which is very pervasive among all of us who operate in the academy. I am not advancing the "reverse discrimination type" argument; instead, I want to point to the dynamics of social oppression. There is another matter, too. It goes to the heart of what it sometimes takes to go through smoothly in the academy. We criticize those pedagogues and educators who become part of the "establishment" and lose a critical perspective of social issues by operating in various capacities to maintain that status quo. But there are also students who play this game, too. I am not saying all students are like this. But there is an increasing number that, one can conveniently argue, do this all the time, sometimes without being aware of it or more so being critical of themselves. We always say students are powerless in much of their dealings with authority and teachers, that students cannot confront established authority without bearing the consequences or a huge academic and social cost. Sure, I know it has happened to some students who have been critical of their teachers. But the fact is many students are able to play the game well, as you know. These students relinquish their critical stance on issues once they are in the room with a professor or someone they are working with, such as a supervisor. How many times has a student said what the teacher wanted to hear? I did that as a student. I am talking about a case where the student may not want to offend or upset his or her supervisor or the teacher who has the power over the student in many ways. The student wants the degree, diploma for sure. The student wants the accreditation, the student wants validation. The student wants affirmation and legitimation. It depends on how you read these desires. The reality is this, students know the academic game and the politics so well, such that they can play it to perfection and sail through very smoothly. Don't get me wrong here. I am not talking about knowledge and expertise in a chosen field or topic. I am talking about the politics that students engage in within the academy. Some students learn to pick the "right" fights, that is, fights that least threaten their positions, goals, or ambition. They will kiss the right spots, even when deep in their hearts they would normally be doing something else. Sure, not all students do that, but for those who do, do we simply explain this politicking by reference to the enormous power of teachers/pedagogues over students? Do we simply say there is much "fear" among students and they learn to play the game or whatever it takes to "succeed" in the academy? I understand how institutional power structures manifest themselves in the lived experiences of a student in the

school system. But can we in any way critique those students who use the system in this way to satisfy their personal goals? How can we engage in transformative learning
if students are going to use the very institutional underpin-
nings of the academy to foster such myopic goals?

AS: Learning to play the game as you have indicated is partly
about survival, but it is survival for those who have some
kind of class, race, gender, and/or sexual privilege. Those
students who enter academia with all or any one of these
privileges are more capable of "mastering" the game than
those for whom these sites operate as oppression. But mastering the game does not, as Audre Lorde reminds me, "dismantle the master's house." I have never taught a class as a
faculty member, so all of what I have to say in this context
is traceable to my position as a student (albeit a Ph.D. student). I do agree we need to critique the practices by which
each of us puts our words out into the world. I do not mean
to be flippant. But it is a bit ironic that these questions per-
sist even though the postmodern academics are telling us
that there is no original text, which of course means that
even Marx's critique against the ownership of ideas is circu-
lating somewhere, undergoing some kind of identity crisis.
Perhaps this condition can be named the "crisis of copies."
The point is not who said it first, literally, or who said it most
recently, or who said it clearly, and so forth. It is I think a
question of who has publishing power and/or the power to
intellectualize in the academy. To some extent it is a claim
to knowledge, to know first, but in an industry that expects
its members to publish or perish, you can understand why
this kind of competition would set in. Surely, this occurs not
only between some students and faculty, but also and more
frequently, between faculty members. In any event, I would
like to say that you will find those students who do speak
up, who take risk, who do not care who took an idea from
whom, but who are pleased that an idea, and a revolution-

ary one at that, is held in common by more and more people and is almost there, finally awaiting its test in and
through practice.

GD: If we are going to talk about who has the power to intellectualize, and put faculty on the side of the dominant
power relations, then you are marginalizing students even
further, which is not what I think you want to do. The question is not simply describing the relations of power but
changing the very dynamic in which these questions are
engaged. Further, I want to critique the notion of intellectu-
alizing power and edge forward in the debate of knowledge
production in the academy, literally reentering the question
of who has the power to produce and who does not. I think
it will take further collaboration not only with other students
but with colleagues to really tackle the kernel of change that
is already occurring in the academy.

ACKNOWLEDGMENTS

George Dei thanks Nigel Moses and colleagues (students, faculty, staff, friends, and family) for their critical engagement with him as pedagogues, learners, and activists. Anita Sheth thanks George Dei for sharing so generously his invitation/opportunity to publish with her. It must be said, at the risk of being so obviously redundant, that without this collaboration across difference, a dialogic engagement of the issues as Freire intended it would not have been possible. Anita also thanks Kelly McDowell for occasioning an unforgettable learning about the importance of the self-reflective and the power of dialogic listening. As well, she thanks Tony Xerri for his help in clarifying some of the ideas and checking the spelling in the document, Rinaldo Walcott for asking important questions, and Arleen Schenke, who constantly encouraged her to keep at it, despite frustration and silences. George and Anita thank Adrienne Churchill for transcribing the audiotapes, and Olga Williams for her assistance in putting together this chapter from its various computer versions.

REFERENCES

Butler, J., "The Body You Want," *Artform*, November, 1992. New York.

Deleuze, G., in C. Owens, "The Indignity of Speaking for Others: An Imaginary Interview," *Beyond Recognition: Representation, Power and Culture* (Berkeley: University of California Press, 1992).

Estrada, K, and P. McLaren, "A Dialogue on Multiculturalism and Democratic Culture," *Educational Researcher*, vol. 22, no. 3, pp. 27-33 (1993).

Freire, P., *Pedagogy of the Oppressed* (New York: The Continuum Publishing, 1988).

Foucault, M., *Foucault Live* (New York: Semiotext(e), 1989).

hooks, b., and M. Childers, "A Conversation about Race and Class," in M. Hirsch, and E. Fox Keller, eds., *Conflicts in Feminism* (New York: Routledge, 1990).

Lorde, A., *Sister/Outsider* (New York: The Crossing Press, 1984).

Minh-ha, T., *Framer Framed* (New York: Routledge, 1992).

Tolmach Lakoff, R., "The Grooves of Academe" in *Talking Power: the Politics of Language* (New York: Basic Books, 1990).

Taylor, S., "Skinned Alive: Towards a Postmodern Pedagogy of the Body," *Education and Society*, vol. 9, no. 1, pp. 61-71 (1991).

Xerri, T., in conversation. OISE, Toronto, 1993.

CHAPTER NINE

LOVE AND HISTORY IN THE WORK OF PAULO FREIRE

James W. Fraser

There is in Paulo Freire, in his writing, his speaking, and his personal presence, a profound sense of love, humility, and rootedness in life and in the present historical moment.[1] In other times and traditions, Paulo Freire would be seen as not only a great teacher but also a spiritual guide.

For very understandable reasons, most North American educators ignore this aspect of Freire's life and work. We are uncomfortable with "religious" language, we have fought too many battles to keep a range of religious dogma out of the schools, and we have seen the escapism and the sheer mean spiritedness of much of what passes for religiosity in this country, whether of the fundamentalist, mainstream, or the New Age type. But ignoring spirituality, ignoring Freire's own power as a "spiritual guide" is both a distortion of his work and an unnecessary impoverishment of our own understanding of the world.

The purpose of this chapter is, then, to engage in a dialogue with Paulo Freire about faith and spirituality—about love and history. The goal is not to "baptize" Freire or to impose a religious theme on his writings that he would not own. Nor is the goal to apply the work of Paulo Freire to the specific educational concerns of churches; that is a different, although also useful task. The focus of this chapter, however, is to seek an understanding of the sense of the spirit—the sense of love and history—that runs through all of Paulo Freire's work.

There is always danger in this undertaking—a danger with which all great teachers have had to contend. On the one hand, there is the danger of mushy sentimentality. Love in the writing of

Paulo Freire is a very different and much tougher force than love in popular culture; it is an active commitment and not a passive and often selfish emotion. On the other hand, there is the danger of making Freire a saint, cut off from human reality. There is a long tradition of this sort of division between symbolic leaders and the movements with which they are connected. Indeed, such a split is one of the primary ways the dominant culture tames revolutionary individuals and movements. No one would insist more strongly than Freire himself that we must beware of this reality. As Stanley Aronowitz notes, "The name of Paulo Freire has reached near iconic proportions in the United States, Latin America and, indeed, in many parts of Europe."[2] The point of this chapter is not expanding any sense of Freire as icon but on the contrary with learning from Freire and engaging with Freire in terms of ways of living in and viewing the world that can serve the process of individual and political liberation in the North American context at the end of the twentieth century.

In spite of these dangers, let me proceed then with the discussion of three significant points that run through all of Paulo Freire's writings: his deep respect for every person, evinced in his insistence that the oppressed never be seen as a group to be led nor as individuals in need of salvation by a vanguard, but rather as creators of their own liberation; second, his call for humility on the part of all educators in light of this need for mutual respect between teacher and learner; and finally, the deep rooting of his pedagogy in history, and in the flesh and blood reality of human existence.

For Paulo Freire, Revolutionary Pedagogy Begins with a Profound Sense of Respect and Love.

The Cuban revolutionary Che Guevara once said, "Let me say, with the risk of appearing ridiculous, that the true revolutionary is guided by strong feelings of love. It is impossible to think of an authentic revolutionary without this quality."[3] Commenting on this statement in *Pedagogy of the Oppressed*, Paulo Freire notes:

> I am more and more convinced that true revolutionaries must perceive the

revolution, because of its creative and liberating nature, as an act of love...The distortion imposed on the word "love" by the capitalist world cannot prevent the revolution from being essentially loving in character, nor can it prevent the revolutionaries from affirming their love of life.[4]

To miss this powerful understanding of love and a love of life is to miss the heart of Freirian pedagogy. In Freire's work, love is always a matter of agency—of commitment and action for justice. Neither sympathy nor mere concern nor resignation is an ingredient in this kind of love.

Paulo Freire's sense of love and respect for all people, so evident in his personal presence, is stated most clearly in *Pedagogy of the Oppressed* as he insists, "No matter where the oppressed are found, the act of love is commitment to their cause—the cause of liberation. And this commitment, because it is loving, is dialogical. An act of bravery, love cannot be sentimental; as an act of freedom, it must not serve as a pretext for manipulation."[5] This commitment to a love that demands a dialogue of mutual respect is at the core of his pedagogy of liberation.

In Freire's work, this notion of loving pedagogy demands that the teacher always begin with a deep respect for all students, for what they can bring to the dialogue that will make it richer for everyone. At the same time, the teacher must begin with a commitment to social and political liberation that will change the objective conditions of the world. Hence, the use of dialogue does not merely support individual growth in a given context but also the growth of a more democratic society.

For Freire, this level of respect and love for all means that each individual must be the maker of her or his own liberation. There can be no liberation—that is truly liberating—that is imposed from above, no matter how good the intentions. There can be no statements like, "we need to educate people so that...." It is reasonable to say that we will join with others in a mutual process of education, and it is reasonable to say that we will bring our special skills, perspective, and ideology to the educational dialogue. But we cannot bring an "agenda" that excludes the agendas of others, nor can we fail to see the essential contribution others will make to the very content of liberation in a given historical context.

Long before Paulo Freire, an ancient Chinese sage wrote:

Can you love people and lead them
without imposing your will?
Can you deal with the most vital matters
by letting events take their course?
Can you step back from your own mind and thus understand all things?
Giving birth and nourishing,
having without possessing,
acting with no expectations,
leading and not trying to control:
this is the supreme virtue.[6]

In these words the author of the *Tao te Ching* summarized a very Freirian approach to life, and to education.

The failure of many well-intentioned pedagogical projects is based on the failure of their initiators to "act with no expectations," or "lead without trying to control." It is a healthy part of human nature that most people resent imposition, even the imposition of very well-intentioned programs for their own uplift by people who are not in true solidarity with them. Freire gives an excellent example of this kind of resentment when he tells the story of an educator working in the rural northeast of Brazil who long sought an invitation to join the weekly meeting of a group of peasants in the area. Finally one day, the invitation came and with it the following introduction from the leader of the group:

We have something very important to tell you, new friend. If you're here to teach us that we're exploited, don't bother. We know that already. What we don't know...and need to know from you...is, if you're going to be with us when the chips are down.[7]

Thus solidarity must precede intellectual analysis and the willingness to listen and learn must always be part of any effort to teach, much less lead.

At the same time, it is essential to note that Freirian education, while it leaves no room for imposition, also does not mean that the educator is in any way passive. It has become popular in some circles to embrace a pedagogy that seems to begin with the question, "So what do you all think?" It has even become popular at times to call this a Freirian approach. Some educators seem reluctant to own their own voice at all. This is not at all what Freire means. In his autobiographical reflections, *Letters to Christina*, he returns to his insistence that while teachers and learners must maintain a mutual respect and a mutual willingness to listen to the other, their roles are different. The fact that educators and learners must share a mutual commitment to expanding knowledge and to building a better world, "does not nullify the specific role of each one. The former are subjects of the act of teaching; the latter are subjects of the act of learning. The former learn as they teach; the latter teach as they learn. They are all subjects of the knowing process, which involves teaching and learning." And, at the same time, the process of teaching and learning is an ethical process and not a "neutral endeavor." Nevertheless, it "must not lead educators to impose, subliminally or not, their taste on learners, whatever those tastes may be. This is the ethical dimension of educational practice." And without the ethical dimension there is no respect or ultimately any meaningful education.[8]

From the beginning of his work, Freire has insisted, "It is not our role to speak to the people about our own view of the world, nor to attempt to impose that view on them, but rather to dialogue with the people about their view *and ours*" (emphasis added).[9] The failure to own one's own voice is as demeaning as it is to demand that all buy in to one's own agenda. Both perspectives are based on a kind of elitism in which the educator sees himself or herself as quite separate from, and very much above, the students. Freire is very clear in his criticism of educators who speak passionately about their concern to go to the community or to the poor, but do so in a way that always reinforces their own separate position above and apart from "the people."[10]

An education that preserves the educator's "objective distance" can never be loving in the way Freire describes it, for it is not based on respect. Such an education fails to see that "Dialogue, as the encounter of men [and women] addressed to the common task of learning and acting, is broken if the parties (or one of them) lack humility."[11] Freirian education takes courage and real humility—not an artificial mask of humility—so that a mutual dialogue of authentic speaking and listening is possible.

There have also been others who gave voice to a similar approach to love, to revolution, and to education. There are points when Paulo Freire begins to sound very much like the great Jewish philosopher mystic Martin Buber when he asks:

> How can I dialogue if I always project ignorance onto others and never perceive my own? How can I dialogue if I regard myself as a case apart from other [women and] men—mere "its" in whom I cannot recognize other "I"s? How can I dialogue if I consider myself a member of the in-group of "pure" men, the owners of truth and knowledge, for whom all nonmembers are "these people" or "the great unwashed"?[12]

There is in this discussion of dialogue a strong sense of what Buber calls an "I-Thou" relationship. For Buber, "Relation is mutual. My Thou affects me, as I affect it. We are moulded by our pupils and built up by our works....We live our lives inscrutably included within the streaming mutual life of the universe."[13] And if we chose to cut ourselves off or set ourselves above the "streaming mutual life of the universe," we have cut ourselves off from what is most basic to our humanness.

While Buber writes of many kinds of relationships, he, like Freire, pays special attention to the relationship of teacher and pupil. And, in words that sound much like Freire, he says:

> In order to help the realisation of the best potentialities in the pupil's life, the teacher must really mean him as the definite person he is in his potentiality and his actuality; more precisely, he must not know him as a mere sum of qualities, strivings and inhibitions, he must be aware of him as a whole being and affirm him in this wholeness. But he can only do this if he meets him again and again as his partner in a bipolar situation. And in order that his effect upon him may be a unified and significant one he must also live this situation, again and again, in all its moments not merely from his own end but also from that of his partner: he must practise the kind of realisation which I call inclusion.[14]

Thus for both Freire and Buber, the student must always be seen as a whole person and never as a bundle of needs or potentialities. The student can never be used, can never be managed in the service of some greater end. For Buber the true "I-Thou" relationship is one in which the dialogue includes a love and mutuality between teacher and student.

Given this respect for the divine in each person, given the call for all educational dialogue to be an I-Thou relationship, education for liberation also precludes education for other lesser aims. It also precludes a relationship in which the educator refuses to enter into the lived situation of the student. We cannot educate for liberation and at the same time educate for regaining America's competitive edge in world markets. We also cannot educate for liberation and at the same time educate for a particular political perspective, even our own carefully worked out progressive agenda. We certainly bring all of our concerns and commitments, economic and political—and spiritual—to the educational process. We do not deny our own voice in the educational dialogue. But we cannot impose even the best of what we hope to offer. To do less is in Buber's words, to step back from the world of the "met" to the world of the "used." And at that moment education has lost its ethical referent and become something less.[15]

Lawrence Cremin was also challenging an impositional form of education when he wrote in *Popular Education and Its Discontents*:

> John Dewey liked to define the aim of education as growth, and when he was asked growth toward what, he liked to reply, growth leading to more growth. That was his way of saying that education is subordinate to no end beyond itself, that the aim of education is not merely to make parents, or citizens, or workers, or indeed to surpass the Russians or the Japanese, but ultimately to make human beings who will live life to the fullest, who will continually add to the quality and meaning of their experience and to their ability to direct that experience, and who will participate actively with their fellow human beings in the building of a good society. To create such an education will be no small task in the years ahead, but there is no more important political contribution to be made to the health and vitality of the American democracy and of the world community of which the United States is part.[16]

While I suspect Freire would always want to push Cremin to see more clearly the dangers of words like "education for growth" slipping into a comfortable acceptance of individual development within the context of privilege in North America, both would ultimately agree that education can never be used as a process of imposing an agenda—even a progressive agenda with which they might agree—on others. Education for Freire and Cremin is ultimately a political activity: a matter of constantly reinventing the meaning of power and democracy at a given time and place. Education as this kind of political activity is the opposite of ideological imposition. It is an activity in which teacher and learner share the task of building a new social order in which the very nature of power and politics is constantly being reconsidered.

When asked recently about the difficult issues facing a liberation movement that comes to power, Freire insisted: "We cannot merely take power, we must constantly remake the meaning of power with and for the people."[17] The educational nature of revolutionary struggle thus remains equally important at all stages of the process of liberation.

It has become popular to say, "we don't need to love each other, as long as we respect each other's rights." At the level of many daily interactions, of course, this is true. But in a larger sense, we cannot build the world we want if we do not love each other.

- We cannot deal with the sickness of a nation in which children go to bed hungry every night, if we do not love each other.

- We cannot deal with the wrong of a society that condemns certain groups of citizens to homelessness and unemployment, if we do not love each other.

- We cannot deal with an ecological crisis brought on by greed and over-consumption, if we do not love each other.

- We cannot deal with the fear and violence and prejudice that lurk in our cities, if we do not love each other.

There are, of course, social programs that are based on creating employment or feeding the hungry that are based on the self-preservation of an elite rather than love. There are also many who seek to solve poverty, homelessness, and crime by inducting a widely diverse range of people into a single Western way of living in the world. But these programs will ultimately fail, for they do not represent a society that is fueled by the strengths of its culturally diverse citizens.

A society worth living in must, in the long run, be a society that is truly built on the strengths and contributions of all of its citizens, in which the range of cultures contributes to the building of a new whole that is richer than even the best that any one part has to offer. But the building of that kind of culture demands that all citizens see in each other people who have important elements to contribute. And the building of that kind of culture also demands a clear recognition that not all players enter the dialogue with an equal share of power. Until power is redistributed, until power inequities are changed, and until the contribution of every citizen is valued, the major social problems of the day cannot be addressed in any fundamental structural way. To talk of the redistribution and redefinition of power in fundamental ways, to talk of building a new culture based on the contribution of every citizen, is to talk of revolutionary change. Thus the theme does remain the same. The true revolutionary is motivated by love.

Freire's understanding of the nature of pedagogy offers the potential to help progressive educators avoid two of the greatest pitfalls facing those who seek to build a better and more just world through education.

One of the tragedies of many twentieth-century revolutionary movements is their failure to attend to the fact that, "an act of freedom...must not serve as a pretext for manipulation." Thus, "Propaganda, management, manipulation—all arms of domination—cannot be the instruments of their rehumanization."[18] This theme has far too often been forgotten or temporarily put aside by revolutionary movements as they consolidate power in the name of the people, but not with the full participation of the people.

In his insistence on a dialogue of liberation, Freire is challenging one of the tragic flaws of much of twentieth century communism—its belief that a vanguard, which stands above the people and understands the revolutionary situation better than the people—will lead the rest to liberty. During the forty years after World War II, the educational systems in much of eastern Europe modeled this vanguard philosophy. The schools taught the "truth" to students. Often the textbooks—in their critique of capitalism and imperialism, in their sophisticated approach to anti-Semitism, Fascism, and revolutionary struggle—represented a very liberating view of the world and of human beings in the world. But sadly the pedagogy was as repressive as the content was liberating. Students were expected to take the texts as received truth, to learn the "right" answers, and to avoid questioning the truth whether or not it made sense to them. In these settings, the guiding assumption of the educators seemed to be that the youth, like the masses, were both ignorant and largely incapable of self-determination.

George Counts, a radical educator of the first half of the twentieth century, noted with irony the pedagogical approach which teaches the "truth" to the people. In 1932, describing one of his own visits to the new Soviet Union in the 1920s, he wrote of a conversation with:

> Mr. Lunacharsky, Commissar of Education in the Russian Republic until 1929, [who] assured me on one occasion that the Soviet educational leaders do not believe in the indoctrination of children in the ideas and principles of communism. When I asked him whether their children become good communists while attending the schools, he replied that the great majority do. On seeking from him an explanation of this remarkable phenomenon he said that Soviet teachers merely tell their children the truth about human history. As a consequence, so he asserted, practically all of the more intelligent boys and girls adopt the philosophy of communism. I recall also that the Methodist sect in which I was reared always confined its teachings to the truth![19]

Clearly confining teachings to the "truth" is not sufficient for a liberating pedagogy.

A tragic result of this misguided pedagogy is that, with the end of communist regimes throughout eastern Europe at the end of the

1980s, the students who were never given any chance for dialogue with the world view presented in their texts are now—in an act of personal liberation but political folly—rejecting all of what was taught. If a liberating subject matter was taught through a highly repressive pedagogy, many now seem to argue, the only solution is to reject all of what was called "truth"—including the critique of the dehumanizing effects of capitalism and imperialism, including also the critique of anti-Semitism and fascism. All of this is, as Freire insists, a byproduct of "The mistake of the Left, or a sector of the Left, today and yesterday," which is "the desire for authoritarianism, a by-product of the Left's dislike for democracy, which it views as incompatible with socialism."[20] The results for the world may yet be tragic indeed.

Eastern Europe today is going through many of the psychological aspects of decolonization experienced in much of Asia and Africa during the last several decades. A ruling power has been totally discredited. The situation in some parts of the former Soviet world resembles that described by Frantz Fanon: "without any period of transition, there is a total, complete, and absolute substitution...[a] *tabula rasa* which characterizes at the outset all decolonization."[21] But the parallels with decolonization also have their limits. How would Fanon have described a colonial class which used an ideal of human liberation in the process of subjugation? How can a people free themselves of the psychological curse of living under an oppressive system of government and education yet hold to some of the liberating ideals and resources of that same world view?

If only the communist leaders had heeded Freire's warning, "In the revolutionary process, the leaders cannot utilize the banking method as an interim measure, justified on grounds of expediency, with the intention of later behaving in a genuinely revolutionary fashion. They must be revolutionary—that is to say, dialogical—from the outset."[22] But then to have done so would have threatened their power base and their own central—and privileged—role as the vanguard.

It is essential, in this context, to note the fact that regimes of the right, including those in the United States and other so-called democracies, use much of the same type of pedagogical imposition in which "democracy," meaning free market capitalism, replaces socialism as the sacred truth to be taught to all. And, as Freire also notes, there is an increasing tendency in capitalist democracies to insist that no questioning of the dominant order be allowed, in which schooling becomes technical training focusing on "production without any preoccupation about what we are producing, who it benefits, or who it hurts."[23] And as with the pedagogy of imposition practiced by much of communism, so the pedagogy of imposition of capitalism cannot ultimately succeed.

There is a second, seemingly opposite, pitfall which Freire warns equally against: the focus on liberating method at the expense of liberating content. Freire's rejection of "banking" education is based on something much more profound than a preference for different pedagogical methods, although there have been many attempts to domesticate it to this. For Freire, decisions about pedagogy are a reflection of one's fundamental stance in relation to one's fellow humans. Merely pouring information into another person is fundamentally disrespectful of that person. On the other hand:

> Information is communicative, or generates communication, when receivers learn the content of what was communicated in such a way as to transcend the act of receiving. They do this by recreating the received communication and transforming it into knowledge concerning what was communicated. The receiver becomes the subject of the process of communication, which, in turn, leads to education as well.[24]

Only communication that includes this mutual quest to make meaning of the information between teacher and student is truly education in any sense of the word that is liberatory or respectful.

As Stanley Aronowitz has noted, many in the United States have focused on methods, especially Freirian methods, at the expense of all else. Thus Aronowitz elaborates:

> Within the United States it is not uncommon for teachers and administrators to say that they are 'using' the Freireian method in classrooms. What they mean by this is indeterminate. Sometimes it merely connotes that the teachers try to be 'interactive' with students; sometimes it signifies an attempt to structure class time as, in part, a dialogue between the teacher

and students; some even mean to 'empower' students by permitting them to talk in class without being ritualistically corrected as to the accuracy of their information, their grammar, or their formal mode of presentation. Or to be punished for dissenting knowledge. All of these are commendable practices, but they hardly require Freire as a cover.[25]

The heart of Freire's commitments is thus masked in the adoption of what are called his methods.[26]

Freire himself is quite well aware of this problem. Thus he warns of the danger of attempting to remove the political project that is at the heart of his pedagogy and "convert the well known education for liberation into a purely methodological problem, considering methods as something purely neutral." He warns:

> Actually, insofar as this type of education is reduced to methods and techniques by which students and educators look at social reality when they do look at it—only to describe it, this education becomes as domesticating as any other. Education for liberation does not merely free students from blackboards just to offer them projectors. On the contrary, it is concerned, as a social praxis, with helping to free human beings from the oppression that strangles them in their objective reality.[27]

The content of liberation—engagement in real action for social change—and not only the methods of dialogue, is central to Freire's enterprise.

The pretense of neutrality regarding pedagogical content often leads to a "subtle and more attractive means of serving the interests of the powerful while appearing to favor the oppressed...I refer again to what we might call anesthetic or aspirin practices, expressions of a subjectivist idealism that can only lead to the preservation of the status quo."[28] At the end of the twentieth century, one of the most popular versions of these "aspirin practices" is the renewed emphasis on technical training which avoids all questions of the meaning and purpose of education. To be liberating, education must include reflection, "which asks the following: for whom, for what, against whom, and against what will these technical instruments work?"[29] But including those questions moves far beyond the agenda of those who want, above all, to maintain the current distribution of power and privilege.

In making his critique of reformism in pedagogy, Freire is also attacking all projects of mere social amelioration. Freire is—as he clearly notes—following in the train of Reinhold Niebuhr who wrote in *Moral Man and Immoral Society* in 1932 that "Teachers of morals who do not see the difference between the problem of charity within the limits of an accepted social system and the problem of justice between economic groups, holding uneven power within modern industrial society, have simply not faced the most obvious differences between the morals of groups and those of individuals."[30] For both Niebuhr and Freire, the avoidance of justice and the focus on the aspirin of reformism is one of the clearest ways of preserving both the benevolence and the privilege of the wealthy.

Within the context of his commitment to liberatory education, Freire always refuses to make a choice between politically neutral pedagogical methods linked to a modest reform agenda on the one hand, or the imposition of a revolutionary social order by an elite vanguard out of touch with the lives of people on the other. Rather Freire demands a revolution made with the people, an alternative that takes seriously both pedagogy and politics. "The true revolutionary [who] is guided by love," never forgets, "the eminently pedagogical character of the revolution." For Freire, the centrality of pedagogy is essential, "unless one intends to carry out the transformation for the oppressed rather than with them." But at the heart of his work is Freire's insistence that, "only the latter form of transformation is valid."[31] It is in transformative struggle that the world itself is remade and renamed. And "naming of the world, which is an act of creation and re-creation, is not possible if it is not infused with love."[32] In committing themselves to a transformation "infused with love," to finding the means of truly making the revolution with rather than for all people, educators and other cultural workers must turn their attention to the problem of their own role, their own power and authority.

Given This Understanding of the Purposes and Goals of Education, the Role of the Teacher Becomes Problematic Yet Very Significant

That old reactionary W. H. Auden did capture something of what is wrong with much of traditional radicalism when he had the shepherds in his Christmas oratorio, "For the Time Being," say:

> Nor can we help noticing how those who insist that
>   We ought to stand up for our rights,
> And how important we are, keep insisting also
>   That it doesn't matter a bit
> If one of us gets arrested or injured, for
>   It is only our numbers that count.
> In a way they are right,
> But to behave like a cogwheel
> When one knows one is no such thing,
> Merely to add to a crowd with one's passionate body,
>   Is not a virtue.[33]

For Freire, asking one's students, asking the oppressed to "merely to add to a crowd with one's passionate body," is neither virtuous nor loving, nor educational. Human beings can neither be objectified nor used as means to an end when recognized as fully human. "My respect for people's rights prevents me from allowing my collaboration to become a disguised 'invasion' or imposition."[34] Freirian education avoids any of the notions of manipulation or propaganda that can happen with other kinds of political education. Yet at the same time, Freire's approach to education is clearly and powerfully political, for it is based on a true understanding of liberation; and it is equally clearly and powerfully spiritual in that it is based on seeing and respecting the divine in everyone.

From this perspective there is no role for a vanguard who will "serve the people." Freire rejects vanguardism, especially on the part of the middle class who would join the revolutionary struggle as teachers, leaders, and theoreticians. He tells of a letter he received from a group of workers in São Paulo who had read a smuggled copy of *Pedagogy of the Oppressed* soon after its publication. After many kind words they concluded:

> Paul...keep on writing—but next time lay it on a little thicker when you come to those scholarly types that come to visit as if they had revolu-

tionary truth by the tail. You know, the ones that come looking for us to
teach us that we're oppressed and exploited and to tell us what to do.[35]

Freire is, in fact, both far too confident that the oppressed know the
nature of their own oppression—and liberation—and far too dis-
trustful of the elitist tendencies within those who have received a
middle class education to ever forget that lesson.

In his essay, "Education, Liberation, and the Church," Freire
warns of the pitfalls still facing those who, recognizing the failure of
simple moralisms of much church work for the poor, turn to a struggle for real liberation. Freire says, this kind of turn is not a one time
conversion experience. It is only the beginning of a long dialogue.
He elaborates:

> In committing themselves to the oppressed, they begin a new period of
> apprenticeship.... This new apprenticeship will violently break down the
> elitist concept of existence they had absorbed while being ideologized.
> The sine qua non the apprenticeship demands is that, first of all, they real-
> ly experience their own Easter, that they die as elitists so as to be resur-
> rected on the side of the oppressed, that they be born again with the
> beings who were not allowed to be.[36]

In his call for a new experience of Easter for those who would move
from oppressor to ally of the oppressed, Freire is echoing his earlier warnings in the *Pedagogy of the Oppressed* to those who would
join the revolutionary struggle.

Early on Freire issued a stern warning to those "certain members
of the oppressor class," who join in the revolutionary struggle. They
do bring important information to the dialogue, they do play an
important role, but "they almost always bring with them the marks
of their origin: their prejudices and their deformations, which
include a lack of confidence in the people's ability to think, to want,
and to know." We have all seen the results, many of us in ourselves,
as we struggle with an authentic role. At the heart of this struggle is
the kind of trust that comes with love and its attendant vulnerability. Freire warns:

> Our converts...truly desire to transform the unjust order; but because of
> their background they believe that they must be the executors of the

transformation. They talk about the people, but they do not trust them; and trusting the people is the indispensable precondition for revolutionary change. A real humanist can be identified more by his trust in the people, which engages him in their struggle, than by a thousand actions in their favor without that trust.[37]

If heeded, these words would have saved many from grief and from rejection from the very people they have sought to serve.

In an extraordinary critique of those who wish to "serve the people" without consulting with the people, who want to make a revolution for rather than with the people, Ram Dass and Paul Gorman warn of the degree to which people, especially those in the so-called "helping professions," often cut themselves off from people by hiding in a role. Thus they warn that even "if we may momentarily be secure in our chosen roles, they can still impede the quality of our service at the deepest level." They tell the story of a chronically ill man who speaks with great appreciation of his caregivers, but who also says:

They're very dedicated. I have nothing but respect for them. But I must say this: I have never, ever, met someone who sees me as whole.... Can you understand this? Can you? No one sees me and helps me see myself as being complete, as is.[38]

When the educator, when the helper in whatever form, fails to see others as a whole person, then the liberating nature of the work has been lost.

Once again, the *Tao te Ching* summarizes the truth:

If you don't trust the people,
you make them untrustworthy.
The Master doesn't talk, he acts.
When his work is done,
the people say, "Amazing:
we did it, all by ourselves!"[39]

In the *Tao*, and in the work of Paulo Freire, the "Amazing, we did it all by ourselves," is not a trick put over on the people by a wily leader. It is rather a statement of the truth. When teacher and student become one in a common struggle, when political leader and the people become one, then all can celebrate and all can benefit from the common victory which is achieved by all for the benefit of all. At this point, as Freire says so clearly, there is no more,

> "I am" or the "I know," the "I free myself" or the "save myself;" nor even the "I teach you." "I free you," or "I save you," but the "we are," "we know," "we save ourselves."[40]

At that point, distinctions and roles, teachers and learners, have disappeared in a mutual quest for liberation.

For Paulo Freire, Education Is Always Located in History and in the Current Historical Moment, in the World and in the Flesh and Blood of Human Reality

Just after he stepped down as Secretary of Education, or superintendent, of the city of São Paulo, Brazil public schools in 1991, Paulo Freire was asked what he thought about sex education in the schools. He responded, "Of course, I support sex education. But I have a different understanding of it than many people do. As Secretary, I insisted that our sex education program in São Paulo begin with the sacred right of orgasm." He was right. This is a very different understanding of sex education than many people have. And in that difference is a key to understanding not only Freire's evident joy in his own life and sexuality, but also his understanding of human rootedness not only in history, but in the flesh and blood reality of a human body.[41]

In this short answer, Freire displays what many theologians refer to as an "incarnational approach" to life: a recognition that the divine is indeed in every person and is to be honored, respected, and loved "in the flesh." This commitment to living fully "in the flesh" and in the flesh and blood struggles of peoples for liberation is at the core of Freire's work. Thus he calls for people to "hold history in their hands," and to "experience death as an oppressed class and be born again to liberation." And he insists that this is a struggle in the world and in history:

We must stress yet again that this journey cannot be made within their consciousness. It must be made in history. No one can make such a journey simply in the inside of his [or her] being....

Important as the intellectual enterprise is for Freire, and it is very important, it is also not enough:

Being revolutionary implies struggling against oppression and exploitation, for the liberation and freedom of the oppressed, concretely and not idealistically . . . it is not sufficient to give lip service to the idea that men and women are human beings if nothing is done objectively to help them experience what it means to be persons. They learn that it is not through good works (Niebuhr's phrase here was "humanitarian") that the oppressed become incarnate as persons.[42]

This commitment, this difficult and continuing commitment by and with the oppressed to "become incarnate as persons," is what liberation means in the world and in history.

Many in today's churches and other spiritual communities are not calling on people to live in the world and in history, but to escape from both. Freire provides a very thoughtful analysis of the destructive role of escapist churches and sects that provide a "haven for the masses," through a rejection of the world. He notes that:

In despising this world as a world of sin, vice, and impurity, they are in one sense taking their revenge on their oppressors, its owners. It is as if they were saying to the bosses, "You are powerful—but the world over which your power holds sway is an evil one and we reject it."...Thus, seeing the world itself as the antagonist, they attempt the impossible: to renounce the world's mediation in their pilgrimage. By doing so, they hope to reach transcendence without passing by way of the mundane; they want metahistory without experiencing history; they want salvation without knowing liberation. The pain of domination leads them to accept this historical anesthesia in the hope that it will strengthen them to fight sin and the devil—leaving untouched all the while the real causes of their oppression.[43]

By locating the powerful attraction of escapist religious movements in the very reality of domination, Freire avoids the victim-blaming that is all too common in the sociology of religion. At the same time, in insisting that a theology of liberation must be based in the mundane and in history, he roots the religious struggle for faith and the political struggle for liberation in the same moment and the same set of events—the historical reality of conscientization for political involvement.[44]

In Freire's writings, salvation is in history and not in escape from history. It is in fully embracing the world that the world and individuals can be transformed. Thus it is necessary, as Freire says of the literacy programs in São Tome and Principe, that people, "taking more and more history into their own hands...can shape their history. To shape history is to be present in it, not merely represented in it."[45] Again and again this theme emerges, it is essential to be an actor in history not merely a witness of the drama.

Freire is very clear in what he means to be present in history and to build a system of education that is located in the world and in the current historical moment. Thus:

> The starting point for organizing the program content of education or political action must be the present, existential, concrete situation, reflecting the aspirations of the people. Utilizing certain basic contradictions, we must pose this existential, concrete, present situation to the people as a problem which challenges them and requires a response—not just at the intellectual level, but at the level of action. We must never merely discourse on the present situation, must never provide the people with programs which have little or nothing to do with their own preoccupations, doubts, hopes, and fears...[46]

In this statement Freire sums up much of his approach. The dialogue does not begin with an "agenda" apart from the people; the dialogue must be one of mutual respect and it must be located in history, in the "present, existential, concrete situation."

All of these points are fundamental to Freire's view of the world, none more so than the emphasis on the present and concrete. It is this location in the historical present that, for Freire, represents so much of what is both practical and utopian in his work. It is in history, in the immediate concrete historical moment, that hope comes alive. As the Tao says, "The Master gives himself up to whatever the moment brings."[47] And in this surrender there is a new hope and sense of opportunity. Thus Freire responded to a question from

Donaldo Macedo, "What do you think about the role of human agency..." by noting:

> Your question brings to mind a statement by Marx. When he referred to the making of history he said that man makes history based on the concrete conditions that he finds.... It is from concrete conditions, or more accurately, from the relationship between the concrete and the possible.[48]

It is this very base in affirming human agency in the midst of the concrete conditions where human beings live that Freire finds the condition for hopefulness. Because he has such deep trust in people, Freire sees hope and possibility in the midst of oppressive situations that would lead others only to despair. His hope is not based on an easy optimism but on a deeply held confidence in the link of the concrete and the possible.

Freire writes with appreciation of the work of Henry Giroux, "I think Giroux understands this perfectly when he asserts that outside the present it is impossible to make history.... When Giroux says that the present is a present possibility, not determinism, he is situating human agency in a key way...."[49] Thus Freire, and Giroux, find hope for change in the exercise of human freedom in the concrete historical situation.

In his hopefulness, Freire has escaped from the determinism which has infected some Marxists, and some Calvinists before them. Where some see history as a predetermined unfolding, requiring and allowing little in the way of human agency, Freire places human agency in a central position. It is in the struggle for liberation that humans become fully human and it is equally in the process of becoming fully loving human beings that liberation is built.[50]

It is Freire's view of people as "active subjects of history," as makers of a new history in the immediate concrete historical situation that leads Cornel West to say:

> In this way, he adds new meaning to Marx's famous eleventh thesis on Feuerback, 'the philosophers have only interpreted the world in various ways; the point, however, is to change it'. This new meaning consists of recasting philosophical reflection among subaltern peoples in their everyday life-settings and of reconceiving change as the creation of new col-

lective identities and social possibilities in history over against vicious
forces of dehumanization. Paulo Freire dares to tread where even Marx
refused to walk—on the terrain where the revolutionary love of struggling
human beings sustains their faith in each other and keeps hope alive within themselves and in history.[51]

Thus, "Freire's genius is to explicate in [his writing] and exemplify
in his life the dynamics of this process of how ordinary people can
and do make history in how they think, feel, act and love."[52] And
thus Paulo Freire represents an approach to education that is filled
with hope and love concretely located in action in the historical present.

REFERENCES

1. For a wonderful description of Paulo Freire's personal impact on people, see bell hooks, "bell hooks Speaking About Paulo Freire—the Man, His work," in Peter McLaren and Peter Leonard, *Paulo Freire: A Critical Encounter* (New York: Routledge, 1993), pp. 146-154.

2. Aronowitz, Stanley, "Paulo Freire's Radical Democratic Humanism," in Peter McLaren and Peter Leonard, eds., *Paulo Freire: A Critical Encounter* (London: Routledge, 1993), p. 8.

3. Che Guevara, Venceremos—*The Speeches and Writings of Che Guevara*, edited by John Gerassi (New York, 1969), p. 398, cited in Paulo Freire *Pedagogy of the Oppressed* (New York: Seabury Press, 1970), pp. 77-78.

4. Ibid.

5. Freire, Paulo, *Pedagogy of the Oppressed* (New York: The Seabury Press, 1970), p. 78.

6. *Tao Te Ching*, 10, A New English Version, with Foreword and Notes by Stephen Mitchell (New York: Harper Perennial, 1988). All citations from the *Tao Te Ching* in this essay are from the Mitchell edition.

7. Freire, Paulo, *Pedagogy of Hope: Reliving Pedagogy of the Oppressed* (New York: Continuum, 1995), p. 70.

8. Freire, Paulo, *Letters to Christina: Reflections on My Life and Work* (New York: Routledge, 1996), p. 127.

9. *Pedagogy of the Oppressed*, p. 85.

10. Freire, Paulo, Conversation with the faculty of the Division of Cooperative Education, Northeastern University, Boston, Massachusetts, March 17, 1994.

11. *Pedagogy of the Oppressed*, p. 78; I have cited Freire as originally published throughout this essay. Many, most notably Freire himself, have noted the sexist use of the word "man" in Pedagogy of the Oppressed. Freire is clear that he has learned from his mistakes and his later works reflect both an inclusive language and a deeper level of inclusivity in his approach to the role of women and men in the process of liberation. See especially the essay by hooks and the dialogue of Freire and Macedo, where he says, "since the publication of *Pedagogy of the Oppressed* I have attempted to rid my language of all those features that are demeaning to women." in McLaren and Leonard.

12. *Pedagogy of the Oppressed*, pp. 76-77.

13. Buber, Martin, *I and Thou*, 2nd ed. Ronald Gregor Smith, trans. (New York: Collier Books, 1958), pp. 15-16.

14. Buber, p. 132.

15. See Ronald Gregor Smith, "Translator's Preface to the Second Edition," in Buber, *I and Thou*, p. ix.

16. Cremin, Lawrence A., *Popular Education and its Discontents* (New York: Harper & Row, 1990), pp. 124-125.

17. Freire, Paulo, Public Dialogue, Northeastern University, Boston, Massachusetts, March 14, 1993.

18. *Pedagogy of the Oppressed*, p. 55.

19. Counts, George S., *Dare the School Build a New Social Order?* (1932) revised with a new perfect by Wayne J. Urban (Carbondale: Southern Illinois University Press, 1978), pp. 7-8.

20. *Letters to Christina*, p. 84.

21. Fanon, Frantz, *The Wretched of the Earth* (New York: Grove Press, 1963), p. 35.

22. *Pedagogy of the Oppressed*, p. 74.

23. *Letters to Christina*, p. 84.

24. *Letters to Christina*, p. 99.

25. Aronowitz, in McLaren & Leonard, p. 8.

26. See also Donaldo Macedo's chapter, "An Anti-Method Pedagogy: A Freireian Perspective," in this book

27. Freire, Paulo, *The Politics of Education: Culture, Power, and Liberation* (South Hadley, Mass.: Bergin & Garvey, 1985), p. 125.

28. *The Politics of Education*, p. 122.

29. *Letters to Christina*, p. 100.

30. Niebuhr, Reinhold, *Moral Man and Immoral Society* (New York: Scribner's, 1932), p. xxii.

31. *Pedagogy of the Oppressed*, p. 54.

32. *Pedagogy of the Oppressed*, p. 77.

33. Auden, W. H., "For the Time Being: A Christmas Oratorio," in *Collected Longer Poems of W. H. Auden* (New York: Vintage Books, 1975) pp. 165, 166

34. Freire, Paulom and Donaldo Macedo, *Literacy: Reading the Word and the World* (South Hadley, MA: Bergin & Garvey, 1987), p. 64.

35. *Pedagogy of Hope*, p. 63.

36. *The Politics of Education*, pp. 122-123.

37. *Pedagogy of the Oppressed*, pp. 46-47.

38. Dass,Ram, & Paul Gorman, *How Can I Help? Stories and Reflections on Service* (New York: Knopf, 1991), p. 27.

39. *Tao Te Ching*, 17.

40. *The Politics of Education*, p. 138.

41. Freire, Paulo, Public Lecture, (Lesley College, Cambridge, MA, July 25, 1991); see also hooks in McLaren and Leonard.

42. *The Politics of Education*, p. 128.

43. *The Politics of Education*, p. 132.

44. *The Politics of Education*, p. 125.

45. *Literacy*, p. 65.

46. *Pedagogy of the Oppressed*, p. 85.

47. *Tao Te Ching*, 50

48. *Literacy*, p. 60.

49. Ibid.

50. For a detailed analysis of Freire's understanding of history as possibility, see *Letters to Christina*, pp. 81-88.

51. West, Cornel, "Preface," McLaren and Leonard, pp. xiii-xiv.

52. Ibid.

CHAPTER TEN

PROGRESSIVE TEACHER EDUCATION
Consciousness, Identity, and Knowledge

William T. Stokes

Nearly one hundred years ago, John Dewey[1] observed that the "goals and process of education are one and the same thing." In the enforced tedium and oppressive harshness of the typical common schools of the day, he saw that pupils were treated as laborers facing tasks and conditions in schools that would mold them into adults suitable for employment in the factories of the early twentieth century. In opposition to this reality, he and others sought to articulate a democratic, socially progressive vision of teaching and learning wherein all children would become active and critical participants in the making and reshaping of their own educations. Only then would the public schools become an essential part of the ongoing struggle for inclusive democracy, social and economic justice, and cultural transformation. Democratic schools would prepare citizens for a democratic, pluralistic society. If, however, the practices of schools remain antidemocratic, uncritical, and narrowly focused upon the mastery of basic skills for lives as compliant workers and consumers, then the outcomes cannot be otherwise.

Today the struggle to sustain a progressive vision for public education remains as much a challenge as it was a century ago. What dominates the public discourse on the conditions of schools in the popular media is the concern for economic competitiveness. Schools are seen primarily as sites for training workers and consumers who will compete with other workers and consumers all over the world. As the United States has fallen from its former preeminent position in the global economy, the schools have been accused of failing this essential mission and there have been urgent demands to restructure the schools, most of which are fashioned in accordance with the conservative programmatics emphasizing increased privatization, exclusivity, and, for the public schools, greater control, authority, and discipline (e.g., tighter budgets, more tests, easier expulsions). The schools are to be held accountable for greater efficiency and productivity as assessed by emphasis upon basic skills, test scores, and the graduation of workers who will meet the requirements of multinational corporations. The process and the goals are one.

Another central feature of the debate on restructuring American education has been concern for the nature of teacher education, or "teacher training." From the perspective that the schools are the cause of weakening economic competitiveness, the immediate source of the problem is the incompetence of the teachers who cannot exert discipline or ensure basic literacy. Thus, in turn, the schools of education are found wanting for not having adequately trained the teachers. What conservative reformers demand are new regulations, requirements, credentials, and evaluations that would ensure that teachers have acquired the essential "skills" necessary to fulfill their responsibility to prepare the next generation of workers. In consequence, teacher training programs are expected to emphasize methods, techniques, and skills. Teachers are to be trained as technicians prepared to acquiesce uncritically to the decisions of supervisors, experts, and textbook publishers. Teachers' work becomes managerial at the lowest level possible—managing the behaviors of children, who in turn are compelled to acquire skills that can be evaluated efficiently through standardized tests. The study of methods and materials to teach skills to children dominates the training of the teacher. The prevailing models are managerial, medical, and scientist; and the language of teacher training is the language of methods, materials, objectives, skills, schedules, grouping, tracking, discipline, tests, diagnosis, disabilities, deficits, interventions, remediation, and so on.

In this chapter I will examine the dominance of "methods" in "teacher training" programs. I will argue that the emphasis upon methods places teachers and students as consumers of knowledge created by remote theorists, researchers, and experts who design "teacher proof" materials and procedures. Because reflection and critique are discouraged, novice teachers lose a sense of their own agency, and become most anxious about the loss of control over their own students. They become focused upon management and discipline, and their greatest anxieties center upon those children who are "different"—children of color, speakers of languages other than English, the culturally different, the poor, the "disabled," and those "at risk." To borrow Paulo Freire's term, it is the banking model of education that dominates teacher training. The "capital" accumulated by student teachers consists primarily of skills in the methods of teaching children another array of skills identified in the predetermined curriculum deemed to be appropriate to that group. The consequence is a mystification of professional competence, with teaching and learning viewed as profoundly difficult. Join these pressures with those of limited resources, limited time, and a climate of desperate competition, and what is created are conditions that effectively prohibit critical reflection upon practice. Several years ago a student of mine, who was preparing to become an elementary school teacher, offered the following assessment: "the adherence to a skills-oriented method of teacher education and the refusal of some teachers to consider student inquiry that challenges their own assumptions creates an environment in education schools that squelches critical thought. We are not expected or encouraged to challenge our teachers, and by extension we are not really encouraged to challenge ourselves. The teaching that is modeled for us is skills-and methods-oriented and discounts intellectual inquiry." When teacher education programs emphasize methods and marginalize reflection, critique and teachers' roles as "transformative intellectuals,"[2] then the outcomes cannot be otherwise—the process and the goals remain one and the same.[3]

Paulo Freire and Critical Consciousness

When I began teaching twenty-five years ago, it was in a city high school in which all the students were African-American males who had been suspended from other schools in the system. As I tried to make sense of that experience, the first writers I encountered were Herbert Kohl[4] and Jonathan Kozol.[5] Their experiences spoke immediately to my own and gave me hope. Through them I first learned of progressive practices and understood that education might be transformed and thereby join the broader purposes of social movements for civil rights, equality, and peace. It was in 1973 that I first read *Pedagogy of the Oppressed*,[6] and it forever changed my understanding of teaching and learning. Paulo Freire offered a truly democratic vision of education based on experience, dialogue, reflection, and critique. I had been charged with teaching my students to read, but it was Freire who taught me that to read words is bound up with reading the world. Literacy is not owning certain skills; it is that which enables us to more fully read and to transform (to write) the world, to recognize injustice, to create democracy in collective action against forces that oppress and marginalize the lives of the poor, of racial, ethnic, and linguistic minorities, and of women and men throughout society.

Through *Pedagogy of the Oppressed*, I tried to understand my role as teacher and my relation to the community of which my students were members. To give focus to my explorations, I returned again and again to critical consciousness, to *conscientização*, in hope of understanding teaching and learning. Throughout the 1960s and 1970s my consciousness regarding gender, class, race, language, religion, and sexuality had undergone continual transformation. It was through reflection on those changes that I began to understand my own cultural experiences and those of my students. By offering a language of critique, Freire taught me about myself and my relation to the world and the historical forces that have shaped my consciousness. In the analysis of the "banking" approach to schooling and the accumulation of cultural capital, I saw my own schooling and my own initial teaching. In the analysis of oppressor and oppressed, I began to understand my position of privilege and the capacity to become critically conscious through examining oppression. I am a white male and though my childhood was lived in poverty and family violence, I have lived within the privileges of the middle class throughout my adulthood. To cross the borders of privilege, to participate in liberatory education, and to struggle for *conscientização*, these are the lessons of Paulo Freire—as offered in *Pedagogy of the Oppressed* and reoffered in the recent *Pedagogy of Hope*[7] and *Pedagogy of the City*.[8]

Freire makes clear that consciousness of oppression, alone, does not create freedom; and education, alone, does not transform society. The means to liberation, however, require an understanding that is "steeped in the dialectical movement back and forth between consciousness and world" (*Pedagogy of Hope*, p. 104). Liberation from oppression through resistance and struggle depends, Freire argues, upon the capacities to dream and hope: "There is no change without dream, as there is no dream without hope" (p. 91). The transformation of reality depends upon first "reading the world," that is awareness, consciousness, and an understanding of ourselves as historical and cultural beings. Hope then lends direction to possibility, to the dream, to the "untested feasibility" (p. 91); "my utopian dream has to do with a society that is less unjust, less cruel, more democratic, less discriminatory, less racist, less sexist" (see *Pedagogy of the City*, p. 115).

My teaching had begun in the most traditional style. I taught— my students did not learn. It was only when I listened and asked them to teach me that we began teaching each other. We studied three domains: mathematics (especially probabilities), English (especially language varieties), and social studies (especially the history of Black Americans). In each a genuine dialogue emerged. We all learned. To illustrate briefly: the mathematics text (as authority) called for teaching ratios and probabilities, building upon fractions and percentages. My students had been failing for three or more years to make any progress in this text. However, as I discovered one day by finding them and watching them play craps in a basement stairwell, they fully understood the laws of chance in the form of odds on wagers. I had never understood gambling or how gamblers calculated and expressed odds on throws of the dice. I asked my students to teach me and together we taught each other and dis-

covered the commonalities in the meeting of our disparate discourses. Once I learned the system, I guided an investigation of the
corresponding representations in ratios, fractions, and percentages.
They discovered that they had long ago mastered the conceptual
relations hidden within the language of the text. We had crossed
borders separating our modes of discourse. Implicitly, the authority
of the text was inverted. They were agents of their own meanings.

Of far greater significance were the more complex explorations
of language and history we undertook. To understand language differences and to discover the histories omitted from the standard
texts required setting aside the authority of the dominant discourses of schooling. The principal of our school had obtained, without
authorization from central administration, a collection of materials
on the history of African-Americans. As we worked from these, we
became agents of our own learning and our every conversation an
implicit critique of the approved texts. This language of critique, that
I use now, was not part of the experience at that time, but reading
Freire provided new possibilities for understanding what had
occurred. I understood that in that school we were beginning to create a language of critique and possibility.

Reading Freire, encountering his words, opened new ways of
seeing my world. I did not at first understand how this was possible—what did reading about adult literacy campaigns in northeast
Brazil have to offer to a teacher of teenage Black males in central
New York? By offering a new language, Freire offered a new literacy—a critical literacy, and new ways of seeing. Foucault[9] offers an
analysis of the role of the writer that is relevant to this experience.
He argues that a too-simple postmodernist critique of the modernist
tendency to valorize the author—who is the center of meaning and
"authority"— proclaims the death of the author and identifies the
reader-text relationship as the exclusive crucible of meaning. This
view is too simple, Foucault argues, because it neglects the author's
role in sustaining and extending discourses ("author," through Old
French, is derived from the Latin, *auctor*, increaser or grower, and
augere, to increase or to enrich). While there are authors who mere-

ly participate in and are fully embedded within a given historical discourse, there are others who significantly extend or open a new discourse, and a very few who open multiple discourses—Freire, in my view, stands among these very few.

Foucault argues that the significance of the author lies with the possibilities available to the reader within the discourses to generate new meanings: the possibilities for "the proliferation of meanings...the free circulation, the free manipulation, the free composition, decomposition and recomposition of [meaning]" (p. 119). Such discourses are generative and may be judged by possibilities within them: "What are the modes of existence of this discourse? Where has it been used, how can it circulate, and who can appropriate it for himself? What are the places in it where there is room for possible subjects? Who can assume these various subject-functions?" (p. 120). The author stands within history—as a confluence of historical discourses. If the author is viewed as the defining creator of a text or discourse, then all others must submit to that authority. Meaning would reside only with the author. But if the author is viewed as one who contributes to and enlarges the historical discourses, then the possibilities of subjectivity and meaning reside with the reader who can appropriate the discourse as a historical agent also. It is the essence of Freire's postmodern discourse that meaning, possibility, and democratic action are created, through the project of critical dialogue, multiple subjectivities, and agency. The discourse taken and enlarged by Freire allows me to make it my own, to appropriate it as I reflect upon my own teaching and the design of the elementary teacher education program I participate in. These questions arise: Who is the teacher? From what historical and cultural position does the teacher act? What is the authority of the teacher? Does the teacher create, define, and delimit discourses? Does the teacher (as author) legitimate and privilege certain meanings and interpretations over others? If so, then are some voices silenced or marginalized? And, how may the teacher participate in the creation of critical dialogue within which the learner becomes a historical agent of his or her own learning? To begin addressing these questions it may be useful to examine the conditions that subvert critique and agency in teacher education.

Domestication of Teachers

In the United States, 90 percent of those who enter programs leading to teacher certification in elementary education are middle-class,
monolingual, white women. These prospective teachers tend to
view their career choice as an opportunity to help children—to nur-
ture their development and supervise their learning in ways that will
excite their curiosity and enhance their self-esteem while also ensur-
ing that each child acquires the expected basic skills. They tend to
be liberal and progressive in the tradition of Parker and Dewey that
extended the child-centered movement in elementary education.
However, they do not, and have not been encouraged to view
themselves as intellectuals. There is indeed a resistance to viewing
their work as being political or concerning knowledge as socially
constructed rather than as merely given. They are concerned with
skills and processes of instruction that are uncritically derived from
the research literature dominated by psychological studies of learning and development. They see only the benign aspects of their
work with children and there is strong resistance to any investigation of ideological foundations of their professional knowledge.

In most states, prospective teachers are required to have com-
pleted a baccalaureate program in a liberal arts discipline; thus they
are presumed to "possess" the required "knowledge" of what to
teach—the so-called "knowledge standard." Schools of education
are then expected to emphasize pedagogy, narrowly interpreted for
the most part as methods and materials—the how of teaching. The
college faculties have been judged, through periodic review, to
already possess the required expertise, their professional "capital,"
and thus their responsibility is to transmit what they can of this to
their students—those being "trained" to be teachers. Teaching is
presented as a great challenge, as indeed in one sense it is; but
moreover it is presented as extremely difficult, requiring almost
unimaginable skills of organization and discipline. Novice teachers
become anxious about their abilities to maintain control, to organize
and manage, to follow defined procedures, to arrange schedules, to

write lesson plans, to fulfill curriculum objectives, to use required texts and materials, and to carry out evaluations. These emphases place teachers as consumers of procedures and techniques created by experts. Then they are judged on their willingness to carry out the orders of supervisors, and become especially focused upon management and discipline. This is the banking model of education that dominates teacher training and effectively domesticates teachers. The mystification of method and management encourages teachers to uncritically focus on skills and behaviors. Indeed, recent legislation in Massachusetts, in its effort to raise standards and ensure that undergraduates complete a liberal arts program, has stipulated that prospective teachers cannot major in education—one consequence of this regulation is that education programs are understood to be "vocational" and to be outside the "liberal arts." Pedagogy is effectively declared absent of intellectual content and reduced to mere methods. While the schools of education are mandated by regulation to meet a lengthy set of "standards" for teacher competencies, demonstrated largely through facility with methods, there is little if any requirement that teachers engage in serious study of the history, philosophy, or sociology of education. Nor is it required that teachers have seriously studied ethnography or language. Critical pedagogy and cultural theory are inserted only at the margins, if at all. These are among the institutional and political barriers that encourage mystification and resistance to critique, and powerfully obstruct pedagogies of hope and possibility.

Further contributing to the antiintellectualism of teacher training is that since the founding of the common schools and the normal schools for teacher training in the mid-nineteenth century, the curriculum presented to students has been directed toward establishing consensus and a "common" national identity. One manifestation of this purpose is the avoidance of controversy in the domains of study. The objects of knowledge (whether mathematics, literary interpretations, historical events, or the law of gravitation) are presented as given, as merely factual matters—about which there can be only right and wrong answers. The avoidance of serious debate, coupled with the commercial intentions of publishers to sell as many books as possible (without offending potential buyers), leads to the circumstance that textbooks, especially for the elementary schools, are designed to be "neutral" or "objective" and "value-free"—all of which only serve the uncritical acceptance of the dominant ideologies hidden therein—and in consequence the curriculum becomes essentially content free, preferring skills instruction to the serious study of content. What is denied or avoided is that knowledge has historicity, ideology, and is "socially created, invented, and reinvented and is learned. Knowledge is produced" (*Pedagogy of the City*, p. 117).

This is not to suggest that there is an absence of fierce debate in the education literature. However, the debates that receive attention tend to be limited to disputes concerning which methods are most effective for the greatest numbers of children in various circumstances. For example, there is the "great debate" concerning approaches to the teaching of reading and writing.[10] Hundreds of books, thousands of articles, and many careers have been shaped by the stance taken on approaches to the teaching of reading and writing in the elementary schools. While these conflicts have historical, ideological, epistemological, and scientific significance, many teachers are left to conclude that only the experts understand these theoretical matters and that all they should be concerned with are questions of practice. Should one adopt a "phonics" approach, or "whole language"—and how should spelling be taught? Or, should "learning disabled" children be "grouped" with "regular education" students?

Despite the appearance of debate between alternative approaches and despite efforts to "empower" teachers, the dominant effect of the debates is to convince teachers of the authority of method. The effort to link theory and practice has the effect of establishing the legitimate authority of this or that method. Science becomes the authority—the deep separation between researchers and practitioners, and between universities and schools (having dimensions of class and gender divisions), only further strips teachers of agency. The expert, through the textbook publisher, is the author of meanings and procedures that learners must accept. The reproduction of method becomes the dominant rationality of teacher education and the processes of induction into the profession encourages teachers to become progressively more blind to the ideological foundations of the dominant discourses by the very process of acquiring them. Whether authoritative and committed to "structure" and skill instruction or child-centered and tending toward "natural" learning, domesticated teachers view method as the "solution" to the "problem" of the child's learning. The discourse defines ways of knowing so as to delegitimize other ways of knowing or even the possibility of other ways of knowing. Those students who share or adopt that discourse are rewarded, others are silenced, and others who resist are marginalized. That teachers may be contributing to silencing and marginalizing their students is unexamined, because the teachers themselves have been silenced. Domesticated teachers resist analysis and critique of power relations in schools, as the following example of examining discipline reveals.

Critical Thinking and Critical Literacy

As a teacher educator, I had the occasion to enter a conversation about critical thinking and discipline, both topics that my students were studying in other courses. Regarding critical thinking, there was considerable enthusiasm for the curricular materials they were exploring. The prevailing view was that these were an improvement over skills based curricula, even though these materials were filled with lists of "thinking skills" that the children would be expected to learn. Moreover, it was expected that only the older, more advanced, or "high track," students would be prepared to truly benefit from the curriculum, though, if they were especially skilled teachers, they might reach some of the "lower" students. I shared my uncertainty about the meaning of "critical thinking:" In what sense is it critical? Where is the critique? Similarly, I hoped to raise questions about discipline. While they were most concerned with how to discipline, I wanted to ask, toward what end? To weave both issues I drew upon Burbules' wonderful deconstruction[11] of a picture book entitled, *Tootle*.[12]

I asked my students to read *Tootle* and another picture book, *Ferdinand*.[13] I explained that I had also done this with a group of children to hear their impressions of the contrasting images of growing up and adulthood that the books contained. *Ferdinand* is a well known and much loved story about a young bull who wishes to live in peace and succeeds in doing so despite being carted off to fight in the bullring. In *Tootle*, a "child" engine is attending school in hopes of becoming an "adult" locomotive, who will pull long trains and be called the "Flyer." His schooling is entirely devoted to the learning of rules such as "Always Stop for a Red Flag Waving" and "Stay on the Rails, No Matter What." As Burbules points out, these lessons consist entirely of the constant repetition of the rules. However, Tootle, who has been playing in the meadow, is caught disobeying the central injunction to "stay on the rails, no matter what." The climax of the story is the moment when Tootle is cleverly guided to give up his childish play and return to the tracks. In the final scene, Tootle has become the Flyer and is offering his achieved wisdom to the next generation of baby engines, that is, of course, to "stay on the rails, no matter what."

I shared with my students the informal conversations I had had in 1987 with a group of elementary and high school students, and especially one with a third grader, Anna, who had a great deal to say about both stories, but was most affected by *Tootle*, which she thought to be the more realistic, because "you have to learn all the rules." Anna offered this final observation as she tried to explain what she thought the rules meant. She had heard a report on the radio that to her was the best example of "Stay on the Rails, No Matter What." A ten-year-old girl, a year older than she was, had been hit by a car while riding her bike. Because the girl's injuries were obviously serious, her mother had called an ambulance. When the ambulance arrived, however, the mother would not allow her daughter to be taken to the hospital in this ambulance. As a result of the delayed treatment, the girl died of her injuries. The events had occurred in a white suburb of Johannesburg, South Africa. The daughter and mother were white. The ambulance that first arrived was a Blacks' ambulance. This, said Anna in utter seriousness, was an example of "Staying on the Rails No Matter What." Anna recognized in the education of Tootle an essential correspondence to the mechanisms that reproduce the social order, including those of apartheid. Though only nine years old, Anna's literacy was a critical literacy.

In the current discourse on teaching so-called "critical thinking skills" (putting aside the fact that as conceived these "skills" have nothing to do with critique), it is presumed that children must be trained in "critical thinking." Here the correspondence to Tootle is indeed close. Children must be trained to adopt the ideology of the dominant social order and to give up their "childish" understandings of the world. The hidden curriculum underlying "critical thinking skills" instruction is the replacement of children's naturally developing understanding of the world with the conventional construction of reality.

Critical literacy, such as Anna's, is a natural adjunct of emerging literacy. However, it can be suppressed and corrupted by the pressures, gradually internalized, to restrict thought and behavior to conform to dominant social rules and expectations. We have only to see the susceptibility of the young television viewer to the seductions of advertisers to know that their judgment withers under the onslaught of ready-made attitudes, expectations, and beliefs. One consequence of the internalization of the dominant discourse is the tendency to resist any genuine attempt to critique or deconstruct that discourse.

After hearing Anna's critique and reading Burbules' analysis of *Tootle*, my students resisted taking the matter at all seriously: "It is only a children's book. Aren't you reading too much into it? That can't be what the author meant." To reawaken critical literacy, to progress toward critical consciousness, these become struggles to reexamine the internalized dominant discourse. Those who are relatively privileged are correspondingly more resistant. Their discomfort with critique prepares them to substitute method for theory. How to teach skills replaces serious critical examination of what is taught.

From Children's Books to the Supreme Court

Teachers are domesticated by their own schooling, and by the contradictory positions of powerlessness and privilege they occupy. They resist problematizing their positions of privilege relative to the many poor and marginalized communities within which they work. Simultaneously, teachers in public schools face tremendous pressures to avoid controversy and to conform to the expectations of supervisors, principals, superintendents, local school boards, and all the municipal, state, and federal agencies that involve themselves in regulating the schools. Academic freedom, as practiced in the universities, does not exist in the public schools, yet these same teachers are expected to teach "critical thinking" and prepare students for citizenship in a pluralistic democracy. They are expected to present the approved curricula and to fulfill the promises made by politicians that the schools will accomplish larger social aims of eradicating drugs, ending violence, reducing teenage pregnancy, and solving deep economic problems by training workers who would compete with workers of other nations. Moreover, they are to do this while avoiding controversy, and therefore, genuine critical consciousness. To illustrate:

On January 13, 1988, the Supreme Court of the United States handed down a decision in the case of *Hazelwood School District* v. *Kuhlmeier* et al.[14] that concerned the First Amendment rights of both students and teachers. In a 5-to-3 decision the Court ruled in favor of the school district in its decision to censor a group of controversial articles about divorce and teenage pregnancy that were to appear in the student newspaper. In the opinion written by Byron White it was stated that the high school principal was justified in censoring the student press if such action was "reasonably related to legitimate pedagogical concerns"(at 273). One of these concerns was that "readers or listeners are not exposed to material that may be inappropriate for their level of maturity"(at 271). A second and more fundamental concern was that a "school must also retain the authority to refuse to sponsor student speech that might reasonably be perceived...to associate the school with any position other than neutrality on matters of public controversy" (at 272). The effect of the decision may be to convince teachers that public debate on controversial issues should be kept safely out of the schools. Furthermore, it was reported that the teacher who had been the advisor to the student newspaper was threatened with the loss of his position and teaching credential if he did not successfully redirect the student editors to safer topics.[15]

For purposes of comparison, consider this section of the "common rules for all professors of higher faculties" as appeared in the *Ratio Studiorum* of 1599 prepared by the Jesuit Order during the Counter-Reformation:[16]. "Avoiding New Opinions—Even in matters where there is no risk to faith and devotion, no one shall introduce new questions in matters of great moment, or any opinion which does not have suitable authority, without first consulting his superiors; he shall not teach anything opposed to the axioms of learned men or the general beliefs of scholars." In an earlier section, it stated "if there are any too prone to innovations, or too liberal in their views, they shall certainly be removed from the responsibility of teaching." The rules and penalties were unambiguous.

Teachers today face subtler pressures. The public schools were established to assure literacy and prepare citizens for their responsibilities in a democracy—including the exercise of freedom of speech and press. Yet, the Supreme Court has ruled that the schools should avoid "any position other than neutrality on matters of public controversy." In the case in question, that meant that the teacher, the principal, and the school would have been taking a "position" had the students been allowed to print that issue of their school newspaper. One is left to wonder what is required to achieve "neutrality on matters of public controversy." It may be obvious that it is essential that public schools should not endorse candidates in elections, nor should they seek to influence the votes taken on specific pieces of legislation. Schools hold authority and power to influence the opportunities and future prospects of their students through the regulative mechanisms of discipline, evaluation, promotion, and graduation. It is indisputable that schools should not exert pressures on students, parents, and their communities in order to influence public debate. Schools would become the explicit instruments of political persuasion. To do so would destroy any remnants of academic freedom and reduce schools to serving the immediate demands of current political interests and powers. However, it should be perfectly obvious that schools are inescapably institutions of control and regulation. "Every pedagogical project is political and filled with ideology" (*Pedagogy of the City*, p. 47). Both the manifest, explicit curriculum and the "hidden" curriculum are historical and ideological constructs. What counts as knowledge, truth, reasoning, or inquiry are all matters of historical formulation. To assert that an argument is "objective" or a position is "neutral" is possible only within an ideological context. The overt censorship practiced in the Hazelwood case fosters self-censorship: the avoidance of controversy, debate, dialogue, or critique. Not only are teachers to keep their students quiet but they are to remain silent themselves. In this respect the public schools can operate like the mainstream press to manufacture consent; debate and critique are only permitted within narrowly acceptable limits. Students and teachers are discouraged from genuine dialogue, inquiry, and critique that does not have "suitable authority" from "superiors...or the general beliefs of scholars."[17,18]

Teacher Education for Transformation

Why teach? Each year, at the beginning of the term, I ask my students this question. Why be a teacher? What purposes are served by teaching? Their initial responses typically range from "always wanted to be a teacher" to "wanting to work with children" to the most hesitant and vague assertions that it is "something important." All readily agree that elementary-school children need to learn to read, write, and "do math." They express commitment to children achieving a love of learning, discovery, and creative activity—coupled with problem-solving and self-esteem. Occasionally a woman will offer a tentative analysis of the limited professional career options available to women. And a few speak with pride that they are the first in their families to attend college and therefore entering teaching represents partial fulfillment of family dreams. Only once in ten years, however, have I encountered an elaborately developed progressive vision: an African woman visiting from Nigeria intended to complete the program and return to the poorest state in Nigeria and through establishing new schools, not based on British colonial models, to transform that impoverished society.

Teacher education, if it is to be consistent with a progressive, democratic vision, must create the conditions of critical dialogue that challenges prospective teachers to examine their cultural identities and promotes the development of critical consciousness of their racial, ethnic, linguistic, and class positions. Teachers tend to be conscious of their own lower and gendered position in the hierarchy (patriarchy) of the public school systems, and they are conscious of some of the pressures that tend to silence them or pressure them toward conformity; but they resist examining their positions of privilege relative to the many poor and marginalized communities within which they work, and they are unconscious of or unwilling to examine their own contribution to the silencing of their students.

A critical teacher education should problematize the lived experience of children, women, and men throughout this society, and simultaneous positions of domination and subordination—contradictory experiences of oppression and complicity with privilege. At the intersections of race, class, and gender, each participates in multiple positions of power and powerlessness. What is required is a teacher education that carries forward "a critical and revealing reading of reality" (*Pedagogy of the City*, p. 49). Teachers must educate themselves about domination and subordination or inevitably their part will be to contribute to the reproduction of the present conditions. Despite their expressed intentions to work with children, to teach them reading, writing, and arithmetic, to help them "learn to learn" and all the rest, including "self-esteem," the greatest effects will emerge through the hidden curriculum, and "the most hidden aspects of the hidden curriculum are found...in the social, historical, cultural and class-based experiences of the society of which teachers are a part" (p. 120).

A radical teacher education program must be founded on the belief that the fundamental purpose of education in a democratic society is to provide opportunities for all citizens to participate fully in the cultural, political, and economic life of the nation and the world; that the essential goals of elementary education are to enable children to become full participants and to develop all their talents and competencies needed to meet the social, historical, and material challenges that they will encounter throughout their lives; and that the teacher's role in education, therefore, is to guide, support, and engage all children, as active learners and makers of meaning, in the discovery and exploration of all aspects of the natural world and their cultural heritages. It should be understood that knowledge and understanding are socially constructed, and that children can be and must be coproducers of meanings who, as active participants (agents) in their own education, become competent to think for themselves, to exercise critical judgment, to solve problems, and act as responsible citizens in a just and democratic society.

Teaching and learning are inseparable components of the process of education. As teachers and learners encounter a particular content, problem, or object of study, they engage as agents, as subjects in the creation of knowledge. The teacher may know more, but does not know everything, and is therefore also a learner. The learner may know less about that particular content, but the learner is never completely ignorant, and is therefore also a teacher. The teacher must fundamentally respect the learner's knowledge derived from the learner's experiences, and the teacher must act to guide the learner to new understandings through serious, critical study and reflection. Moreover, teachers must reflect critically upon the cultural sources and conditions of their own knowledge, that is, as reflective of their own lived experiences and cultural identities. In this fashion the process of education is child-centered—it begins with the knowledge and interests of the child, but it does not remain there. Rather, education so conceived is constructive and elaborative—moving both learners and teachers to new understandings and competencies. The teacher can be neither authoritarian nor a romanticist about "natural learning" who would deny a role for serious teaching. "We need neither authoritarianism nor permissiveness, but democratic substance" (*Pedagogy of Hope*, p. 113). A critical educator must be prepared to intervene, but also to repudiate the banking approach. "What is ethically required of progressive educators is that, consistent with their democratic dream, they respect the educands [learners], and therefore never manipulate them." (p. 80). He or she is never authoritarian, and "never cancels, crushes or hinders the development of the educands thinking" (p. 117).

A radical, liberatory education in the United States is impossible without the capacity to more truly read the realities of pervasive and systematic racism, sexism and class oppression. It is a feature of our national myths to profess to aspire toward equality and the end of discriminatory practices (to have constitutional and legal protections), but to simultaneously remain blind to the "savage inequalities" that exist.[19] In the context of the United States, unmasking the mechanisms of domination and subordination depends upon recognizing that race, gender, culture, and language remain the central regimes of representation in struggles for identity and liberation. The naming of the systematic marginalization of people of color is essential to the reconstruction of the existing power relations.

The dominant ideologies operate to render racism and sexism both visible and invisible. That one is male or female and white or black are immediately visible and enduring features of identity; but systematic discrimination is reduced to a problem for litigation. Among Americans of European origins, there is a nearly complete failure to examine the historical construct of "whiteness" as an identity and access to privilege (I write from the position of being white and male and middle class). New generations, rather than learning from the struggles of their parents and grandparents, are recruited into the experience of being "white." What has been perfected in this society, for the privileged middle class, is the comfort of not seeing, of not knowing. The public schools, which represent white middle-class discourses and positionality, have perfected pedagogies of ignorance. Teachers, as products of these schools, are easily recruited in the reproduction of such schools. By means of the introjection of the dominant ideologies, the objectified learners (those who are not agents) participate in their own subordination. A critical pedagogy (for schools and for teacher education) that reveals and challenges can intervene by respecting the learners as subjects and thereby contribute to the transformation of present realities.

"In a progressive educational practice…one searches, through the teaching of content, to unveil the reasons behind [social] problems…to make the students unquietly critical, challenging them to understand that the world that is being presented as given is, in fact, a world being made and, for this very reason, can be changed, transformed, reinvented" (*Pedagogy of the City*, p. 24). Educators are also producers of knowledge. They are potentially transformative intellectuals, cultural workers, and border-crossers. The contradiction of schools lies in the possibilities for both reproduction and reconstruction, for both colonialization and liberation. "The fundamental issue is politics. It has to do with which content gets taught, to whom, in favor of what, of whom, against what, against whom, and how it gets taught. It has to do with what kind of participation students, parents, teachers, and grassroots movements have in the discussion around the organization of content" (p. 40).

Elementary teacher education must be viewed critically, ideologically. Just as children acquire their first language and discourse patterns without conscious reflection or intentional instruction, children also acquire, from earliest childhood, the ready-made categories of experience—the regimes of truth: what it is to be male-female, black-white, rich-poor; one learns "place" or position without conscious or critical reflection at an age when possibilities for resistance are least available.[20] Thus, the conditions of oppression are naturalized through the mechanisms of identity formation and the naming of reality as simply given, rather than as constructed. However, a critical pedagogy for elementary schools, as a form of political struggle, can begin a critique of language and the categories of experience so as to undertake a new reading of reality. This is essential to protecting and extending a critical literacy such as Anna's.

Conclusion

To create a critical pedagogy for elementary teacher education will require fundamental change in (1) the intellectual preparation of teachers, (2) the serious study of and reflection upon pedagogy and practice, (3) the nature, duration and variety of field-based experiences, and (4) the permanent professional development of teachers.

It is absolutely essential that teachers in this society be seen (and see themselves) as intellectuals. Through serious and competent study in the liberal arts and sciences, prospective teachers can come to understand the construction of knowledge and experience in diverse domains of interest encompassing the social and physical world, human histories and cultures, as well as distinct modes of human expression from languages and the arts to mathematics. Unless teachers are serious (and joyful) learners, who have achieved competence in domains of interest, they cannot share that experience with young learners. If the dignity, respect, and autonomy of the teaching profession can be positively influenced by the adjustment of teacher certification requirements, perhaps by imposing specific undergraduate degree requirements (e.g., recent regulatory changes in Massachusetts require teachers to have majored not in education but in some domain of the liberal arts), then such changes should be introduced nationally.

It is important, however, to recognize that typical liberal arts major requirements are no guarantee that the student has achieved competent understanding of any but the most general sorts of "cultural literacy" or the narrowest of academic specializations. The intellectual development of teachers must be a component of their professional training at both undergraduate and graduate degree levels. It is doubtful that all liberal arts majors would have engaged in serious study of history, culture, or critical theory—which must be regarded as essential to critical pedagogy.

Although there are pressures that tend to define schools of education as places for vocational training, and therefore primarily concerned with practice, the serious study of pedagogy and schooling must not be placed outside the liberal arts—in the broadest sense of disciplined inquiry.

> Teachers who fail to take their teaching practice seriously, who therefore do not study, so that they teach poorly, or who teach something they know poorly, who do not fight to have the material conditions absolutely necessary for their teaching practice, deprive themselves of the wherewithal to cooperate in the indispensable intellectual discipline of the students. Thus, they disqualify themselves as teachers. (*Pedagogy of Hope*, p. 82)

Pedagogy, understood as the joining of theory and practice, cannot be reduced to method, materials, techniques, or skills. But neither are theoretical understandings of human learning, social organization, or discipline-based inquiry sufficient to effect competence in teaching. While I argued before that "methods" dominates too much of teacher education, I do not want to make the complementary error of dismissing their significance. As I learned when trying to "teach" ratios and probabilities, my own "competence" in solving given problems in the conventional fashion prepared me not at all for teaching and learning with my students. Pedagogy depends upon competent improvisation, creativity, and, above all, a willingness and readiness to learn. Moreover, pedagogy should be understood as specialized and advanced study of complex, natural systems. For example, the so-called basic (laboratory) research into the nature of human learning may inform teaching, but cannot guide it. Natural social environments, with all the variables and constraints of time, space, participants, and institutional structures, are many orders of magnitude more complex than anything controlled research has begun to understand. Competent teaching is not just a matter of discipline, scheduling, and curriculum "delivery" as some who dismiss the efforts of teachers seem to think it is. Only in the joining of theory and practice can the education of teachers be advanced.

The worst possible circumstance for elementary teacher education would be to spend little or no time in real classrooms with children and competent mentors. Under previous teacher certification regulations in Massachusetts, it would have been possible, with a bachelor's degree, say in geology, to enter a graduate teacher education program without any classroom experience, then complete a series of "foundations" and "methods" courses before finally undertaking a "300 hour" student teaching practicum. At the end of that time one could be certified as a teacher. Recent changes in regulations have mandated nearly twice the time in supervised classroom experience, but even that is too brief. No one learns to teach in the college classroom. Teaching is a craft learned in doing, as all natural learning is. One learns to teach in context, on site, in collaboration with other teachers, professionals, and all the workers in schools and associated agencies—and most fundamentally one learns to teach and learn with the students, their families and communities. Wherever possible, teacher education programs should have begun during undergraduate programs, perhaps comparable to so-called "pre-med" programs. Both intellectual preparation (e.g., in cultural theory) and diverse field-based experiences (e.g., in schools, day-care centers, recreation centers, hospitals, shelters, courts, prisons, etc.) should begin at the earliest opportunity to allow sufficient time for study, experience, and reflection upon theory and practice. Graduate teacher education should entail both rigorous intellectual study and concentrated field-based experience in order to intensify reflection on pedagogy and practice.

Another consequence of recent changes in state certification requirements is the opportunity for prospective teachers to enter the profession very quickly. By creating the category of "provisional teacher" certification, it may be possible to begin teaching (if one holds a bachelor's degree or relevant work experience) after an intensive training period of as little as six weeks or a few months. While there is ample reason for wanting to lengthen teacher education, doing so necessarily increases the cost of preparation and thereby the likelihood that economic obstacles to becoming a teacher would become even greater. As implicit throughout the argument presented earlier, it is essential that a more diverse teacher corps evolve to more closely reflect the diversity of children and adolescents in the public schools. Creating alternative paths to certification (within the credentialing system), allows greater opportunity for more qualified people to enter the profession. This raises the need for the "permanent professional development of teach-ers"—a phrase that Freire uses throughout his reflections on his efforts to transform the schools of São Paulo, Brazil, during his tenure as superintendent for a metropolitan area that includes three million school-aged children. He described his efforts to bring together universities, schools, unions, government agencies, par-ents, and community groups in a coalition to "change the face of the schools"—to make true reform. The partnerships so formed would provide teachers with the support, encouragement, and collabora-tions necessary to their continuous professional development and to the on-going transformation of the schools. In the context of edu-cation reform in the United States, the professional development of teachers must also be made "permanent," through the formal mech-anisms of advanced degree and recertification requirements, as well as through social and cultural partnerships between schools, com-munities, and other social service agencies.

These reflections upon my own professional practice are shaped by my encounter with Paulo Freire. It is fitting perhaps to conclude with a few more comments from his recent book, *Pedagogy of the City*:

> The education worker, as such, is a politician, regardless of whether he or she is aware of it or not. (p. 44)

> Only within a dialectic understanding of the school-society relationship, is it possible not only to understand but also to develop the fundamental role of school in the transformation of society. (p. 49)

> I think the role of a consciously progressive educator is to testify con-stantly to his or her students his or her competence, love, political clari-ty, the coherence between what he or she says and does, his or her tol-erance, his or her ability to live with the different, to fight against the antagonistic. It is to stimulate doubt, criticism, curiosity, questioning, a taste for risk taking, the adventure of creating. (p. 50)

> To change the face of schools implies also listening to the children, to ghetto societies, parents, school directors, instructional coordinators, supervisors, the scientific community, janitors, cafeteria workers, etc. It is

not possible to change the face of schools through an act of the secretary's [superintendent's] goodwill. To conclude, I would say that we are engaged in a struggle for schools that are competent, democratic, serious and happy. (p. 30)

REFERENCES

1. Dewey, John, "My Pedagogic Creed," *The School Journal*, Vol. LIV, No. 3, 1897; reprinted in Martin Dworkin, ed., *Dewey on Education* (New York: Teachers College Press, 1959), p. 27.

2. Hendrix, Julia, "Democracy in Schools and Teacher Education," unpublished paper, 1992.

3. Giroux, Henry, *Teachers as Intellectuals: Towards a Critical Pedagogy of Learning* (South Hadley, Mass.: Bergin and Garvey, 1988); Henry Giroux, *Border Crossings: Cultural Workers and the Politics of Education*, (New York: Routledge, 1992).

4. Kohl, Herbert, *36 Children* (New York: New American Library, 1967).

5. Kozol, Jonathan, *Death at an Early Age: The Destruction of the Hearts and Minds of Negro Children in the Boston Public Schools* (Boston: Houghton Mifflin, 1967).

6. Freire, Paulo, *Pedagogy of the Oppressed* (New York: Continuum, 1970). (My first copy available from Herder and Herder, New York, 1972. Original Portuguese manuscript, 1968.)

7. Freire, Paulo, *Pedagogy of Hope: Reliving Pedagogy of the Oppressed* (New York: Continuum, 1994).

8. Freire, Paulo, *Pedagogy of the City* (New York: Continuum, 1993).

9. Foucault, Michel, "What is an author?" *Language, Counter-Memory, Practice: Selected Essays and Interviews*, D. Bouchard, ed. (Ithaca, N.Y.: Cornell University Press, 1977).

10. An especially interesting and fierce exchange of views appeared in *Phi Delta Kappan* from November 1988 through November 1989. Marie Carbo, "Debunking the Great Phonics Myth," *Phi Delta Kappan*, November 1988, pp. 226-240; Jeanne Chall, "*Learning to Read: The Great Debate 20 Years Later.* A Response to 'Debunking the Great Phonics Myth,'" *Phi Delta Kappan*, March 1989, pp. 521-538; several further responses and counter-responses appeared in the following months; see also, Frank Smith, "Overselling Literacy," *Phi Delta Kappan*, January 1989, pp. 353-359; and Denny Taylor, "Toward a Unified Theory of Literacy Learning and Instructional Practices," *Phi Delta Kappan*, November 1989, pp. 184-193.

11. Burbules, Nicholas, "Tootle: A Parable of Schooling and Destiny,"

Harvard Educational Review, vol. 56, no. 3, pp. 239-256 (1986).

12. Crampton, Gertrude, *Tootle* (New York: Golden Press, 1946).

13. Leaf, Munro, *The Story of Ferdinand* (New York: Viking Press, 1938).

14. Hazelwood School District v. Kuhlmeier et al., 484 U.S. 260, 1987.

15. *The Nation*, editorial, January 30, 1988.

16. Ulich, Robert, ed., *Three Thousand Years of Educational Wisdom: Selections from Great Documents* 2nd ed., (Cambridge, Mass.: Harvard University Press, 1954).

17. Chomsky, Noam, *Necessary Illusions: Thought Control in Democratic Societies* (Boston: South End Press, 1989).

18. Macedo, Donaldo, *Literacies of Power: What Americans Are Not Allowed to Know* (Boulder, CO: Westview Press, 1994).

19. Kozol, Jonathan, *Savage Inequalities: Children in America's Schools* (New York: Crown, 1991).

20. Gore, Jennifer, *The Struggle for Pedagogies: Critical and Feminist Discourses as Regimes of Truth* (New York: Routledge, 1993).

CHAPTER ELEVEN

DILEMMAS OF LITERACY
Plato and Freire[1]

James Paul Gee

In 1988, in a paper entitled "Legacies of Literacy," I proposed what I called a "problem/question"—one to which I admitted I did not then (and do not now) have *the* answer. I attempted to make the case that this problem/question ultimately requires an answer from each reader in the form of his or her own "theory of literacy." My paper started with Plato and ended with Paulo Freire. Although the paper was meant to raise questions, not to lodge criticisms, several of the editors of the journal where my paper originally appeared read my questions as criticisms and told me that it was inappropriate to criticize Freire. In fact, they asked me to change the ending of the paper so as to "soften" it. Since the paper has appeared, I have, in conversation with some who claim to be "Freirians," found the same attitude, namely, that questions are criticisms and criticisms, of Freire show a lack of sympathy for his political project and for the liberation of oppressed peoples.

This response is not one I imagine Freire himself would make—consider, for instance, the following remark Freire made about one of his books: "...here are a few brotherly suggestions. First, start rereading this book. Your second reading should be far more critical than the first. I suggest this not only for this book but for all your reading," Freire (1985, p. 198). However, this response does exemplify part of the "problem/question" I was trying to raise: What are the conditions of real dialogue, and why is it so hard to differentiate dialogue and criticism?

---

1   This paper is a revised version of a small portion of my paper, "Legacies of Literacy: From Plato to Freire through Harvey Graff." I thank the *Harvard Educational Review* and the *Journal of Education* for permission to rework some of this material.

With these remarks serving as an interpretive framework, I will rehearse here a version of my problem/question, because I believe it an important one, all the more so in our "new world order," both within the United States and outside it. The question today of how we work together to make real local and global change—in a world where some countries are actually engaging in revolutions in order to obtain some fantasy version of an "American style" capitalism that, at home, is choking to death on its own social, economic, and political processes—is all the more pressing.

So, I start with Plato, because, like Freire, he was a revolutionary thinker and doer with strong views on literacy. He was, as well, like Freire, a champion of dialogue. Although it is another story, for another place, Plato has also been responsible, in the history of Western culture, for much of the thinkings, doings, and institutions that Freire has worked so hard to save us from. Plato was, in fact, one of the first great literate figures in Western culture (his dialogues are both great literature and great discursive, expository writing). He has also the distinction of being the first writer to attack writing in writing, primarily in his brilliant dialogue, the *Phaedrus* (Rowe, 1986; see Derrida, 1972; Burger, 1980; De Vries, 1969; Griswold, 1986).

To start with, Plato thought writing led to the deterioration of human memory and a view of knowledge that was both facile and false. Given writing, knowledge no longer had to be internalized, made "part of oneself." Rather, writing allowed, perhaps even encouraged, a reliance on the written text as an "external crutch" or "reminder." For Plato, a people knew only what they could reflectively defend in face-to-face dialogue with someone else. The written text tempted one to take its words as authoritative and final because of its illusory quality of seeming to be explicit, clear, complete, closed, and self-sufficient, that is "unanswerable."

In addition to these flaws, there are two other problems with writing that were far more important to Plato. To cite the dialogue, the first of these is:

Socrates: I think writing has this strange feature, which makes it like painting. The offspring of painting stand there as if alive, but if you ask them something, they preserve a quite solemn silence. Similarly with written words: you might think that they spoke as if they had some thought in their heads, but if you ever ask them about any of the things they say out of a desire to learn, they point to just one thing, the same thing each time. (275 d 4 - e 1)

Socrates goes on immediately to the second charge:

And when once it is written, every composition is trundled about every-where in the same way, in the presence both of those who know about the subject and of those who have nothing at all to do with it, and it does not know how to address those it should address and not those it should not. When it is ill-treated and unjustly abused, it always needs its father to help it; for it is incapable of defending or helping itself. (275 e 1 - 275 e 6)

These charges are connected. What writing can't do is defend itself; it can't stand up to questioning. For Plato true knowledge comes about when one person makes a statement and another asks "What do you mean?" Such a request forces people to "re-say," say in different words, what they mean. In the process they come to see more deeply what they mean, and come to respond to the per-spective of another voice/viewpoint. In one sense, writing—unlike face-to-face speaking—can only respond to the question of "What do you mean?" by repeating what it has said (the text). It is at this juncture of the argument that Plato extends his charges against writ-ing to an attack also on rhetoricians and politicians (he referred to both as "speech writers"). They sought, in their writing and speech-es, to forestall questioning altogether, since their primary interest was to persuade (through language that claimed to be logically complete and self-sufficient, standing in no need of supplement or rethinking, authoritative in its own right), not to mutually discover the truth in dialogue.

However, there is a sense in which writing *can* respond to the question "What do you mean?" It can do so by readers "re-saying," saying in other words, namely *their own* words, what the text means. But this is a problem for Plato. It is, in fact, part of what he has in mind when he says that writing "does not know how to address those it should address and not those it should not." By its very nature writing can travel in time and space away from its "author" (for Plato, its "father") to be read by just anyone, interpreted however they will, regardless of the reader's training, effort, or ignorance (witness what happened to Nietzsche in the hands of the Nazis; to the Bible in the hands of those who have used it to justify wealth, racism, imperialism, war, and exploitation). The voice behind the text cannot respond or defend itself. And it cannot vary its substance and tone to speak differently to different readers based on their natures and contexts.

Plato was too sophisticated to make a crude distinction (so popular today) between speech and writing, orality and literacy. He extended his attack to the poets, and in particular to Homer, the great representative of the flourishing oral culture that preceded Greek literacy. The oral culture stored its knowledge, values, and norms in great oral epics (e.g., the *Iliad* and the *Odyssey*), passed down from generation to generation. To ensure that these epics were not lost to memory, and with them the cultural knowledge and values they stored, they had to be highly memorable. Thus, they were highly dramatic (built around action) and rhythmical (a species of song), features that facilitate human memory. That is, they had to be a form of poetry (Havelock, 1963; Ong, 1982). But, Plato argued, the oral tradition via its very drama and poetry lulled the Greeks to sleep and encouraged them to "take for granted" the contents of the epics, thus allowing them to accept uncritically the traditional values of their culture.

The oral epic could not stand up to the question "What do you mean?" either. Such a question was a request to poets to re-say their words in a different form, to take them out of poetry, and put them into prose, and the words thereby lost the power that had lulled the Greeks into a "dream state" (Havelock, 1963). In fact, *here* writing facilitated the critical process. Once written down, the epics could be scanned at leisure, various parts of the text could be juxtaposed, and in the process contradictions and inconsistencies were all the easier to find, no longer hiding under the waves of rhythm and the limitations of human aural memory (Havelock, 1963, 1986; Ong,

1982; Goody, 1977, 1986).

Plato's deeper attack, then, is against any form of language or thought that cannot stand up to the question "What do you mean?" That question is an attempt to unmask attempts to persuade (whether by poets, rhetoricians, or politicians) based on self-interested claims to authority or traditionalism. Plato, then, thought only dialogic thought, speaking, and writing authentic, with the proviso that writing was inherently prone to antidialogic properties. Plato's own resolution to this conflict, as a writer, was to write dialogues and to warn that writing of any sort should never be taken too seriously. It should never be taken as seriously as the "writing" that is "written together with knowledge in the soul of the learner, capable of defending itself, and knowing how to speak and keep silent in relation to the people it should" (276 a 5 - a 8). In fact, for Plato, authentic uses of language were always educational in the root sense of "drawing out" of oneself and others what was good, beautiful, and true.

All this may make Plato sound like a progressive, modern educator defending "open classrooms" and "process" approaches to writing and speaking. He was no such thing. Plato's concerns about writing had a darker, more political side, one auspicious for the future of literacy. Both Socrates and Plato were opponents of the traditional order of their societies, and in that sense revolutionaries. In the *Republic*, Plato drew a blueprint for a utopian, "perfect" state, the sort that he wished to put in the place of the current order. Plato's perfect state was an authoritarian one based on the view that people are (by and large) born suited for a particular place in a naturally given hierarchy with "philosopher-kings" (i.e., Plato or people like him) at the top (or, at least, people are given differential access to higher places in society based on inherent characteristics and various tests). The philosopher-kings rule in the best interests of those below them, many of whom have no actual say in government, the philosopher-king knowing their interests better than they do.

In this light, Homer, the rhetoricians, and the politicians, can be seen as Plato's political opposition, competitors to the philosopher-king's assertion to power. In the case of Homer, as long as Greek culture was swept away in rhapsody by Homer's epic verse, its members were not listening to either the oral or written dialogues of Plato. Plato's tactic (originated by Socrates) of confronting the poets with the question "What do you mean?"—forcing them into prose—was both an intellectually and a politically motivated assault, an attempt to break the power base of Homer and traditional culture (Havelock, 1963).

This question ("What do you mean?") has a related effect when asked of the politicians, speechwriters, and lawgivers, those who control the new Greek literacy. It is a request for them to say what they have just said over again, but in less rhetorically persuasive language. Once stripped of its "rhetoric," the power-seeking, lack of critical thought, and self-interest that lies behind their language is exposed. And in the process they are also rendered vulnerable to a political assault by Plato's dialectic and its assumptions about what is right and just (in other words, the invitation to "dialogue" with Plato, given his skills, is not likely to be one that will show the politicians and rhetoricians to their best advantage).

In the preceding light, Plato's attack on writing takes on additional meaning. His objection that the written text can get into the wrong hands, that it cannot defend itself, is an objection to the fact that the reader can freely interpret the text without the author ("authority") being able to "correct" that interpretation, that is, to stipulate the correct interpretation. In this sense, Plato wants the author to stand as a voice behind the text not (just) to engage in responsive dialogue, but to enforce canonical interpretations. And these canonical interpretations are rendered correct by the inherently higher nature of the philosopher-king, backed up by the advantages (which the *Republic* ensures) of socially situated power and state-supported practice in verbal and literacy skills.

As a writer, Plato also had a resolution to this problem, the problem of how to enforce "correct" interpretation. First, he believed that his writings should by and large be restricted to his own inner circle of students and followers. Second, it appears he may not have actually written down his most serious thoughts, but only spoken them (none of his dialogues contain a discussion between two mature philosophers). And, finally, he built into his written dialogues various layers of meaning such that they announce their deeper message only to those readers skilled enough to find it, where this skill is tied to being trained (or "initiated") so as to interpret the way one is "supposed" to (Griswold, 1986: 221; the same strategy is used in many sacred writings, e.g. the New Testament—see Kermode, 1979).

His ultimate solution, however, would have been the instantiation of the society delineated in the *Republic*, where the structure of the state and its institutions would have ensured "correct" interpretations. This last solution is the one that has, in fact, been realized most often in history (though not by states realizing all the other aspects of the Republic).

There is a contradiction here. In Plato we see two sides to literacy: literacy as liberator and literacy as weapon. Plato wants to ensure that there is always a voice behind the spoken or written "text" that can dialogically respond, but he also wants to ensure that this voice is not overridden by respondents who are careless, ignorant, lazy, self-interested, or ignoble. One must somehow empower the voice behind the text, privilege it, at least to the extent of ruling out some interpretations and some interpreters (readers/listeners). And such a ruling out will always be self-interested to the extent that it must be based on some (privileged) view of what the text means, what correct interpretations are, and who are acceptable readers (where acceptable readers will perforce include the one making the ruling).

The ruling is also self interested in that it has a political dimension, an assertion to power, a power that may reside in institutions that seek to enforce it (whether modern schools and universities or Plato's governing classes in the *Republic*). But then we are close to an authority that kills dialogue by dictating who is to count as a respondent and what is to count as a response.

There is, however, no easy way out: if all interpretations (re-sayings) count, then none do, as the text then says everything and therefore nothing. And if it takes no discipline, experience, or "credentials" to interpret, then it seems all interpretations *will* count. If they can't all count, then someone has to say who does and who does not have the necessary "credentials" to interpret. A desire to honor the thoughtful and critical voice behind the text, to allow it to defend itself (often coupled with a will to power), leads us to Plato's authoritarianism. In fleeing it we are in danger of being led right into the lap of Plato's poets, speechwriters, and politicians. For them, all that counts is the persuasiveness or cunning of their language, its ability to capture readers, to tell them what they want to hear, to validate the status quo (and therefore the views readers in all likelihood already hold and that form the basis for their interpretations). There have been many facile attempts to get out of Plato's dilemma. But there is no easy way out.

Up to this point, however, I have built a somewhat one-sided case, concentrating on the authoritarian side of Plato's dilemma. But there is another side, the liberating side of the dilemma, that is, the use of an emancipatory literacy for religious, political, and cultural resistance to domination. No name is more closely associated with emancipatory literacy than that of Paulo Freire (1970, 1973, 1985). Like Bakhtin (e.g., 1981), and to a certain extent like Plato, Freire believes that literacy only empowers people when it renders them active questioners of the social reality around them:

> Reading the world always precedes reading the word, and reading the word implies continually reading the world.... In a way, however, we can go further and say that reading the word is not preceded merely by reading the world, but by a certain form of *writing* it or *rewriting* it, that is, of transforming it by means of conscious, practical work. For me, this dynamic movement is central to the literacy process. (Freire and Macedo, 1987: p. 35)

In a chapter entitled "The People Speak Their Word: Literacy in Action" in his 1987 book with Donaldo Macedo, Freire discusses and cites material from learner workbooks he helped design for a national literacy campaign in the republic of São Tome and Principle, a nation that had recently freed itself from "the colonial yoke to which it was subjected for centuries" (p. 65). He calls attention to the way in which "the challenge to the critical perception of those becoming literate gradually grows, page by page" (p. 72). The second notebook begins by "provoking a debate" (p. 76), and goes on to say to the learner: "To study is not easy, because to study is to create and re-create and not to repeat what others say" (p. 77). The notebook tells the learner that education is meant to develop "a critical spirit and creativity, not passivity" (p. 91). Freire says that in these materials "one does not particularly deal with delivering or transferring to the people more rigorous explanations of the facts, as though these facts were finalized, rigid, and ready to be digested. One is concerned with stimulating and challenging them" (p. 78).

All this sounds open and liberating, much as Plato initially did, and in not dissimilar terms. But there's another note here as well. Freire comes up square against Plato's problem: What is to ensure that when people read (either a text or the world) they will do so "correctly"? Thus, the second notebook also reads:

> When we learn to read and write, it is also important to learn to think correctly. To think correctly we should think about our practice in work. We should think about our daily lives. (p. 76)

> Our principal objective in writing the texts of this Notebook is to challenge you, comrades, to think correctly... (p. 87)

> Now try to do an exercise, attempting to think correctly. Write on a piece of paper how you see this problem: "Can the education of children and adults, after the Independence of our country, be equal to the education that we had before Independence?" (p. 88)

> Let's think about some qualities that characterize the new man and the new woman. One of these qualities is agreement with the People's cause and the defense of the People's interests... The correct sense of political militancy, in which we are learning to overcome individualism and egoism, is also a sign of the new man and the new woman.
> To study (a revolutionary duty), to think correctly...all these are characteristics of the new man and the new woman. (p. 92)

It is, at first sight, perhaps, startling that a pedagogy that Freire says is "more a pedagogy of question than a pedagogy of answer," that is radical because it is "less certain of 'certainties'" (p. 54), in fact knows what it is to think *correctly*. Students are told not to repeat what others say, but then the problem becomes that in re-saying for themselves what they read, they may say it "wrong," that is in conflict with Freire's or the state's political perspective. Thus, the literacy materials must ensure that they think correctly, that is, re-say or interpret text and world "correctly."

Freire is well aware that no literacy is politically neutral, including the institutionally based literacy of church, state, and school that has and continues to undergird the hegemonic process in Western society. Freire has his *Republic* too. There is no way out of Plato's dilemma. Literacy always comes with a perspective on interpretation that is ultimately political, ultimately a view about how the world *ought* to be. One can hide that perspective the better to claim it isn't there, or one can put it out in the open. There is no way out of having an opinion, an "ideology" (in the sense of a theory of how social goods and power *ought* to be distributed, see Gee, 1990/1996: chapter 1), and a strong one, as did Plato, as does Freire. Literacy education is not for the timid.

Before concluding, there is one objection that has been made to my previous remarks about Freire's "correct way of thinking" that should be mentioned. The objection runs as follows: There is a difference between "correct way of thinking" as a universal dilemma in the interpretation of texts and "correct way of thinking" as individual peoples' processes of attempting to think clearly *for themselves* in the specific context where they are learning to throw off the internalized voice of the oppressor. While this objection misses my point, it actually does get us to the heart of the matter. It is clear in the material I cited earlier that any thoughts that do not fit "the new man and the new woman," that do not agree with "the People's cause," will count as "misinterpretations," as the internal voice of the oppressor, and thus false. But this is, I have argued, the *normal* case with any literacy practice, whatever your politics: any literacy (any practice of interpretation) comes with built-in perspectives and assumptions that serve as a test as to whether one is correctly practicing that literacy.

There is no honest way to evade "owning up" to your perspectives and assumptions (which in one sense constitute your "politics"); to leave them implicit is to pretend they don't exist and to allow them to serve your political purposes covertly. Indeed, much of the literature on school-based literacy makes just this point: the perspectives, values, and assumptions built into school-based literacy practices are often left implicit, thus empowering those mainstream children who already have them and disempowering those children who do not and for whom they are never rendered visible, save in the negative evaluations they constantly receive (Cazden, 1987; Cook-Gumperz, 1986; Heath, 1983).

In the end, the problem/question I have posed by thinking about Plato and Freire in juxtaposition suggests, to me, at any rate, that work on literacy (or, better, sociohistorical, sociocultural, politically situated literacies) must be inherently tied, not simply to rhetoric about democracy and liberation, but to *specific* arguments about what social, cultural, educational, and political institutions ought to look like, and how they could actually be realized. Plato did so; so, too, Freire in the learner workbooks cited earlier. The question of how interpretations are to be "enforced" ("socialized," "communalized")—a question that, I have argued, cannot be evaded (other than by a facile and complete relativism)—ultimately becomes the question of what will constitute social wealth in common ("commonwealth") in modern institutions and states.

REFERENCES

Bakhtin, M. M., *The Dialogic Imagination*. M. Holquist, ed. (Austin: University of Texas Press, 1981).

Burger, R., *Plato's Phaedrus: A Defense of a Philosophic Art of Writing* (Alabama: University of Alabama Press, 1980).

Cazden, C., *Classroom Discourse: The Language of Teaching and Learning* (Portsmouth, N.H.: Heinemann, 1987).

Cook-Gumperz, J., *The Social Construction of Literacy* (Cambridge: Cambridge University Press, 1986).

Derrida, J., La pharmacie de Platon, In *La Dissemination* (Paris: Seuil, 1986), pp. 69-198.

De Vries, G. J., *A Commentary on the Phaedrus of Plato* (Amsterdam: Hakkert, Adolf M., 1969).

Eagleton, T., *The Function of Criticism: From the Spectator to Post-structuralism* (London: Verso, 1984).

Freire, P., *Pedagogy of the Oppressed* (New York: Seabury Press, 1970).

Freire, P., *Education for Critical Consciousness* (New York: Seabury Press, 1973).

Freire, P., *The Politics of Education* (South Hadley, Mass.: Bergin & Garvey, 1987).

Freire, P., and D. Macedo, *Literacy: Reading the Word and the World* (South Hadley, Mass.: Bergin & Garvey, 1987).

Gee, J. P., Legacies of Literacy: From Plato to Freire through Harvey Graff, *Harvard Educational Review*, vol. 58, pp. 195-212 (1988), (reprinted in special issue of *Journal of Education*, vol. 171, pp. 147-165 (1989), and in Masahiko Minami and Bruce P. Kennedy, eds., *Language Issues in Literacy and Bilingual/Multicultural Education*, Reprint Series No. 22 (Cambridge, Mass.: *Harvard Educational Review*, 1991), pp. 266-285.

Gee, J. P., *Social Linguistics and Literacies: Ideology in Discourses*, 2nd ed., (London: Falmer Press, 1996)

Goody, J., *The Domestication of the Savage Mind* (Cambridge: Cambridge University Press, 1977).

Goody, J., *The Logic of Writing and the Organization of Society* (Cambridge: Cambridge University Press, 1986).

Griswold, C. L., *Self-knowledge in Plato's Phaedrus* (New Haven: Yale University Press, 1986).

Havelock, E. A., *Preface to Plato* (Cambridge, Mass.: Harvard University Press, 1963).

Havelock, E., *The Muse Learns to Write: Reflections on Orality and Literacy from Antiquity to the Present* (New Haven: Yale University Press, 1986).

Heath, S. B., *Ways with Words: Language, Life and Work in Communities and Classrooms* (Cambridge: Cambridge University Press, 1983).

Kermode, F., *The Genesis of Secrecy: On the Interpretation of Narrative* (Cambridge, Mass.: Harvard University Press, 1979).

Ohmann, R., *English in America* (Cambridge and Oxford: Oxford University Press, 1976).

Ong, W., S. J., *Orality and Literacy: The Technologizing of the Word* (London: Methuen, 1982).

Rowe, C. J., *Plato: Phaedrus,* translation and commentary, (Warminster, Wiltshire, England: Aris & Philips, 1986).

CHAPTER TWELVE

AFRICAN WOMEN AND REVOLUTIONARY CHANGE
A Freirian and Feminist Perspective

Asgedet Stefanos

Encountering Freire: A Personal Note

In 1974, I came to Cambridge, Massachusetts to pursue my doctorate in education. A few months earlier, Paulo Freire had visited. His new book *Pedagogy of the Oppressed* had ignited enormous interest among graduates raring to learn an alternative approach to literacy education. For those of us from the Third World societies, *Pedagogy* provided a welcome perspective on education by a person who came from that part of the world. *Pedagogy* did not hand us a prescription for literacy training, but rather delineated a philosophical and theoretical orientation to this project. We grappled with Freire's theory, its interrelationship with his experience (practice), and an abundance of new terms and concepts. Some of my peers faulted *Pedagogy* for failing to spell out concrete techniques in literacy education. These critics were frustrated by Freire's concentration on theory, which they found inaccessible. Still others (and I count myself among these) felt that *Pedagogy* catalyzed a sense of mission and a myriad of vital insights.

Those of us inspired by Freire began to recognize that to understand fully his ideas, we needed a process to "work" and "confront" them. Taking our cue from our mentor, we needed to shift the power and control of knowledge creation to our own hands.

We formed an informal group. The group consisted of both women and men originating from diverse countries, including Columbia, Brazil, Chile, the United States, Somalia, Eritrea. Its members had different political orientations, class affiliations and racial identities. Some of us studied Freire for his philosophical approach to education and learning, others for his theory of knowledge and politics, and still others for his commitment to activism and community development. The interplay between major ideas in *Pedagogy* and our diverse work interests became an avenue to gain a deeper understanding of Freire's thinking. We valued that Paulo Freire stepped beyond the analysis of oppression, to conceptualize the constituents of and catalysts for empowerment. This proactive orientation was inspiring and mobilizing.

As for me, it was a distinct moment in my life. I was returning to the university with a felt need to weave my political and personal selves. As a student in the United States, I had been politically active in supporting the ongoing Eritrean revolution and in articulating solidarity with other African anticolonial movements. I had also been in the United States long enough to feel engaged by and situated within the struggles of African-Americans and other peoples of color. I was initially led into activism through my experience of and opposition to oppression based on nationality and race. At the time in the Boston area, I was one of only a handful of Third World women participating in progressive organizations supporting national liberation struggles. It was abundantly and painfully clear that issues of gender permeated and constrained our activism. Feminism became an important personal and political frame of reference. My scholarly interest in women and education is rooted in my own individual history and journey. I am a first generation woman to achieve higher education. It was a path actively resisted by my parents, who viewed it as a tragic detour from an early and successful marriage. My mother was nonliterate, in a context where participation in education was not allowed for females.

During the initial year of graduate study, I examined Third World revolutionary thinkers. My political and social concerns were primarily shaped by the voices of Paulo Freire, Franz Fanon, Albert Memmi, and Amilcar Cabral. Each emphasized and provided insights on the nature of subjugation, the relationship between the oppressed and oppressor, and the role of culture in curtailing or promoting freedom and empowerment.

In the preface to *A Dying Colonialism*, Franz Fanon gives a voice to the reawakening African masses: "This is what we want and this is what we shall achieve. We do not believe that there exists anywhere a force capable of standing in our way" (Fanon, 1965). Yet, Fanon gave much attention to what holds the subjugated back. In a society where social groups are ranked and accorded vastly unequal resources and treatment, people develop deep insecurities about their own status within the system. These insecurities produce a need to emulate those above and derogate those of or below one's own strata. Accordingly, Fanon noted that race prejudice often binds the moderately oppressed to ruling elites. Albert Memmi indicates that social elites employ not only direct force to maintain their power and privileges, but also utilize indirect methods to make the oppressed believe and collude in their own oppression (Memmi, 1967). The oppressed have to break the cycle themselves and achieve inner freedom, through social and cultural transformation. Amilcar Cabral emphasized that "culture is thought" and that "culture is also a product of history—just as a flower is a product of a plant—and is also a determinant of history by positive or negative influence it exerts" (Cabral, 1973). During the long campaign for national liberation in Guinea Bissau, Cabral proclaimed that resistance is a cultural act, and that it must promote cultural change which enables the colonized people to "return to the source," to reassert their own history, and recapture their own identity. Cabral said, "cultural transformation becomes possible only when men and women fight their mental battles for themselves." He placed supreme value on developing the masses as an active conscious subject: "political preparation is extremely important, without it, nothing of lasting value can be done. [It] is the toughest, most daunting, but also most important aspect of the whole campaign for national liberation" (Davidson, 1969).

Paulo Freire brought rich understanding about education and learning to the dialogue on how the oppressed forge and solidify change. He was a major influence in my effort to become an educator and to integrate my political, social, and intellectual concerns.

In the late 1970s, Freire became directly involved with the Guinean revolution in which he put into practice his concept of education during national reconstruction. I set out to do research on how and why African women are oppressed; how do women get emancipated; and, what's the role of education in this.

During my graduate studies, I struggled to establish a theoretical framework to ground and guide my analysis of the realities of Third World women. Although they provided relevant concepts and methodological guidelines, Cabral, Freire, and my other mentors did not give adequate focused attention to women's oppression and female emancipation.

I was frustrated by the inadequacies of Western economic development theories. These approaches (modernization, dependency, developmentalist, female spheres) marginalize women and focus on Third World men as the key subject (or object) of change. Both modernization theorists and their critics, dependency theorists (many of whom are Third World men) share the view that social power is fundamentally derived from economic dominance. Patriarchy and gender relations are absent from these analyses. Women enter only on the periphery; the emphasis is on how women can "contribute" to development, rather than how notions of economic development need to be reframed so that women's needs can be fully included.

By contrast, the three broad themes of Western feminism—classical Marxist, radical feminist, and socialist feminist—put women in the center. I considered the strengths and weaknesses of each orientation in addressing the historical and contemporary realities of African women. Generally, I concluded that while Western feminism has supplied a range of notions pertinent to gender oppression in the Third World, Third World women themselves need to broaden feminist thinking so that it is thoroughly inclusive.

An important element of my work was my view that education serves as a vital catalyst in the emancipation of women from class, national, and gender oppression. Through education, women can transform their material conditions, social relations, and consciousness. It facilitates the creation of the "new woman" by raising consciousness and skill-building. Education enables women to articulate how change occurs and what kinds of change should occur.

A campaign to provide emancipatory education for Third World women does not occur in isolation. It requires the support of a national liberation struggle and/or progressive nation building. I wanted to assess how a liberation struggle against colonial and imperial aggression—through its political leadership and also by the people's initiatives—tackled the problem of women's subordinate position within the family and the society. I was particularly interested in examining those Third World national liberation struggles that made a strong philosophical and practical commitment to combating women's oppression.

Women and Education in Guinea Bissau: An Analysis of Theory and Practice

In 1978, I wrote my qualifying paper for a doctoral dissertation, *Women and Education in Guinea Bissau: An Analysis of Theory and Practice* (Stefanos, 1978). In 1974, Guinea Bissau had achieved its independence after 500 years of colonial rule. I studied Guinea Bissauan women for four reasons: Partido Africano Da Independencia da Guinea é Cabo Verde (PAIGC), the national vanguard political party, had made an explicit commitment to include women in its campaigns for liberation; Guinea Bissau, like my homeland, Eritrea, is a small African country, with diverse class, national, and religious groups; Portugal (Guinea Bissau's colonizer) like Ethiopia (Eritrea's colonizer) was itself a client state for more powerful imperial powers; and Amilcar Cabral,[1] PAIGC's leader, was

---

[1] Amilcar Cabral, born in Guinea Bissau in 1925, was an agronomist who studied in Lisbon with Africans from other Portuguese colonies. His contemporaries included Agostinho Neto and Mario de Andrade (founding members of the Popular Movement for the Liberation of Angola—MPLA), and Eduardo Mondlane and Marcelino dos Santos (founding members of Mozambique Liberation Front—FRELIMO). Cabral went back to Guinea Bissau and worked as an agronomist from 1952 to 1954. He traveled throughout the country and acquired a detailed knowledge of its people and their situation. Based on this knowledge, he prepared a detailed analysis of the social structure of different ethnic groups, the revolutionary poten-

an outstanding and complex revolutionary thinker, and in addition, Paulo Freire had actively participated in Guinea Bissau's national reconstruction planning and programs (Freire, 1978).

My research delineated and evaluated what changes have occurred for women in the realm of education in Guinea Bissau since the launching of a national liberation struggle against the Portuguese colonialists and after independence was achieved. The study offered a description of the experiences and efforts of Guinean women themselves, since change was determined, not only by PAIGC's political leadership but also by the people's initiatives. This study had three major parts. First, it presented a historical analysis of Guinea Bissau and explicated PAIGC's broad social vision and specific theories that underpin the education of women. Second, it examined the educational policies and programs that defined the PAIGC's approach to female members of the society. The third section concentrated on outcomes. It assessed how education of women had effected change in their roles and status within both the family and the job market. These changes were measured against the ideals of the philosophies and goals of PAIGC's programs explored in the two preceding sections.

Philosophy: Theoretical Perspectives of PAIGC and the Guinean Revolution
Vision of the New Social Order

The basic principles of PAIGC were to end colonialism, advance economic development, create democracy, develop a cohesive national identity, raise political consciousness, and become active subjects. The struggle against colonialism was only a subcategory within a broader vision. There was much stress on the long-term goal of ending economic underdevelopment, with agricultural production emphasized. Cabral stated, "we are fighting to make the

---

tial of each group and the revolutionary strategy to be used against the Portuguese colonialists. In 1956, Cabral, with a small number of comrades formed PAIGC in Bissau. He went on to become the party's secretary general, primary theoretician, and political organizer. He was assassinated by Portuguese agents in 1973, several months before independence was achieved.

people's labor benefit people with…a full stomach"—but, then quickly added, "with health…and an open enlightened mind" (Chaliand, 1969). PAIGC strove for a revolutionary process that was profoundly democratic. Cabral warned, repeatedly, against the possibility of creating an indigenous ruling elite that would simply replace the Portuguese. In the Party's view, change must be inherently cultural. Cultural transformation becomes possible only when men and women fight their mental battles for themselves. Cabral stated that the rural masses had to make profound transition from the world of tradition, religion, and witchcraft to that of thought and political revolution (Davidson, 1969). Supreme value was placed on developing the masses as an active subject through political consciousness. A gut-willingness to fight and work was not enough.

Philosophy of Education

PAIGC viewed education as interdependent with revolutionary struggle and the task of nation building. The system of pedagogy had to be inextricably linked with the interests of Guinean workers and peasants. The fundamental objectives of the new educational system were to combine learning with productive work, eliminate a colonized mentality, expose and demystify elements of the traditional culture that retarded social and economic transformation, value science in the study of nature and society, and promote widespread mass education. The pedagogical approach was to be congruent with the existing social realities and challenges. During the armed struggle, the party set up an educational system designed to advance the goals of national liberation. Nonformal education was given as high status as formal learning. The PAIGC established each level of schooling as self-contained, instead of the conventional pyramidical type (Freire, 1978). The content of education had to be responsive to the masses of the Guineans. The curriculum was to highlight everyday experiences encountered by students. Abstractions were to be avoided. Strict separation between subjects was viewed as artificial and undesirable. Educational content had to be consistent with the development of revolutionary values. For example, students who cultivated their own food would be learning not only the fundamentals of science and biology, but also the principles of collectivity and cooperation.

Theory of Dual Oppression and of the "New Woman"

PAIGC's commitment to egalitarianism promoted the need to change women's subordinate position to men with in the Guinea Bissau society. Women's equal participation in the revolution and in the society at large became a fundamental goal.

PAIGC articulated the notion that Guinea Bissau women suffer dual oppression—"the one of the Portuguese and the other of [their] men" (Urdang, 1979). The subordination of women was discerned in the domestic as well as the public sphere. Within the family, in traditional Guinea Bissau society, women had a distinctly inferior role and status. An unequal division of labor within the household, discriminatory marriage customs, denigrating religious ideologies and practices, biased customary laws, and chauvinistic attitudes of men—were all viewed as contributors to this reality. Western colonialism left undisturbed women's oppression within the family—in fact it added new discriminatory laws. Within the sphere of the economy, in traditional Guinea Bissau society (as in many other parts of Africa) women had the primary responsibility for agricultural production. With the introduction of a cash-crop economy by the Portuguese, women's inferiority was significantly exacerbated. Cash increased women's dependence on men, and men's absorption with cash crops made women the sole burdened producers of subsistence agriculture. Thus, PAIGC asserted that the oppression of women in Guinea Bissau resulted from both traditionalism and colonialism. The party stressed that the creation of a "new woman" largely depended on women, themselves, initiating change, informed by their own experiences. PAIGC recognized that women's liberation must be launched from two fronts—from above and, as well as, from below (Urdang, 1979). From the outset the party stated clearly that women's liberation, like any freedom, was not a given. It was a right, but it had to be taken.

PAIGC Practice: Women and Education

A broad and comprehensive analysis was required to evaluate PAIGC's programmatic effort to support female emancipation through education. Were programs effective and creative? Were they consistent with the larger social vision and values? Was combating women's subordination occurring in other vital fronts in the public and private sectors?

I surveyed PAIGC's programmatic attacks on all aspects of sexual inegalitarianism. As such, I focused not only on the party's promotion of women's right to an education, but also on a broad array of campaigns for female emancipation within the family, the economy, and the political life of the nation. PAIGC viewed education and learning, not as discrete, isolated activity, but as an integral component of all forms of individual and socioeconomic development. Accordingly, in my view, a broad assessment of the party's programs to eliminate male domination was a critical measure of its specific commitment to eradicate sexual discrimination in the realm of education.

The party attacked female oppression vigorously on three basic fronts—ideological, organizational, and legislative. In the area of ideology, it launched an extensive campaign of consciousness-raising around women's issues. On the organizational level, it promoted increasing participation by women in the new socioeconomic and political institutions formed during the national liberation struggle and after independence. The third approach—the legislative—consisted of a series of laws that were designed to eliminate concrete barriers to women's advancement. This extensive campaign for female emancipation was a favorable indicator that the party was serious in its aim to provide women with equal educational opportunities.

The party's effectiveness in creating a system of schooling that corresponded to its revolutionary educational ideals also was specifically relevant for women; many of the broad ideals were aimed at goals that support and facilitate educational opportunity for women. The developing educational system and programs were structured to eradicate the colonized mentality, discourage elitism, instill collectivity, and encourage the student to be an active subject. The new schooling, unlike traditional and colonial education, was accessible to the masses. It was not segregated artificially "within walls," but rather interconnected with productive labor and national development. Since 99 percent of the population was nonliterate, after independence, in May 1975, at the invitation of Guinean government, Paulo Freire led a team to assist in the campaign for literacy (Freire, 1978). Guinean women's hopes to move beyond pervasive nonliteracy were responded to as the nationwide coeducational school system was erected. The curriculum and pedagogical techniques were consistent with revolutionary ideals and concrete socioeconomic goals for national reconstruction. Finally, programs for nonformal instruction had not taken a back seat to the development of a formal school system, but rather were flourishing and expanding.

PAIGC recognized the need to attack material and attitudinal barriers to women's participation in the educational sector. It launched an intensive political education campaign to counteract the strong resistance and opposition by the peasantry to female schooling. The fundamental obstacle was the parental view that a girl's singular goal was to ready herself for and succeed in getting married. However, there was also an economic basis to the resistance; in rural life peasants are constantly in need of extra hands for domestic and agricultural work. So the party began to address this issue by creating programs that accommodated the masses' concerns and anxieties. Teachers made particularly intensive efforts with girls during school hours to ensure that they would keep up with boys. Schools required girls to complete their schoolwork before the end of the school day, so that they would not be in a bind when faced with the necessity of focusing on work, once back at home. Another approach was to place female students in *internatos* (boarding school). This was a major benchmark in the effort to change parents' attitudes—for now they were permitting their daughters to secure an education, separate and often far away from home. The geographical distance also effectively eliminated all forms of parental interference with girls' pursuit of their studies. By the end of 1973, a substantial advance was made in the realm of female education—a third of elementary and high school graduates were female. This ratio was impressive, when placed within the context of the intense traditional resistance and the grueling demands of a protracted national war of liberation. It also represented significant progress, for during the liberation struggle in 1965, only a quarter of those engaged in education had been female (Urdang, 1979).

My assessment of the philosophical tenets and programmatic actions of PAIGC had been consistently positive. The theory that has guided the party's approach to women and education was, in my view, sound and thoughtful. The theories reviewed grew out of the Guinean experiences. Thus, these speculations bear the strength of their primary creator, Amilcar Cabral, who insisted—"it [can] be no good talking about any theory of social change, unless this theory...[stands] firmly on a known and practical reality" (Davidson, 1969). In its practice, PAIGC had been persistent in advancing the right of women to an education and flexible in disarming the masses' anxieties about that right.

An Encounter with Revolutionary Change: A Portrait of Contemporary Eritrean Women

Background and Overview. In 1961, the Eritrean Liberation Front launched a national liberation struggle in response to Haile Selassie's unilateral incorporation of Eritrea as part of Ethiopia. In 1970, a group of Eritrean activists split from the Eritrean Liberation Front and formed a separate organization called the Eritrean Peoples Liberation Front (EPLF), which emerged as the predominant organization to forge a national liberation struggle. This struggle had enormous success in mobilizing and uniting the Eritrean people. Against enormous odds and with no big power sponsorship, it ultimately succeeded. Eritrea won its national independence in 1993.

Early on, the EPLF determined that it was engaged in a liberation struggle that must take the form of a national democratic revolution. It asserted that it represented the interests of the Eritrean working class—generally described as Eritrea's peasants, workers, and petty bourgeoisie. EPLF adopted the idea of self-reliance and took steps to establish people's democracy in areas as they were liberated.

EPLF claimed that there was a dual and interrelated need for both national independence and an egalitarian social revolution. The former could not be attained without pursuing the latter. In 1974, after decades of male predominance in the struggle, EPLF made a major decision to admit women into the organization and to mount policies and programs against gender inequality in Eritrean society.

In 1983, I began a five-year study that resulted in my dissertation, *An Encounter with Revolutionary Change: A Portrait of Contemporary Eritrean Women*. By then, EPLF's campaign against women's subordination had had time to take root. Female membership in EPLF constituted almost 45 percent of the organization. My study featured twenty-four life histories of Eritrean women. The central questions I assessed were: What constitutes equality? Are Eritrean women experiencing equality? What elements promote (or inhibit) change? What's the role of education in this? Four major realms of Eritrean women's lives were explored—education, the family, economic and political life. The field research was conducted during the struggle for national liberation over a period of two months, in eleven towns and villages in the northeastern and northwestern regions of Eritrea. In addition, I conducted interviews with a range of EPLF officials, including members of its central committee. My study contrasted the perceptions of my female subjects with those of EPLF officials as they assessed the significance and impact of the campaign against male domination.

Methodology. My research strategy was to collect data from two principal sources—intensive interviews and documentary materials—and to categorize them into four major themes: women's relationship to politics, economy, family, and education. A third source of data was my own, as a participant observer, which allowed direct observation of relevant events and participation in the life activities.

I interviewed a diverse group of twenty-four women. These "views from below" were essential in examining Eritrean women's position in the contemporary period, their conception of revolutionary life. I utilized these life histories to illuminate women's position within the broader social and cultural structures and themes in contemporary Eritrean society. The interviews largely encouraged women to focus on themselves; what they do within the revolution; how they assess their activities; how they conceive oppression and emancipation; what they identify as core attitudes and behaviors that are oppressive; whether they see shifts in opportunity as a result of their struggle and their participation in it. A major part of the interview was focused on women's encounters with education, how it was valued, assessments of its impact, where it fits in the women's perception of social change.

The documentary materials that I analyzed were a second major source of data. They helped flesh out the EPLF's "view from above" of women's status and effort to achieve emancipation. They delineated EPLF's strategies and programs for eradicating women's inferior position in Eritrean society. These data illuminated both official policies and programs undertaken to bring about women's equality, and the Front's theoretical viewpoint on the nature of women's oppression.

As a participant-observer, I kept a journal and recorded my experiences and perceptions of the overall revolutionary process, women's emancipatory process, and the interview process. I interviewed a certain number, including several Eritrean men, members of the revolutionary leadership, about their conception of women's emancipation. I also discussed my central areas of study with people other than my subjects. My observations and discussions with various individuals helped illuminate the interviewees' data and redirect the inquiry. I participated in group activities and attended special events which enabled me to observe a range of activities.

The interview subjects came from eleven towns and villages,*

---

* The average length of an interview was about 90 minutes, and it was conducted most in the Tigrignia language. On a couple of occasions, I used translators for those who spoke the Tigre and Kunama languages.

and were not necessarily the most active or visible women from their sites. They were diverse in age, educational level, class background, religious affiliation, and ethnic group. They ranged from 12 to 65 years old, nonliterate to college-educated, peasants and factory workers to students and medical doctors. The religious affiliations included Coptic, Catholic, Protestant, Muslim, and African religious orientations. The nationalities represented were Tigre, Sahho, Belen, Denakil, Kunama, and Kebessa. The sample also included varied marital statuses and ideological positions. Levels of involvement with the liberation struggle and the EPLF, itself, also varied greatly.

The interview format was individual and semistructured. I developed an informal interview guide, which consisted of open-ended questions relating to the four themes of politics, economics, family, and education and utilized women's life histories to illuminate their personal position within the broader social and cultural structures. I wanted Eritrean women to speak in their own voices and ascertain what their own ideas of equality were, how they depicted revolutionary change, to hear what changes they valued and what priorities they set. I also wanted my own evaluations to be firmly rooted in the experiences and perceptions of the women I interviewed and observed.

Methodologically, my knowledge of the language and familiarity with the culture provided me with the means to probe for clarification or elaboration, to help detect error or misunderstanding, and to reduce ambiguities and complexities of Eritrean cultural expression into their English equivalents. In addition, my insider role provided knowledge and reduced problems of ethnocentrism. As an Eritrean woman, I was sensitive to how the framing of questions and the style of interviewer would elicit (or inhibit) open communication from my female subjects. My approach was interactive and openly empathetic. The research work was an intensively collaborative effort between the participants and myself. Many of the subjects indicated there were moments during the interview when new insight and understanding emerged. Many participants stated that they had never had such focused and in depth discussions on gender issues and particularly their own personal lives.

View from Above: EPLF's View of Women's Subordination and Strategies for Change

Politics. The dynamics of national liberation struggle generated EPLF's interest in mobilizing the active support of women. Beginning in 1974, women's political mobilization and integration became a major priority of the front. It strove to eliminate obstacles to women's participation in political activity. Concurrently, women became fighters in the revolutionary army (20 percent by 1983). EPLF was clear that women's political involvement strengthened support for the liberation struggle and all initiatives, including an Eritrean women's organization, were geared to this larger instrumental goal. Women's entry into central leadership positions was not highlighted as particularly desirable. It was not necessary to mobilize effectively on lower levels. While grassroots changes proliferated, the highest strata of leadership were exclusively male.

Economy. EPLF viewed the economy as the critical realm in which to advance women's emancipation. The underlying assumptions of this point of view were: (1) the oppression of women was held to derive from class relations, and men were regarded just as victimized by it as women; (2) economic transformation was key to eliminating women's oppression; and (3) the mobilization of women into the labor force was seen as a means to enhance the drive for national economic development and, at the same time, women's inferior status dissipated through wage labor. Thus, production and development are primary goals. Women's equality, while desirable, was subordinate to economic transformation. Economic activity is stressed as the most vital pathway for women to achieve liberation. Productive labor, according to EPLF, promoted transformations in both women's consciousness and material circumstances.

Family. The EPLF's concept of the family was informed by the view that public and private power are linked, that social liberation was fundamental and necessary to generate gender equality within the personal realm of the family. Since the oppression of women was held to derive primarily from the overall societal oppression, evidence showed that EPLF's policies underplay the noneconomic, primarily familial elements of Eritrean women's inequality.

There was very little official strategy to alleviate women's domestic work within the family. The study found that institutionalizing childcare through communal parenting was given precedence over programs to equalize household labor between the sexes. There was new legislation to abolish restrictive customs and traditions against women, such as granting the right of women to choose their marriage partner, the right of divorce, and of equal legal status. EPLF had cautiously disseminated information questioning discriminatory customs, such as female seclusion, polygamy, and female circumcision.

Education. Education was viewed as critical in EPLF's broader vision of the imperatives for national liberation. The official ideal of education was the linkage of a system of pedagogy to the interests of peasants and workers in Eritrea. EPLF's ideal of education was to create or reinforce a nonhierarchical society. The system of education included formal and nonformal schooling and consciousness-raising. Education was viewed as an important vehicle for the elimination of social inequalities through the creation of capabilities for skill acquisition and consciousness. Educational policy was therefore regarded as central in helping women prepare to build the kind of society EPLF envisions. Accordingly, females were extensively given access to education, a nonformal literacy campaign had major impact on women, women's oppression was addressed by the curriculum, and male and female teachers modeled emancipated gender relations.

View from Below: Eritrean Women's Perceptions of Oppression and Emancipation

I interviewed Eritrean women who chronicled major events in their lives that caused changes in their material condition, social relationships, and ideas. They revealed their lived reality and perceptions of their position within the society. I analyzed the interview data using the four major themes in women's lives: public life, which includes political activities; work; private family life; and education, which included formal and nonformal schooling and consciousness-raising.

Politics. The women placed high value on their participation in the national liberation effort. By and large, political activity was conceived as a duty to their country. For example, involvement in the revolutionary army was a highly regarded political activity. Further, many women pointed out that political participation was a rapid means of achieving equality with men. They said political activity helped create new values, images, and mobility. All women interviewed indicated that the political situation had made their integration in such public spheres as the economy and education possible; enabled them to become involved in activities traditionally perceived as being exclusively for men; and developed their awareness of the need to change women's unequal position within the society. Upon reviewing women's representation at different levels of the political structure, the analysis indicated that women's participation in top leadership positions was nonexistent, although 20 percent of the revolutionary army was female.

The National Union of Eritrean Women was viewed as an organization whose primary purpose was to mobilize women for participation in political, economic, and educational activities. The organization did not concern itself with women's issues specifically. In addition, the organization had very little influence and independence from the EPLF leadership. Women insisted upon "proving themselves" in political activities (through deeds) and "sacrificing their lives for the national cause, just like men" in order to claim equality to men.

Economy. While they did not stress it as strongly as political participation, few women viewed full involvement in the labor force as an important means of attaining their equality. Many reported that official encouragement of women's right to work outside the home was critical to accessing the kinds of jobs that were previously unattainable to them. They asserted that integration in the work force enhanced their capabilities to learn new skills and thereby move into jobs previously defined as being exclusively male.

For the most part, women maintained that they had to prove themselves, work hard, and improve their capabilities in order to claim their equality. The majority declared that participation in the economy enhances women's personal autonomy and self-worth. Some, but not the majority, also shared the official view that over-all economic development precedes and makes possible female emancipation.

Family. Eritrean women stressed that women's oppression stems from both the economy and the family. In contrast to the official view, most women asserted that women's equality can be achieved only when the unequal sexual division of labor is abolished within the private as well as the public sphere. They deplored the enor-mous burden of domestic labor and childcare on women in Eritrean society. They also maintained that regressive beliefs and attitudes of men toward women that upheld discriminatory customs and tradi-tions had to be abolished. While viewing childcare services as nec-essary to alleviate domestic labor, they asserted that men should assume equal responsibilities for household labor and raising chil-dren. The respondents rejected all the customary discriminatory laws and practices with regards to women, such as limitation of choice in marriage, lack of divorce right, female seclusion, female circumcision, and lack of legal rights.

Education. The Eritrean women respondents perceived educa-tion (formal, nonformal, and consciousness-raising) as a critical means of achieving equality. They believed that education fostered individual betterment by attaining higher consciousness and an improved material position for women in society by providing skills necessary to become equal members in public life. They believed that education would enable them to become equal participants in political and economic activities.

Women's participation in education and other activities with men had enhanced their ability to be equally active in public life and to change the images of women as intellectually inferior, pas-sive, and worthless. Schoolbooks and lesson materials included women as active members of society—they recounted women's achievements and showed their inferior positions in the previous social order. Contemporary women were represented in a positive manner—as active participants in all areas of life including warfare, wich was traditionally a male preserve. However, these new images of women had some ambiguities in them that do not challenge some basic assumptions about women's role and status. The notion that women had special relationships to children continued to be unchallenged. For example, there were themes of mother's brigade, mother's day, or working-mothers, and the portrayal of women in official iconography "with a gun in one hand and a baby in the other" that are promoted as manifestations of interest in women's issues. However, there was no similar representation of men hailed as images of "fathers work-brigade," or "fathers with a child in one hand and a gun in the other." The respondents pointed out the importance of encouraging females to enter the educational arenas, traditionally reserved for men. Many stated that the educational disparities between the sexes were a reflection of Eritrean women's subordinate social position.

Western Theories of Women's Oppression

I analyzed a variety of Western Marxist and feminist theories to assess their ability to engage the realities of Third World women, in general, and of my Eritrean female subjects, in particular.

The *classical Marxist* concept of women's emancipation is rooted in Engel's work, *The Origins of the Family, Private Property and the State* (Engels, 1972). He argued that the oppression of women began with the rise of capitalism, which transformed not only economic and social relationships but also the relationships between men and women within the household. In this view, women's suppression by men derives from workers' oppression by capitalists. Accordingly, women achieve emancipation through a successful class struggle for massive economic reorganization. In order to fully participate in this core effort and terrain, women must move out of the domestic realm into full participation in wage labor. Education is important only as it provides necessary work skills for women.

Radical feminists argue that the primary oppression of women is patriarchal oppression. They assert that division of labor by gender preceded division of labor by class and that capitalism and socialism oppress women equally. As in the classical Marxist analysis, the character of all social relations is seen flowing from a single primary dynamic. However, patriarchal, rather than capitalist, domination is viewed as central. This construction of male domination is rooted in procreative biology, which is the root cause of women's oppression. Radical feminists substitute gender for class, race, and nationality as a prime motor in the materialist account of history. Education is important to the extent that it changes women's consciousness and enables them to be free from men.

The *socialist feminist* approach to women's oppression accepts class as the correct framework within which to understand women's positions, but also stresses the significance of patriarchy. Both the economy and the family are viewed as vital determinants of women's positions. Socialist feminists argue that class is a primary contradiction and that revolutionary change of the economic system is necessary, but not sufficient to liberate women. They place great value on autonomous women's organizations as vehicles for change. In addition, new modes of organizing all forms of production are needed, and patriarchy must be explicitly attacked. Since the family is the cornerstone of women's oppression, immediate, consciously designed changes in living arrangements should be a significant part of a change strategy. In this perspective, education is important since it enables women, through changed consciousness and learned skills, to participate fully in society, and, also, it diminishes men's oppositional attitudes toward gender equality.

Western Theories and Eritrean Realities

Although I encountered their limitations (and parochialisms), these three Western theories of women's oppression enriched my study of contemporary Eritrean women. I needed to discern variations between these perspectives. The major difference between the classical Marxist approach and that of radical and socialist feminism is the field of vision. For classical Marxists, economic reorganization is the singular vehicle for women's emancipation. In contrast, feminists open up an examination of problems within the family system, the institution of marriage, reproductive activities, and relations between men and women. They also focus on the significance of ideology and psychology, viewed as independent social factors in the oppression of women.

Historically, the radical feminists were the first to view the subordination of women as a central concern that should be in the foreground of emancipatory politics. Radical feminism provocatively breaks with orthodox Marxism's tendency to place women's liberation on the "backburner." However, radical feminism overemphasizes biology and reproduction, ignoring other forms of gender oppression. As my interviews reveal, Eritrean women articulate diverse obstacles to liberation, many of which are ignored by the radical feminist perspective. Radical feminist theory universalizes the experience of women, abstracting from historical and cultural differences. The rich voices of Eritrean women indicate that their oppression—and avenues for change—require an appreciation of historical, national, and cultural specificity. Viewing one's menfolk as oppressors can minimize other forms of oppression, as evidenced by the history of the Eritrean people. For these reasons the radical feminist approach does not contribute to a comprehensive understanding of Eritrean women's inferior position and to strategies for change.

The socialist feminist approach is a more expansive and totalist perspective. While it views the family as a central institution where women's emotional, sexual, and material subordination is maintained, it also acknowledges the differences generated by class, nationality, and race. It also views the complex relationships among gender, economic, political, and community affiliations. While socialist feminists recognize the need for restructuring both economic and family life, they emphasize the need for women to demand change for themselves and advance women's issues through an autonomous organization.

The socialist feminist approach was useful in assessing Eritrean women's contemporary position. Further, it presented a contrasting perspective to the EPLF's official view on gender oppression. EPLF theoretical orientation was grounded in classical Marxism, regarding gender relations as a by-product of class relations. EPLF consistently stressed that women's emancipation can be achieved only as part of wider goals of social and economic transformation. Accordingly, the dismantling of the feudal and colonial orders and their replacement with a centralized, secular, and more egalitarian social order was depicted as the fundamental solution to the problem of women's subordinate status. Thus, women's vigorous participation in larger social change—in politics, production, and education—also will ease and eliminate their oppression. As socialist feminists correctly note, this orientation is top-down and narrow, while it is pitched as comprehensive. While women's involvement in socially productive labor and political activities may terminate some of the most extreme forms of female exploitation, other cultural practices and attitudes that are resistant to change may still limit women's liberation. Without the inclusion of the feminist point of view, patriarchal tendencies remain locked and unchallenged within the official policies and programs.

Socialist feminists are better able to depict obstacles than to delineate a route toward emancipation. They are effective in establishing that economics, politics, family life, and culture must all be taken up by an effective campaign to emancipate women. Only Eritrean women themselves can identify which specific conditions to contest and determine how to prioritize targets. The areas for change stressed by my twenty-four interviewees, particularly those minimized by EPLF, suggest the themes of an independent Eritrean women politics.

Towards an Autonomous Women's Politics

The evidence suggested that the women respondents felt they had achieved significant positive change in their status. (This assessment was in some tension with what would be the expectation of each theory that I have discussed.) Women had assumed important positions within the revolutionary movement. Their activity in economics and education had grown steadily since 1971. Women had been granted equal legal status. The effort to abolish some oppressive customary practices within the family, coupled with the availability of institutional services for household work and child care, had lessened burdens women encounter in the domestic realm.

Those interviewed highly valued their political involvement in the national liberation struggle. They viewed the EPLF's recognition of women's individual right to participate in politics as a milestone in the history of the Eritrean nationalist struggle. They perceived their participation in *politics* as a right to defend themselves and their country militarily. Interviewees stated that full participation in *economic* activity was fundamental to the achievement of women's equality. They indicated that equal access to resources and the right to engage in productive activity increased a woman's personal awareness, self-worth, and economic autonomy. In addition, on the societal level, women valued the opportunity to enhance the economic development and well-being of the country. These women believed that equalization of women within the *family* required a complete transformation of gender roles, personal status, and legal rights. Underlying ideologies and beliefs that sustain prejudicial attitudes and values toward women must also be rooted out. Eritrean women viewed *education* as a means of gaining understanding and acquiring the skills that enabled them to improve their material well-being within the private and public spheres. They believed that education opened the way for women to understand the need for change and enhance their control over their lives. Until joining the national liberation struggle, women had been discouraged from getting formal schooling.

However, the interviews support the view that Eritrean women's emancipation was possible, not only when women secured their liberation from national and economic oppression but also from inequality between the sexes. The women interviewed declared that *both family and education were the most critical realms in bringing about changes in women's status within society.* The political situation was foremost in their minds, and they directed their energies into political and related work activities. At the same time, they were deeply connected with their own struggle as females and viewed the family as critical in inhibiting their pursuit of schooling and participation in public life. (However, many noted an exceptional family member who sanctioned and facilitated their break with a conventional female role.) They indicated that while access to productive activities was significant, the traditional familial relationships between the sexes and the prevalent cultural notion of female inferiority are vital impediments to equality between genders. In contrast to the official EPLF view that economic change was key to changing women's position in the family, the interviewees added that familial roles and behavior also shape economic and social realities. They imply that the transformation of the family was necessary in itself and could drive societal change. They argued that domestic work should not be relegated to women only and that men were equally capable of performing household activities. Men's prejudice was deeply ingrained and arose from the total culture, but the women did not suggest a clear strategy on how to combat this. They indicated that with the new experience of seeing women in nontraditional roles, men had gradually, if minimally, changed their perception of women.

Eritrean women emphasized and spoke with intense passion about education as a critical means to gain their emancipation. They stated that they were denied employment, income, and social recognition and were consigned to be intellectually subordinate to men due to lack of education. They noted that education promoted both material and nonmaterial change—new knowledge, training, and skills, that facilitated their entry into the public sphere of politics and economy as well as new self-awareness, values, and cultural habits that impacted on women's interpersonal relationships within the family.

EPLF's commitment to overcoming sex oppression has been momentous in the history of the Eritrean nationalist struggle. The official recognition of women's right to equality and subsequent programmatic interventions have brought positive changes in the lives of women. To its credit, EPLF initiated its campaign against women's inequality in the face of material scarcity and famine, while a brutal war of national liberation was being waged. Nevertheless, women in Eritrea have not become equal to men, and their oppression still persists. EPLF's emphasis on nation-building and national unity may prove problematic for the cause of women's liberation. A fundamental attack on tradition—the system of male domination—inevitably causes stress and division. Of course, the freeing up of women can unleash enormous productive economic activity. However, if gender equality is slighted by theory (as it is by current EPLF ideology), its supporters may back off when the campaign for women's emancipation shakes morale and cohesiveness.

It is inevitable that hard choices will be encountered. It is uncertain whether EPLF will have the stamina to resist rationalizing inequalities in the sexual division of labor as productive or political necessities. A focus on juggling scarce material resources and the need to develop the mode of production is already deflecting the policy to lighten household and child-care work.

The participants in my study indicated that Eritrean women shared with male workers and fighters an objective interest in economic development and technological change and an objective political interest in the national democratic revolution. Yet Eritrean women's experience indicates that there is also a genuine female interest in abolishing women's oppression that transcends class lines. This female interest is vulnerable unless firmly embodied in the strategy for national reconstruction, and the blueprint for socioeconomic development. In other countries political power did not necessarily result, when women joined the labor force *en masse*. Although women had achieved significant progress, the firm establishment of both economic and political power was inhibited by the influence of traditional attitudes that confined and subordinated women. Membership on revolutionary committees, the locus of political and economic decision-making, remained largely in male hands.

Finally, women's voices, insights, and strategies are vital to their full emancipation. The best vehicle for synthesizing and mobilizing a "view from below" is an independent and significantly autonomous women's organization. In order for Eritrean women to organize toward full equality, they must be able to grasp and theoretically formulate the nature of their oppression. They must have the organizational means to design and implement strategies for women's emancipation informed by their own experiences. Only thus will EPLF's commitment to women's emancipation be fully achieved.

Reflections

Freire's influence has affected significantly the evolution of my thinking and work. As a young adult, I began a personal quest to transform my life so that I could contribute to the struggle to create a just society. Freire's strong and gentle voice was an affirmation that there must be a convergence of self and work, what is said and what is done, subject and object, theory and practice, ideas and lived reality. Freire's invitation to unlearn years of conditioning has been both energizing and a challenge.

Freire's philosophy, concepts, and methodologies have also informed my studies of women in Guinea-Bissauan and Eritrean society. It has been said that perhaps the greatest difficulty for many of Freire's followers is that "there are no concrete formulas to apply Freire's methodology." However, I have found that the very act of engaging in his approach has provided not only the means to change myself but also to study social problems. Through that process the methodology unfolds.

As a scholar influenced by Freirian thinking, I examined the relationship of gender politics and national liberation movement politics in both Guinea Bissau and Eritrea. Assessing whether women were achieving social equality with men, I examined: women's life histories as told by them; traditional and colonial experiences of women; and, the male movement leaders' ideas and practice in fighting against gender oppression.

I also placed great emphasis on the study of education in bringing about material and attitudinal change. I focused on education as a vital resource to catalyze revolutionary change. As Freire suggests, the revolutionary situation is, in turn, a great stimulus for educational and intellectual development. Freire also indicates that the creation of a new knowledge or new practice demands "an intimacy with reality in order to grasp its internal movements." The comprehension of "internal movement" requires understanding contradiction(s) of reality...(and) grasping the contradictions means to touch problems of power."

My approach to my work was to view the national liberation struggle as lived reality and enter into dialogue with Guinea Bissauan and, more directly, with Eritrean women. I utilized Freire's approach of *seeing* the situation as lived by participants, *judging* it though the assessment of present and historical experiences of women, and enabling myself and the participants in the study to engage in *activities* that enhanced the emancipatory process in these societies.

Freirian analysis of domination and liberation, his approach to building a humanitarian and democratic society are compatible with and relevant to feminism. Women's oppression is connected to injustices embedded in the larger society and to those directed at women in particular. Freire's concepts and strategies concern interpersonal relations and deal with people's lives in concrete ways. They capture realities of both individuals and groups, and, in turn, suggest actions necessary to transform reality. For example, if women are to be emancipated, they must not only achieve equality with men, but also engage in a mutual process with men that transcends oppressive relations. Freire's notion that the process of transformation has to take place through social awareness, critical analysis, and self-reliance contributes to shaping women's struggle for empowerment. His perspective is useful in assessing the kinds of changes that lead to emancipation, the issues that command women's interest, or the causes that change women's status. The reality and the struggle of the oppressed incorporate the "existential duality....[they] are at the same time themselves and the oppressor whose image they have internalized." Another strength of Freirian philosophy lies in his rejection of a rigid hierarchy of what is primary and secondary. He questions all acts of domination or oppression that keep people from becoming more fully human and over time impair their ability to act humanely. The existence of class, nationality, and racial hierarchies demands that women indeed fight on multiple fronts. The weakening of one system of oppression is intimately linked with another.

Despite his avoidance of rigid hierarchical thinking, Paulo Freire nevertheless displays a proclivity to focus most predominantly on oppression based on class. He tends to absorb patriarchal oppression into the class struggle. As my work indicates, his analysis of oppressor and oppressed relationships and his methodology for social change provide essential insight into the root causes of oppression and strategies of change. However, I strove to overcome Freire's limitations by incorporating feminist analyses into Freire—above and beyond my studies of Guinea-Bissauan and Eritrean women. A feminist analysis perceives women's oppression as embedded in the relationship of women to men. As a feminist, I place patriarchy at center stage in my analysis of why and how women occupy an inferior positions in a society. In Eritrea patriarchal practices and attitudes existed well before the emergence of capitalist modes of production. Women's subjugation cannot be subsumed as a subset of general class or economic oppression. In my view, Freire's notion that cultural workers have to "commit class suicide," needs to be expanded. One must also assert that revolutionaries must engage in a "gender suicide" in order to advance the emancipation of women. Feminist, as well as class, cultural and racial analyses must be fully utilized and integrated if we are to grasp the development of Third World societies, the predicament of women within them, and pathways to liberation.

REFERENCES

Cabral, Amilcar, *Return to the Source* (New York: African Information Service and PAIGC, 1973).

Chaliand, Gerard, *Armed Struggle in Africa: With Guerrillas in "Portuguese" Guinea* (New York: Monthly Review Press, 1969).

Davidson, Basil, *The Liberation of Guinea: Aspects of an African Revolution* (Baltimore: Penguin Books, 1969).

Engels, Frederick, *The Origin of the Family, Private Property and the State*, Eleanor B. Leacock, ed. (New York: International Publishers, 1972).

Fanon, Franz, *A Dying Colonialism* (New York: Grove Press, 1965).

Fanon, Franz, *The Wretched of the Earth* (New York: Grove Press, 1965).

Freire, Paulo, *Pedagogy in Process: The Letters to Guinea-Bissau* (New York: The Seabury Press, 1978).

Freire, Paulo, *Pedagogy of the Oppressed* (New York: Seabury Press, 1974).

Memmi, Albert, *The Colonizer and the Colonized* (Boston: Beacon Press, 1967).

Stefanos, Asgedet, *An Encounter with Revolutionary Change: A Portrait of Contemporary Eritrean Women* (Harvard University Dissertation, 1983).

Stefanos, Asgedet, *Women and Education in Guinea Bissau: An Analysis of Theory and Practice* (Harvard University Qualifying Paper, 1978).

Urdang, Stephanie, *Fighting Two Colonialisms: Women in Guinea-Bissau* (New York: Monthly Review Press, 1979).

CHAPTER THIRTEEN

PEDAGOGY, POWER, AND THE CITY
Paulo Freire as Urban School Superintendent

Tim Sieber

Although he had advised literacy campaigns and educational planning in Cape Verde, Chile, Guinea-Bissau, Tanzania, Nicaragua, and
Cuba, and long been a political man, Paulo Freire had never before
occupied a position of formal political or administrative power, particularly in Brazil. Such a responsibility presented itself to him in Fall
1988 when the *Partido Trabalhista*, the Worker's Party, under the
leadership of Luiza Erundina, won a surprise victory in São Paulo
municipal elections. Freire had been a founding member of the
Worker's Party in 1979, even before he ended his long, sixteen-year
exile from Brazil, had acted for many years as the party's secretary,
and been a key member of its education committee. He was the log-
ical choice for appointment as the city's secretary of education, or
school superintendent, and he did not shrink from the responsibility of power or, as he phrases it, the challenge of struggling for
"coherence" between political conviction, pedagogical theory, and
praxis. After he took office on January 1, 1989 he noted, "If I had
not accepted the honorable invitation…I would have to, for a matter of coherence, pull all of my books out of press, stop writing, and
be silent until death…To accept was to be coherent with everything
I have ever said and done" (Freire 1993; 58).

Freire devoted two and a half years to the challenge of directing
the system before resigning to resume the many writing, teaching,
and consulting projects he had abruptly suspended after the elections and his appointment. He left the secretary's position in mid-

1991, having put significant reforms into motion, confident that his transformative work was succeeding, a trusted colleague taking over as secretary, and those in the system empowered through transformed structures to continue the work he had helped to begin.

Freire has commented on these São Paulo experiences in his recent work, *Pedagogy of the City* (Freire, 1993), the English version of *Educação na ciudade* first published in Brazil in 1992. The book collects eleven dialogues that address his hopes, dreams, and ongoing struggles to transform São Paulo's school system. This is not the full accounting of his administrative work that he has promised for a future date, but a statement reflecting his ongoing, incomplete struggles and goals while still in office. His statements nonetheless articulate an extraordinary vision and program of educational transformation, and show that Freire's leadership was marked by energy, ferment, and significant positive change, particularly toward democratization of the schools, both pedagogically and administratively. Freire's program and his leadership were guided by his long-standing liberatory educational vision, his sense of himself first and foremost as a teacher, and his abiding commitment to dialogue, democracy, and socialism. His work in São Paulo suggests a fresh model of how progressives might assume and exercise political power—particularly within administrative contexts—without the seemingly inevitable bureaucratic corruptions that all too often undermine the democratic impulse.

Assuming office in 1989, Freire and the Worker's Party found a school system in utter crisis, understaffed, teachers underpaid and demoralized, with a deteriorating physical plant, high rates of student failure and dropouts (Freire calls them "expulsions"), and a curriculum that manifestly rejected students' lives, cultures, and aspirations. Equipment, books, and furniture were lacking in many schools. In addition to the failures in basic education for children, there were high rates of youth and adult illiteracy. The conditions of the school system only mirrored the broader crisis of services and quality of life in São Paulo, at 11.4 million the world's fifth largest city. The school system served 720,000 children, grades preschool to eight, with almost 40,000 employees, including more than 35,000 teachers, and 657 schools. A million additional children were out of school, however, including 400,000 who had never attended, and another 600,000 excluded for lack of space. Many of the excluded were among the one million children who live in the city's streets. Funds were available under constitutionally mandated funding formulas to accommodate only one third of the city's school-age children. To fully accommodate everyone, Freire found that an impossible 547 additional buildings would be needed. In addition, 60 percent of the existing buildings were dilapidated, including 55 that were so decrepit they had to be immediately condemned.

Freire committed himself to "changing the face of the schools" toward schools that were "serious, competent, fair, joyous, and curious." A major thrust of his work was to expand student access and retention, through reducing failure, retention in grade, and dropouts. He defended the minimum four-hour daily school session against attempts to shorten it, and instituted quadruple sessions in many schools so that idle classrooms could be put to use in the evenings. His administration repaired and adequately furnished existing schools, and built many new school buildings. They also established classes in factories, churches, government offices, and other community settings. His book reports that significant expansion of enrollments occurred at the preschool and adult levels.

Access and retention depended heavily on curriculum and pedagogy, of course, and Freire worked to transform the system's traditional fixed "scope and sequence" curriculum into an interdisciplinary "process curriculum with a perspective of liberating education," one built on dialogue with students' own lives and aspirations, and oriented toward critical learning. His administration put into place an extensive democratic process to rethink curriculum, extending from citywide "pedagogical plenaries" that included student and community voices, to new local school councils, which made final proposals for curriculum transformation at their own schools. The curriculum changes were tied to establishment of a new, permanent system of teacher in-service education that provided time and support for teachers to reflect critically and collaboratively on their own practice. By the time Freire left office, almost half the city's elementary schools had prepared and implemented their own local curriculum plans acting through local site councils that included administrators, teachers, students, parents, and community members.

In a system known for its hierarchy and centralization of administrative power, Freire worked intensively for democratization and decentralization of decision-making, opening up schools and the administrative bureaucracy to popular, grassroots engagement from many constituencies formerly shut out of participation: students, parents, community activists, teachers, and other educational workers. Freire knew that progressive changes in pedagogy and curriculum could not occur, or be sustained, without this broader political commitment to a democratic transformation of governance within the system.

At the same time, he applied pedagogical principles—especially the promotion of courageous, open dialogue among all constituencies—as the key to this administrative transformation. As he notes repeatedly in *Pedagogy of the City*, "no one can democratize the schools from the secretary's bureau" (Freire, 1993; 39). Refusing to impose on schools curriculum models created by academic experts, for example, he noted that:

> For political conviction and pedagogical reasons, we refuse the "packages" with recipes to be followed word for word by the educators who are at the base. For this reason, in the following stages of the curricular reformulation process, we will be speaking directly with principals, teachers, supervisors, cafeteria workers, mothers, fathers, community leaders, and children. (Freire 1993; 38)

Among the new governance developments were creation of the new school site councils already mentioned (recent Chicago school governance reforms in the United States are similar in concept) that allowed for parent, community, teacher, and student input into policy making at the local school level, and a network of subdistrict and citywide education councils linking these across São Paulo. Special efforts were directed at increasing parent involvement and communication with teachers, and forty community groups began collaboration with the school system by offering parent training. Freire also worked with the teachers' union to strengthen the voice of teachers vis-à-vis principals, to increase teacher salaries and benefits to the highest level of any city in Brazil, and to begin compensating teachers for student advising and evaluation, and for collaborative planning. For the first time, student organizations and associations—even at the elementary level—were also encouraged to form and lend their voices to debates over school and system policy.

Freire not only sought to increase the ability of grassroots constituencies to pose ongoing challenges from within the system, but also worked to enlist progressive organizations and individuals from the broader community in efforts to transform the system. Over ninety different compacts were signed between social movements and the Bureau of Education, for example, establishing collaborations as part of the system's youth and adult literacy projects. He also strengthened relations with the city's universities, including Pontificia Universidade Catolica de São Paulo, the University of São Paulo, and the State University of Campinas, whose professors, students, and other workers joined with the system as consultants on a wide range of issues, and who also created ten new pilot schools, with university professors as mentors. Overall, Freire recruited over one hundred specialists from outside the schools to work closely with him and his colleagues in the work of transforming the system.

In exercising leadership, Freire and his associates struggled to sustain the difficult balance between authority and dialogue, between principle and openness to democratic process. As his collaborator Ana Maria Saul remarks, "We could not…run the risk of committing the 'sin of power' obtained through elections only to use this power arbitrarily…" (Saul, 1993; 156). Freire disavowed authoritarianism and what he called "bureaucratism," and rather than sitting in his office and signing directives and memoranda dictating change, spent an extraordinary amount of his time in the schools and community, encouraging discussion and listening and talking with all kinds of people—janitors, cooks, teachers, principals, students, and parents—about his "educational project." He saw these "courageous dialogues" as a central element of his political responsibility:

> ...we accept the fact that there is no reason why we should try to escape the duty of intervening, of leading, of ensuing, always acting with authority, but also respecting people's freedom and dignity. For us, there cannot be a more adequate and effective way to conduct our educational project than the democratic route, than the open, courageous dialogue.... We need above all, to convince, almost convert. (Freire, 1993; 39)

Most of the significant changes introduced under Freire's tenure, in fact, were not quick to occur since they entailed wide, sometimes time-consuming democratic debate among all the involved constituencies.

Freire also worked to permanently institutionalize these forms of dialogue and democratic participation, through rewriting the "Common Constitution and By-Laws" of the school system to incorporate the new forms into the system's everyday governance. Never a careerist himself, he worked even at the system's headquarters, as Ana Maria Saul has remarked, to "democratize the administration of the Department of Education....," so that the reform process did not depend so much on his own leadership (Saul, 1993; 148). Surely, this is why once Freire left office, he could do so with more confidence that his work—fundamentally, defined as democratic dialogue over the means and ends of education—would continue even though he was not himself present to oversee it.

The singularity of Freire's model can perhaps be underscored by comparing him with another notable urban school superintendent in the Americas, New York City's Joseph Fernandez. Many of Fernandez' goals during his 1990 to 1993 tenure—roughly contemporaneous with Freire's—were superficially similar to Freire's, especially the emphasis on "School-Based Management" as a key reform strategy. Fernandez, and his abrupt dismissal, have also become strongly identified in media accounts with right-wing attacks against his advocacy of the multicultural "Rainbow Curriculum," and with the interpretation that Fernandez himself was too progressive politically to succeed.

Fernandez's model of educational transformation, style of leadership, and overall discourse of change, however, contrast dramatically with Freire's: Fernandez's model was predominantly corporate, and emphasized centralization of power. As Superintendent of New York City schools, he defined himself as a "CEO" of the "twelfth-largest corporation in America" (Fernandez, 1993; 21), and argued that schools and school systems "have to look at ourselves more as businesses" (Fernandez, 1993; 21) and "find more ways to get free enterprise keyed into the process" of education (Fernandez, 1993; 22). In his autobiography he defines students as products that the system should "guarantee" for employers' use before they send them into the workforce. His model of "school-based management" involved little actual decentralization of decision-making to the local school level: local councils had no control over budget, personnel, or curriculum.

As for administrative style, instead of disavowing authoritarianism and elitism, as does Freire, Fernandez' autobiography emphasizes how much he likes to "kick" "somebody's rear end" if it "is poised between me and where we have to go" (Fernandez, 1993; 20) and how much he "thrives on being in control" (Fernandez, 1993; 23). His own description of a model Miami school "executive training program" he designed, called "Leadership Experience Opportunity," is telling. He noted that his main message to participants was: "Put yourself in a position to be thought of as the most valuable person in the school so that when you're not there, everyone wishes you were" (Fernandez, 1993; 173).

However progressive his goals may have sounded, Fernandez was often criticized for his "arrogance" and for his failure to cultivate support among grassroots constituencies in the city. His appointment to office was never the result of a popular political process, but instead was brokered by an elite group of political, business, and school reform leaders who welcomed the command-style approach he wished to take toward the problem-ridden school system. Fernandez' failure to cultivate grassroots support with workers, students, and communities, however, was a clear factor in his later vulnerability to abrupt firing, and in the subsequent jeopardy of many of the innovations he worked to introduce within the system. The contrasts with Freire's approaches in São Paulo could not be starker.

"Tell-all" accounts of detailed political and administrative struggles in the genre of Fernandez's autobiographical *Tales Out of School*, however, do raise questions about Freire's experiences in São Paulo. They highlight how much *Pedagogy of the City* is an account of Freire's admitted "pedagogical dreams" and even "utopian" visions, more than an explanation of the practical politics of his work in the schools. Freire alludes a great deal to struggle, and even to some disappointments and defeats in efforts to change the system, but there is no general assessment of these in the book. He variously terms the bureaucracy with which he had to work as "illogical," "threatening," and even "perverse," and while it is noted that his proposals were controversial and sparked opposition, he never reveals from which directions it came, or whose interests were being challenged. Who defined themselves as his enemies? He also never details his daily strategies for resisting cooptation, or the seductions of privilege, bureaucratism, and authoritarianism that overwhelm so many reformers. His book prompts many questions: How much did Freire's critical pedagogy actually guide his broader political project in the schools? In the crucible of intense administrative struggle, was this model adequate? In this struggle, did any contradictions ever emerge for him between pedagogy and power, between discourse and practice? Last, of course, is the issue of results. How much of a difference have Freire's reforms made, and how should their results be defined and measured?

It is clear that something historically unique and path-breaking occurred in São Paulo when Freire was in charge of public schools, and that because of his clear vision of transformative practice he has valuable lessons to offer all progressives on the responsibilities and challenges of assuming power, in educational as well as other arenas of struggle. We eagerly await a fuller accounting from him about these issues of practical politics, and we anticipate learning much from the new reflections and insights he will no doubt share with us.

ACKNOWLEDGMENTS

I thank Norman Fruchter for his insightful help in conceptualizing the issues dealt with here, and in framing appropriate questions for Paulo.

REFERENCES

Fernandez, Joseph, *Tales Out of School: Joseph Fernandez' Crusade to Rescue American Education* (Boston: Little, Brown, 1993).

Freire, Paulo, *Pedagogy of the City* Donaldo Macedo, trans., (New York: Continuum, 1993).

Saul, Ana Maria, "Postscript: São Paulo's Education Revisited," in Paulo Freire, *Pedagogy of the City* (New York: Continuum, 1993), pp. 145-165.

CHAPTER FOURTEEN

THE SUBJECT OF EDUCATION
Paulo Freire, Postmodernism, and Multiculturalism

Ron Scapp

For more than two decades now, multiculturalism has been vociferously debated by politicians, civic leaders, and educators. From pugnacious gatherings dealing with changes in school curricula to emotional confrontations about sexual behavior and identity, the issue of "multicultural" difference among American educators and Americans generally has worked its way into almost every discussion on the subject of education. Yet despite the plethora of news coverage and public name-calling by some of the more celebrated adversaries of multiculturalism, most notably Dinesh D'Souza, William Bennett, and Diane Ravitch,[1] much remains to be discussed and considered: When all is said and done, what is meant by "multiculturalism"?

Conservative commentators and the Christian Right have claimed that diversity consciousness will, if it has not already, fracture and fragment our school districts, cities, and the nation itself into a myriad of distinct and ultimately isolated pockets of *absolute* difference. They agree with their colleague Roger Kimball that "tenured radicals"[2] have taken over American institutions of higher learning, including teacher education programs. According to Kimball's argument, these radical professors are leading our nation's students at all levels of study toward a rejection of their very roots, their profound (metaphysical) connection with the values and accomplishments of Western culture.[3] Thus, the "culture wars" and the crisis of national identity that they have produced as their collateral damage, continue to be a specter haunting the American democratic experiment.

A parallel, if not antecedent, crisis has also developed over the last twenty years or so owing to a variety of theoretical critiques that find themselves grouped together under the rubric of postmodernism: the deconstruction of Jacques Derrida, the genealogical explorations of Michel Foucault, the cultural criticism of bell hooks and Gayatri Chakravorty Spivack, the queer studies of Judith Butler and Eve Kosofsky Sedgwick, and so on. The crisis of postmodernism is one that extends far and wide, ranging from critiques of contemporary liberalism and enlightenment subjectivity to challenges of the notion of Truth with a capital "T" along with many other of the privileged terms, concepts, and values of Western culture. The question here is, what impact do multiculturalism and postmodernism have on the very subject of education, the student whose representation has been historically configured (disfigured?) by the multifarious transformations of subjectivity from Plato through Descartes to Hegel and beyond. In particular, what do these two influential and powerful theoretical modes of thinking offer by way of critique of Freire's work and vision?

Let me begin by stating from the start that I want it both ways. I believe that postmodernism and multiculturalism do in fact offer something valuable by way of critique to any discussion on the subject of education, including Freire's work. At the same time that I want to acknowledge and use the critique of subjectivity offered to us by contemporary critics working within these two theoretical positions, I also want to note that it is precisely, what I will here name, Freire's foundationalism, that is, his committed engagement with the student as *subject* that I want to embrace. It is this complicated and perhaps paradoxical position of the primacy of the subject, of the subject's privileged intentional relationship with the world, taken as a given by Freire, that warrants both rigorous criticism and *critical acceptance*, but acceptance nevertheless. Thus the very thing I draw our attention to as problematic in Freire's work, namely the privileging of subjectivity itself, I also want to empathically endorse. I want simultaneously to criticize and welcome

Freire's subject(s) of education from a multicultural perspective that not only welcomes the philosophical arguments of postmodernism, but also recognizes a plurality of subjectivity rather than the singular representation of it that Freire inherits and accepts. Put bluntly, if also somewhat simplistically: the subject of education is a complicated subject! There's more to it than just "humanizing" people.

A naive embracing of the power of subjectivity, an embracing of subjectivity that ignores postmodernism in favor of a structurally and culturally simpler interaction between "self" and "world" leads to, I contend, the repetition of modes of pedagogical oppression that Freire wants to overcome, modes of oppressive interaction that remain, however, unless confronted by the criticism available to us because of postmodernism and multiculturalism. In short, Freire, for me, becomes an even more profound and useful theorist if his work is read and understood within the context of postmodernism and multiculturalism. Those who refuse to consider Freire, postmodernism, and multiculturalism together in this tripartite relationship, risk limiting the potential genuine transformative power of education that Freire has been offering to us since *Pedagogy of the Oppressed*. The very subject of education is cheated of the possibility of Freire's pedagogy of liberation if that subject is already destined to be overdetermined by a metaphysically laden narrative of the singularity and "complete" rationality of subjectivity that instinctively balks at each and every challenge that postmodernism and multiculuralism confront it with, challenges that offer *counternarratives of identities*.[4]

In *Pedagogy of the Oppressed*, Freire articulates his foundationalism at one point by claiming that

> [t]eachers and students (leadership and people), co-intent on reality, are both Subjects, not only in the task of unveiling that reality, and thereby coming to know it critically, but in the task of re-creating that knowledge. As they attain this knowledge of reality through common reflection and action, they discover themselves as its permanent re-creators. In this way, the presence of the oppressed in the struggle for their liberation will be what it should be: not pseudo-participation, but committed involvement. (Freire, p. 56)

To those theorists who may wince at the very mention of reality, "co-intended" or not, we must acknowledge that such a formulation about the "nature of things" still smacks of the sort of metaphysical indebtedness that Freire's work does not attempt to move us beyond. Freire has in fact an ethical and aesthetic engagement with the world that is metaphysically grounded following the lead of both Hegel and Marx. It is certainly not the case, however, that Freire's work expresses a relationship with the world that, in his own words, is a "naive consciousness" simply attempting to super-impose itself on reality (Freire, *Education*, p. 44). Freire is meta-physical but not uncritical of the relationships existing between oppressor and oppressed. He unfortunately does not extend his crit-ical analysis to include many of the traditional metaphysical oppo-sitions (as well as the potentially reductive opposition of oppressor and oppressed) that make many postmodernists nervous and could be said to help justify and sustain the status quo of power relation-ships existing among different people: Freire, one has to remember, is not the only or the first interpreter of the world claiming to ratio-nally ground his engagement with other humans.

Although one could point to passage after passage throughout Freire's work where he reinscribes the dialectic between the ratio-nal and the irrational always favoring "rationality," it would be to miss something of great importance, in my opinion, if we rejected Freire for simply appealing to rationality in the enlightenment tradi-tion. Freire always gives us much more than just the appeal to ratio-nality: he offers us love. It is his love and respect that challenge and ultimately prevent the surrendering of the subject of education to any dogmatic singular rational prescription of education and libera-tion. Unlike many other enlightenment-influenced thinkers, Freire introduces passion as part of his ethics, that is, as a positive dimen-sion to his ethics of liberation. With this he introduces something other than rationality into the equation of "education as the practice of freedom."

An example of Freire's own undermining of his relationship to rationality can be encountered in the passionate conclusion to his essay "Education as the Practice of Freedom," where he exclaims that

> [o]ne subverts democracy (even though one does this in the name of democracy) by making it irrational; by making it rigid in order "to defend it against totalitarian rigidity;" by making it hateful, *when it can only develop in the context of love and respect for persons,* by closing it, when it only lives in openness; by nourishing it with fear when it must be courageous; by making it an instrument of the powerful in the oppression of the weak; by militarizing it against the people; by alienating a nation in the name of democracy. [emphasis added] (Freire, *Education*, p. 58)

Freire's rejection of the irrational is not an authoritarian attempt to suppress freedom, love, courage, and respect. On the contrary, it is his attempt to stay away from the *rigidity* that sets over communities in the name of governing the people. One encounters the same intensity to fight off such social and political rigidity in the work of Vaclav Havel, for example, but without the (rigid?) rejection of the irrational expressed by Freire.[5] Perhaps this has more to do with a difference in training than temperament: Freire the social scientist, Havel the playwright. In any event, it would be hard to overlook Freire's declaration of and commitment to the importance of passion, love, courage, and respect for the subject of education—the student—if we stopped abruptly at the point at which he articulates and affirms the traditional subordination of irrationality.

Freire's theoretical formulation of the subject of education is open to the criticism alluded to earlier, but his resulting pedagogy ironically benefits from his theoretical orthodoxy because it allows him to consider *the subject* of his efforts first and foremost. It is his expressed commitment to assisting students of all stripes to become critically conscious (*conscientização*, the process of critical engagement with the world) that arises from the foundationalism of a notion of subjectivity as he understands it. Freire is led on to liberate by a process of humanizing the subject, that is, of facilitating the turn from object to subject. For Freire, every student is a potential subject, an individual liberated by dint of *conscientização*. Rather than reject Freire for a move toward totalizing the subject, we could embrace this move as a unifying gesture in the spirit in which I believe it was intended: *solidarity*. This could be theoretically developed with the aid of postmodernism and multiculturalism; Freire's work could benefit by what these two theoretical perspectives offer and they in turn could benefit from Freire.

Anthony O'Brien has argued for acknowledgment of the solidarity of subjects as an important dimension of Freire's pedagogy in his cogent and insightful essay *'Organize and Act': Cultural Rights in South African Communities*. Speaking of the work of Nise Malange, co-director of the Center for Culture and Working Life in Durban and Zakes Mda, a scholar-activist and dramaturgist, O'Brien notes that Malange and Mda working together

> draw on Freire's Pedagogy of the Oppressed ("conscientization"—naming, reflection, praxis)...; its point, Mda says, is not to provide technical solutions to *community problems* but to help develop the *community's* own critical awareness of the structural causes of their problems. The point is the process of understanding and action.... [Emphasis added.] (O'Brien, p. 41)

Freire's pedagogy is about the movement of the community toward consciousness. It is no accident, according to O'Brien, that Freire's work was of importance to the Black Consciousness movement in South Africa, a movement of critical consciousness and a movement toward solidarity (that would eventually involve whites). True that given the complexities of differences existing among various groups of people, it is incumbent upon any one discussing the importance of individuals not to reduce them to some sort of metaphysically transcendent ideal unity (community). The process of "humanizing" people cannot repeat the reductive and, in my opinion, the ultimately oppressive move of rendering *all as one subject*, the historically classic metaphysical mode of appropriation. Instead it must be, following the lead of postmodernism and multiculuralism, an emphasis of *different individuals* moving toward a position of solidarity, of political and ethical union.

Interestingly, it is precisely at this moment of recognizing the full import of difference and resistance to any totalizing act of unification that Freire's work announces its importance to postmodernism and multiculturalism: *real individuals are oppressed*. Engagement with the *real individuals* who are oppressed is predicated on a theory and practice (i.e., pedagogy) being understood more as opposite sides of the same coin than an engagement of (pure?) theory informing a (naive?) praxis. Freire's work demands that postmodernists not remove themselves from *actual, real others*; and that multiculturalists acknowledge the need to understand and embrace *unity as solidarity*, and not to see it solely as an attempt to annihilate the dignity of different peoples. If not, then one could envision a postmodern theorist (many contemporary academics) as a disengaged elitist "fussing" with a nuanced critique of the hegemony of Western metaphysics while being rather oppressive to students, colleagues and others. The multiculturalist, too, could easily be seen as one who merely superficially "celebrates all differences" while ignoring the very *real and concrete obstacles* that separate and keep different people from working, living, and learning together.

Freire's work has always insisted on an engagement with many different people, not just as an abstract (irrational?) exaltation of difference as difference; and he has always confronted power as something more than mere discursive operations occurring on their own. People, for Freire, need to become involved in *the process of critical consciousness* that reveals those social/political/cultural contradictions and structures that *do, in fact*, set different people at odds with each other and even themselves. Freire, postmodernism, and multiculturalism can and, I believe, must come together as a theoretico-practical alliance, forming a unity (solidarity) that joins a valuable and powerful pedagogy with contemporary reflections on the problems of subjectivity conceived within the context of the legacy of the enlightenment. That postmodernism and multiculturalism have the theoretical strategies to push Freire's work to even greater critical importance, for today's educators and students should not make us ignore or underestimate the value or importance of the subject of education that Freire's work dignifies and respects.

NOTES

1. While I refuse to group these conservative commentators with the likes of liberals such as Richard Rorty, it should be noted that Rorty and a fair number of liberals and left-minded intellectuals have done their share of damage concerning multiculturalism and postmodernism. See for example Barbara Ehrenreich, "The Challenge for the Left," in *Debating P.C.*, Paul Berman, ed., (New York: Dell, 1993). pp. 333-338.

2. See Roger Kimball, *Tenured Radicals: How Politics Has Corrupted Our Higher Education*, (New York: Harper and Row, 1990).

3. See Roger Kimball, *ibid.*

4. See Mario Moussa and Ron Scapp, "The Practical Theorizing of Michel Foucault: Politics and Counter-Discourse," *Cultural Critique*, (London: Oxford University Press, Spring 1996).

5. See Vaclav Havel, *Living in Truth*, Jan Valdislav, ed., (London: Farber and Farber, 1986). Also see Havel et al., *The Power of the Powerless*, (Armonk, N.Y., M. E. Sharpe, Inc., 1985).

OTHER WORKS CITED

Freire, Paulo, *Pedagogy of the Oppressed*, (New York: Continuum,1992).
   Education for Critical Consciousness, (New York: Continuum, 1973).

O'Brien, Anthony, "'Organize and Act': Cultural Rights in South African
   Communities," *Radical Teacher*, (Fall 1995), pp. 40-47.

CHAPTER FIFTEEN

THE DILEMMAS OF LIVED MULTICULTURALISM

Tanya McKinnon

A great many dreams are deferred every year in urban public school education: those of the students and those of the teachers. As a teacher of New York public school teachers, every semester I see the ways in which the multicultural dilemmas teachers face continue to make not just classrooms but multicultural theorizing itself a deeply contested terrain. Rarely do people share the same definition or assumptions about what multiculturalism is or how it should be implemented. As a proponent and practitioner of multiculturalism, it is my intention to expand what we currently understand as a multiculturalism to include the lived experience of multicultural diversity from the perspective of urban public school teachers. It is my belief, that the way in which multiculturalism is frequently understood and practiced has focused too narrowly on the politics of diversifying and integrating predominantly White institutions and curricula. This is a focus that neglects the ways in which urban teaching environments are rapidly changing as well as transforming urban multicultural concerns. Many urban public schools are not only integrated, but have evolved into highly diverse and culturally complex settings, producing different notions of identity, creating new concerns for classroom management, and presenting teachers with dilemmas that go beyond curricular guidelines and general counseling. Multicultural theory has failed to keep pace, resulting in an eclipse of the concerns facing already integrated or predominantly marginalized locations. This often unintentional neglect of the confusions, needs, and concerns that communities of color and well-integrated institutions articulate, reproduces the very exclusions that multiculturalism purports to address. Therefore, in the spirit of my most vocal and opinionated New York public school teachers, I ask Freire to help articulate the theory and practice necessary to address the needs of teachers and students who already work and live within a multicultural context. Let me begin by presenting two short case studies by Sue and Helen, both former students of mine.[1]

Sue, a White, college-educated woman, came to teach in New York City public schools last year. The school administration, needing to fill a last-minute vacancy, assigned her to teach science instead of humanities, which was her field. A novice teacher, with a history of science phobia in her own school days, she was anxious about her ability to relearn science while simultaneously attempting to teach it. Removed from her area of expertise, she had little time to engage students interpersonally or attempt innovative teaching techniques. Her uneasiness with science was soon coupled with an inability to control class behavior. Her students, largely Black and Latino, justifiably skeptical about her emotional or intellectual sincerity, challenged her authority, ignored her class rules, and demeaned her with racialized epithets. Into this already charged space was added an additional complication: two of her sixth graders openly identified themselves as gay, becoming the targets of violent homophobia from their heterosexual peers.

Sue ended up having to devote a great deal of class time to negotiating complex and potentially volatile issues of race and sexuality. Teaching content became an absurdly remote problem. The meager multicultural curriculum she was provided was of no assistance, either in getting the lessons across or in helping her understand, manage, or, at least, deal with the challenges she faced with dignity. Sue needed classroom strategies that would enable her to answer difficult questions like: What tactics are there to establish authority in a multicultural classroom without resorting to actions predicated on unjust power and privilege? What do you do when two of your students identify as gay and get bashed by other students? These are questions, not simply about the classroom but about an emerging American—and increasingly global—landscape in which notions of authority and identity, guidance and learning are readjusting themselves. Unfortunately, much multicultural theory does not address itself to providing teachers with support structures, advice, or concrete strategies—in fact, advice is often rare to come by if only because such dilemmas are so recent.

Sue's decision was to confront issues of sexuality in the classroom. From a theoretical multicultural perspective it sounds like the right thing to do. But the right thing to do does not always yield the right results. For one thing, it made her more suspect and further eroded her authority with other students. The decision also had serious repercussions outside the classroom. Both the school administration and her student's immigrant parents disapproved of any engagement with issues of sexual orientation. The gay-bashing did not stop and she was at a loss as to what to do. As she told my class, "How could I teach or mentor my students when I was the one who really needed a mentor?"

Unfortunately, it is frequently the case that literature on multiculturalism written for public school teachers focuses on history, geography, and custom instead of the real on-the-ground issues of difference. Literature on multiculturalism frequently assumes a predominantly White setting in need of being made more inclusive. Sue, however, did not need advice on food festivals or even a workshop on antiracism. She is an English major who specialized in African-American literature as an undergraduate. Working in a primarily Black and Latino classroom she saw race awareness and racial representation as a given. She was not a reluctant multicultural educator and had grappled with and used multicultural theory and subject matter, but in that setting it was of no assistance. What Sue needed was a lesson plan to help her get intellectually disempowered kids to trust her. She needed a community consultant to help her address issues of sexuality without alienating immigrant parents from the Caribbean and Central America. The advice Sue needed was not how to create a multicultural context but rather, how to manage one.

Further emphasizing this point, many teachers talk and think a great deal about how their own and their students' identities are constructed and the ways in which their identities will mutually impact one another. Helen, who is African American, tells the story of her multicultural classroom in which many of the students are biracial, in foster homes, or being raised by adoptive parents. In other words, they are culturally not as they appear. Just last semester she faced a pedagogical conundrum similar to Sue's. Teaching in a predominantly Black and Latino classroom she had three Chinese American students. In a desire to be more multiculturally specific, she incorporated Chinese history into her curriculum. As with Sue, Helen's "right thing to do" did not yield the right—or at least the desired—results.

Other students began focusing attention on the Chinese students in an exaggerated way. During and after class, their "Asianness" became prominent. One of the Chinese children, dismayed by the attention she was receiving from her peers about her "Asianness," complained to her parents. As it turns out, she was adopted by a non-Asian couple who were deeply troubled by their daughters emergent feelings of "not fitting in." They blamed Helen for "confusing" their daughter. The parents of one of the other Asian students also complained. Recent immigrants, they felt Helen spent too much time on China when it was "America" their child needed to learn about. Helen, much like Sue, felt both betrayed by the dearth of theorizing on the vicissitudes of lived multiculturalism and uneasy about the capacity for multiculturalism to address the needs of her classroom.

In the urban multicultural context teachers face daily the reality that a simple category such as "oppressed" no longer serves to explicate the complexity of power relations they face. Nor does the simplistic incorporation of culturally diverse materials address the need young "Americans" have for materials that reflect the imbricated and culturally complex nature of their cultural identifications. Students in urban classrooms no longer passively accept a simplistic pigeonholing of their identities. Certain forms of "multiculturalism" feel as narrow and constricting, in their essentialist assumptions about racial and ethnic identity, as the insular and conservative curriculum they seek to replace.

As Helen stated, "I have to help a kid be a Black, Latino Jew if that's how she identifies and that's who she wants to be. Sometimes it's hard for me, but I can't just assume we're all Black anymore." She goes on to say, "You see an all Black high school and people think great just do some Black history and it will all be fine. But the truth is half our students are from the Caribbean, a fourth are from Africa and the rest are divided between those with immediate southern roots and those who are second- and third-generation urbanites." Obviously, the incorporation of materials on Native American genocide, or the slave trade will only go so far in solving the problems that school faces. Inter-ethnic rivalry and inter-ethnic identity can get completely ignored. I would also add that many young urban teachers are much like their students; culturally mixed and therefore dealing with the same questions of competing identities that they wish to share and explore in their classrooms. A reality that requires a more complex and nonessentialist vision of "cultures" within multicultural curricula.

Many public school teachers resemble Sue and Helen in the problems they face daily. Take for example other questions that were asked in my class:

1. What do I do after earning a student's trust and they tell me they secretly carry a gun to school so they can get home safely? Do I inform the administration or the parents and violate the students trust? Or do I keep my student's secret because I know how dangerous getting to and from school in this particular neighborhood can be?
2. How do I motivate all my students to learn for a "better future" when the majority of Black boys in my classes fear they won't live to their twenty-third birthday?
3. How do I intervene when a student tells me they are being sexually abused at home but beg me not to tell the counselor because they don't want to be placed in foster care?
4. How do I intervene in potentially violent gang conflict between

Jamaicans and Haitians in my predominantly Black school?
5. Should I incorporate the multiple and competing educational expectations of recent immigrant families into the classroom?
6. How do I, an untenured White teacher, effectively challenge the racism of White colleagues who will determine if I receive tenure?
7. How do culturally diverse students affect each other's learning and behavior when sitting and working together in the classroom?
8. Should I risk my job and potentially alienate parents by introducing gay materials to students from communities whose "traditional cultures" oppose public discussions of sexuality?

It is precisely these underlying tensions, controversies, passions, and problems that end up being overshadowed by the very discussions and strategies designed to create and implement multicultural curricula.

Given the way in which multiculturalism is frequently appropriated as a revisionist program rooted in the liberal practice of integration, many practitioners of multiculturalism often end up refocusing attention on the center of power to the exclusion of marginalized communities. In such cases, the educational needs of communities that are already integrated, in other words, comprising primarily people of color, are eclipsed by the concerns of primarily White schools and institutions whose needs are to both integrate and diversify the curricula. Yet it is worth reemphasizing that these primarily White institutions do desperately need revisionist multicultural curricula as well as strategies that assist them in divesting of racism, sexism, classism, homophobia, and ethnocentrism. However, in many communities of color, there may exist a number of teachers of color who teach and have been teaching within a multicultural paradigm for years.[2] For these teachers and these schools there exists alongside the basic need for a more multicultural official curriculum the even greater need for a politics of multiculturalism that takes into account the deeply complex nature of life lived within a diverse cultural context. For instance, a Latina teacher may not need to emphasize Puerto Rican cultural pride; she may, in fact, need ways in which to negotiate an excess of cultural pride which finds expression in violent fights between Dominicans and Puerto Ricans. Like Sue, she may have to deal with the negative consequences of introducing gay subject matter in a community whose traditional cultural mores are homophobic. Like Helen, many of her kids may be culturally mixed necessitating great sensitivity on her part in helping kids articulate an identity that "feels" right for them.

In other words, there exists within the discourse of multiculturalism itself a discourse on multiculturalism that has not been addressed. In those locations where the multicultural struggle is not centered on diversifying alone, there exists within the context of racism the question of African-American boys and a foreshortened sense of future; within the context of gender the question of sexuality and high school date rape; within the context of classism the question of African-American and Latino colorism; within the context of essentialism the question of imbricated cultural identities; and within the context of sexism the question of sexual orientation.

Unfortunately, as I raise these issues I do not necessarily have ready answers. Clearly we must begin to theorize multiculturalism from multiple locations. We must also broaden the scope of multiculturalism to incorporate the concerns of urban public school teachers whose lives attest to the complexity of merging theory with practice. We must, in fact, merge academic theory on multiculturalism with the very real concerns teachers already voice in multicultural classrooms. As bell hooks advises in *Teaching to Transgress*, "There must be training sites where teachers have the opportunity to express those concerns while also learning to create ways to approach the multicultural classroom and curriculum." Perhaps Freire, himself from a country in which many of its citizens are negotiating competing cultural identities, can assist us in this revisioning of multiculturalism. A revisioning that must begin with a greater inclusion of the ideas and voices of urban public school teachers, thereby transforming multiculturalism into a more liberatory site in which theory and practice merge as urban public school teachers formulate and share strategies useful to them in negotiating the complex and ever-changing dynamics of the urban multicultural classroom.

NOTES

1. The names of all teachers in this essay have been changed.
2. In making this assertion I in no way wish to imply that teachers of color constitute a majority in the New York public school system. Nor do I wish to diminish the impact multiculturalism has in increasing awareness of the ways in which the unexamined racism of White teachers serves to disempower and silence students of color.

CHAPTER SIXTEEN

A RESPONSE

Paulo Freire

I can think of no better way to begin my response than by saying how gratified I am that the scholars represented in this volume have taken the time to engage my work in a critical and thoughtful way. I am not going to try to respond to each one of them by name or by chapter. Rather I will respond to what I perceive to be the major themes that emerge from these various chapters, these different thoughtful offerings, so that in the end we may have a critical dialogue with each other around some of the leading ideas represented here. My chapter then will not be Paulo Freire engaging this person or that person, but Paulo Freire engaging the major themes that emerge in this important volume. I have, therefore, organized my remarks around what I see as the most important themes and questions that run through all of these chapters.

The Issue of Methods: Specifically, Do My "Methods" Work in a North American Context?

Every time I am asked this question of methods it seems as if my central preoccupation for thirty-five years had been to work on a method to make possible a quick and easy process of literacy. The question implies that I am being seen as a specialist in the techniques and methods for making possible a much easier way for illiterates to learn how to read and write. Of course, if it was like this, I am sure that I would be very happy because it would imply a certain contribution—an important contribution—that one could have given to facilitate the millions of illiterate in the world coming to literacy. The real question, nevertheless, is not this one.

Of course, it is not possible for me or for you or for no matter whom to think and act on the literacy problems of teaching without attending to technical questions for teaching literacy. They are essential, for without the techniques of teaching we do not achieve literacy. However, the question for me, the question to ask me, is what was the central point when I began to have a concern with the techniques for teaching literacy?

My initial concern was with the process of reading and writing words. But for me, from the beginning, it was not ever possible to separate reading words from reading the world. Second it was also not possible to separate reading the world from writing the world. That is, language—and it is a linguistic question—cannot be understood without a critical comprehension of the presence of human beings in the world. Language is not exclusively a medium for expressing the impressions we have vis-a-vis the world. Language is also knowledge in itself. And language implies the intelligibility of the world that does not exist without communication. What I want to say is that it is impossible to access meaning simply through reading words. One must first read the world in which these words exist. One of the things that human beings did, to the extent that they began to connote the reality through their action, to the extent that they have begun to become able to speak the reality, to speak about the reality, is that they *acted* on the reality. One of the most important things that women and men did was to understand and communicate their understanding. There is no intelligibility of the concreteness of human reality without communicability of the things we understood. Otherwise it is just blah, blah, blah.

My preoccupation then was never to work just on the techniques that are necessarily implied in making possible writing and reading. My preoccupation was not necessarily with the specific techniques that are needed for reading but with the substantivity of the process that requires techniques. That is where many people in the United States and elsewhere misunderstand my work. Technique is always secondary and is only important when it is in the service of something larger. To make technique primary is to lose the purpose of education.

The issue is not the techniques in themselves (not that they are not important), but the real issue is the comprehension of the substantivity of the process that in turn requires multiple techniques to achieve a particular goal. It is the process that led to the need for techniques that needs to be understood.

Thus what challenges me is not so much how to facilitate the reading of various sounds of the language, but how to develop the capacity that human beings have to know. What is important is not the ability to engage the phonemic structure of the language but for teachers to understand how the structures of the language can be used in the meaning-making process. Thus you have a nice marriage between theory and methods, but theory always precedes methods.

For example, one of the issues that challenged me with respect to the process of teaching writing and reading was basically the interrelationship between men and women and their immediate environment in which their language is being constituted while expanding itself. In this way, for me, the basic reading program, or literacy program, that I would have to develop with the peasants, would have to take as a point of departure the capacity of knowing that these peasants had about their context, and the world context, and their ability to express that knowledge through their own language.

I would have to begin any literacy program not from my own language as a middle-class teacher, but by using the student's own language as a means for literacy development. This initial process of using the student's own language as a point of departure for literacy development does not, however, mean that students should not eventually be assimilated into the teacher's discourse. The objective of education is the development of multiple literacies and multiple discourses.

I am talking about beginning, but not ending, with students' literacies. I think the fundamental issue is that the beginning of literacy and the "end" of literacy are not mutually exclusive, but they represent a process. The problem is when one overemphasizes the beginning so as to romanticize the peasants' language so as to keep them ghettoized in that language. In overromanticizing students' language so as to discourage them from acquiring multiple discourses, including the "standard" discourse of the dominant society in which they live, teachers run the risk of becoming entrapped in a "feel good" pedagogy that passes as progressive. If they do this, teachers are not engaging with their students in a mutual process of liberation.

The Key to Critical Dialogue: Listening and Talking

To continue these reflections, when I began with the literacy programs 35 years ago or so, I was already intensely living and experiencing one of the necessary virtues of a democratic educator, which is to know how to listen. That is, to know how to listen to a Black child with his or her specific language with his or her specific syntax, to know how to listen to the Black illiterate peasant, to know how to listen to a rich student, to know how to listen to the so-called representatives of minorities who are basically oppressed. If we don't learn how to listen to these voices, in truth we don't really learn how to speak. Only those who listen, speak. Those who do not listen, end up merely yelling, barking out the language while imposing their ideas. The one who is a student of listening implies a certain treatment of silence and the intermediary moments of silence. Those who speak democratically need to silence themselves so that the voice of those who must be listened to is allowed to emerge. I lived the experience of the speech of those who listened and I perceived that the educational work that must follow required creativity as well as humility. It is also a kind of work that implies taking risks that those who have been silenced cannot take.

In other words, none of this would make pedagogic sense if the educator does not understand the power of his or her own discourse in silencing others. For this very reason, this understanding of the power to silence implies the development of the ability to listen to the silenced voices so as to then begin to look for ways—tactical, technical, methodological ways—that could facilitate the process of reading the silenced word that is in a close relationship with the lived world of the students. All of this means that the educator must be immersed in the real historic and concrete experience of the students, but never paternalistically immersed so as to begin to speak for them rather than truly listen to them.

The challenge is to never paternalistically enter into the world of the oppressed so as to save it from itself. The challenge is also to never want to romanticize the world of the oppressed so that, as a process of staying there, one keeps the oppressed chained to the conditions that have been romanticized so that the educator keeps his or her position of being needed by the oppressed, "serving the oppressed," or viewing him or herself as a romantic hero.

For example, forty years ago, some of my generation—my peers—in Brazil had a great love for the oppressed of that day, a love that was also tainted by a romanticization about the oppressed. As a result, they left their academic settings to go live in the slums. In the end, we lost potentially very good academicians and gained not so good slum-dwellers. They were tourists. They knew—and their poor neighbors knew—that they could leave at any time. They took it upon themselves to speak for the poor without listening to the poor. This is a point that I discussed in the *Pedagogy of the Oppressed* when I critiqued the members of the middle class who came to the revolutionary struggle without first learning to listen to those in whose name the revolutionary struggle must be waged.

What I Can and Cannot Offer to Educators in Other Contexts

I think that another fundamental point that represents the anxiety of many educators, not only with respect to my work but with respect to other thinkers, with respect to Dewey, for example, or Montessori, or Frenet, is that what too many educators expect from these thinkers is that we will provide techniques to save the world. You have to be a superhuman person to be able to provide the correct pedagogical response in all contexts. In truth, in my case, what I have been proposing from my political convictions, my philosophical convictions, is a profound respect for the total autonomy of the educator. What I have been proposing is a profound respect for the cultural identity of students—a cultural identity that implies respect for the language of the other, the color of the other, the gender of the other, the class of the other, the sexual orientation of the other, the intellectual capacity of the other; that implies the ability to stimulate the creativity of the other. But these things take place in a social and historical context and not in pure air. These things take place in history and I, Paulo Freire, am not the owner of history.

I understand history as possibility. I struggle and fight for the respect for people that comes from seeing history as a possibility that could also stop being a possibility. For that very reason, the educator who accepts my ideas and then tomorrow encounters difficulties in that his or her own students assume respect for themselves cannot then say that Freire is wrong. Simply, he or she must say it was not possible to really experience the necessary respect in the particular context. I think this is the real issue in the sense that educators also romanticize my ideas without internalizing a way substantively to understand and apprehend what it means to be Freirian. In short, many of these educators who superficially use me as a way to solve their technical problems pedagogically are in a sense Freirian tourists. They almost become Freirian fundamentalists, and thus the world becomes fixed, eliminating the possibility of history being a possibility. What I propose is precisely the opposite. History is always a possibility and not fixed or predetermined. Also, the progressive educator must always be moving out on his or her own, continually reinventing me and reinventing what it means to be democratic in his or her own specific cultural and historical context.

Responding to Race, Class, and Gender in the United States

Given what we have been discussing, I believe that one could say that I have addressed the issue that has been raised many times about my work, that my ideas "do not address the specificities of race and gender in the U.S. context." I couldn't possibly address the details of race and gender in the U.S. context if I myself did not know the context. What I do provide is a general framework that calls for a deep respect for the Other along the lines of race and gender. What I do provide, while avoiding universalizing oppression, is the possibility for the educator to use my discussions and theorizing about oppression and apply them to a specific context. I have said this many times and I become frustrated when I hear the complaint yet again. I also become frustrated when I hear the opposite complaint, that "Freire is universalizing." I am not universalizing. What I do, in a humble way, is to provide certain parameters in dealing with issues of oppression as these issues relate to the pedagogical context. But I couldn't possibly give you recipes that basically fall into providing a kind of certainty of teacher-proof curriculum or ways of teaching in a Black ghetto in the United States, or ways of teaching in the new communities of color in Europe, or ways of teaching in ethnic neighborhoods anywhere else. It would be dishonest of me to do that without knowing the context. Thus I have to be reinvented and re-created according to the demands—pedagogical and political demands—of the specific situation.

In the various dialogues I have had with Donaldo Macedo we have addressed these issues in more detail that need not be repeated here. Still, even though I may run the risk of repeating myself I would like to reiterate that when I wrote the *Pedagogy of the Oppressed*, I tried to understand and analyze the phenomenon of oppression with respect to its social, existential, and individual tendencies. In doing so, I did not focus specifically on oppression marked by specificities such as color, gender, race, and so forth. I was more preoccupied then with the oppressed as a social class. But this, in my view, does not at all mean that I was ignoring the many forms of racial oppression that I have denounced always and struggled against even as a child. My mother used to tell me that when I was a child, I would react aggressively against any manifestation of racial discrimination. Throughout my life, I have worked against all forms of racial oppression, which is in keeping with my desire and need to maintain coherence in my political posture. I could not write in defense of the oppressed while being a racist, just as I could not be a machista either.

I would also like to point out that I have spoken and written a great deal about the question of race in my continuing quest to fight against any form of discrimination. You need to keep in mind that my work is not limited to the *Pedagogy of the Oppressed*. It is exactly because of my growing awareness over the years concerning the specificities of oppression along the lines of language, race, gender, and ethnicity that I have been defending the fundamental thesis of Unity in Diversity, so that the various oppressed groups can become more effective in their collective struggle against all forms of oppression. To the extent that each specificity of oppression contains itself within its historical location and accepts the profile that was created by the oppressor, it becomes that much more difficult to launch an effective fight that will lead to victory. For example, when the oppressors speak of "the minorities," they hide the basic element of oppression in the process. The label "minority" falsifies reality if we remember that the so-called minorities actually constitute the majority, while the oppressors represent the dominant ideology of a small minority.

Allowing Me Also to Continue Growing and Changing in My Contexts

To reinvent Freire means to accept my proposal of viewing history as a possibility. Thus the so-called Freirian educator who refuses to reinvent me is simultaneously negating history as a possibility and looking for the teacher-proof certainty of technical applications. This educator then has to reevaluate his or her posture vis-a-vis the theoretical proposal that I have been making for the last thirty-five years. This so-called Freirian educator, if he or she truly wants to understand me, must also go beyond reading *Pedagogy of the Oppressed*. He or she must continually be engaged in reading the works I have done since then, including *Pedagogy of Hope, Reading the Word and the World, The Politics of Education, Pedagogy of the City*, and *Letters to Christina*. It seems to me that many educators who claim to be Freirian are only referring to *Pedagogy of the Oppressed*, which was published almost thirty years ago, as if that is the first and the last work that I wrote. My thinking has been evolving and I have been constantly learning from others throughout the world, particularly with respect to questions of race and gender in other societies. As I have said, for me also history is always a possibility, never frozen. The same is true of my ideas. The minute you freeze history, or ideas, you also eclipse the possibility of creativity and undermine the possibility of the development of a political project.

Layered and Multiple Identities: People as Oppressor and Oppressed

In the first place these issues of layered and multiple identities always preoccupied me and I always thought about them. In my political and pedagogical experience I confronted many situations of profound ambiguity. For example, personally, at the beginning of my initial research I worked with a woman who was illiterate. She told me how much she was suffering from having to struggle against her husband and her oldest son because they wanted to keep her from becoming literate. Her husband and her son were as socially oppressed as she was. But in the direct relationship with her at home they developed a machista position through which they became the oppressors. I have also encountered many teachers, some of them friends, who while being oppressed by the political system in which they operated, were in turn oppressors of their students. We could spend an entire morning making reference to these obvious contradictions. What interests me now, in speaking to the probably North American readers of this book, is to ask myself again, what to do?

A first answer that is more or less easy, but that would reveal a lack of motivation to fight in me, would be to say, the reality is just as it is. This is the way human beings are, "let's give up." That would be the easy way out. However, this facile answer is something that I could never accept within the theoretical and practical proposals that I have been making over the years.

By the same token, it seems to me that the answer to this concrete possibility of ambiguity implies an increasingly critical comprehension of human beings as incomplete beings who need to come to know that they are incomplete. The consciousness of incompleteness in human beings leads us to involve ourselves in a permanent process of search. It is precisely this constant search that gives rise to hope. In truth, how can I possibly search without hope that I will find what I am looking for. But this incompleteness as human beings also pushes us toward action and thus makes us beings with options, beings who have the possibility of decisions, beings who have the possibility of rupture, and finally beings who have the possibility of being ethical. But in becoming ethical we engender a probability of transgressing the ethical. For example, if we had not become ethical beings, we would not know what it means to be ethical in that we would lack that point of reference. One of the ethical requirements that we have as historical beings is the search for coherence. It is precisely the lack of historical coherence that explains the machismo of the oppressed man I was discussing who would forbid his oppressed wife from learning how to read. Thus the question of complex identities is not only a technical one or political or pedagogical one; it is also an ethical one.

And, if I may say so, it is this ethical dimension to which teacher preparation programs in the United States, and in other countries, need to attend. It is essential to create a situation where future teachers can engage in a meaningful discussion about the ethics of education. It is not only knowing a theory of the oppressed with its various multiple identities; it is also knowing how to position oneself—ethically—vis a vis the layered and multiple identities engineered by the history of oppression that is needed.

The Ethical Requirements for Teachers

One of the dangers of this time in history, which is referred to in different ways in several of these chapters, is precisely the danger of the narrow understanding of ethics that is the perspective of neoliberalism. Ethics for the neoliberal teacher is something that is reduced to merely the ethics of the market. For us, no. For example, how is it possible for us to accept the fact that millions of people are without jobs? Is it just a fatality of the end of the century? It is not a fatality. It is one of the results of the ethics of the market. It needs to be understood that this so-called fatality is also a social construction informed by the ethics of the market. Thus it has become necessary for teachers, especially critical teachers, to deconstruct the social construction of this fatalism so as to unveil the inherent ideology that informs and shapes and maintains an ethic of greed. It is for this reason that we democratic educators must struggle so that it becomes clearer and clearer that education represents formation, and not merely training. And there is no possibility of having human formation without ethics. For me, then, one of the requirements of the present historical context is that the ethical formation of teachers has to accompany, has to go hand-in-hand with, the professional preparation of scientifically and technologically literate future teachers. The ethical requirements are becoming more and more critical in a world that is becoming less and less ethical. Thus we can never really solve the problem of teacher preparation with mere technicist proposals, which is what everyone is asking me to give. I surmise that some people, some questioners, are expecting me to give simple answers so as to address problems engendered by a context that requires ethical intervention and not technical responses. However, because in our preparation as teachers we were denied access to dialogue about the nature of ethics, we have been handicapped in our ability to confront and clearly address the specificity of a context that in its nature is ethical, because we do not know the ethics.

The Absence of Attention to Ethics in the Preparation of Educators

It is not a coincidence that the curriculum of most professional programs—in our case, teacher preparation—often does not include the opportunity for future professionals to engage in a serious and profound discussion about what it means to be ethical in a world that is becoming more profoundly unethical to the extent that human beings are becoming more and more dehumanized by the priorities of the market. This is one of my fights, my struggles, in working with those who dare to challenge the historical fatality imposed by the neoliberalist thinking. In this manner it becomes fundamental that a biologist discuss the nature of the life-forms that he or she is analyzing, but it is also fundamental for him or her to also discuss solidarity, ethics, love, dignity, respect of others, the nature of democracy. These issues that I have just mentioned are considered by the materialists as expressions of an inoperative romanticism or idealism. You often hear, "I was also an idealist, you'll grow up." This is a profoundly short-sighted view that only strengthens the hand of the neoliberal, market-driven people who want no ethical questions posed that might get in the way of their accumulation.

The Need to Maintain Ethical Clarity

Those of us who propose posing ethical questions at the heart of the debates about education often hear that we are soft and "political." The neoliberals view themselves and are viewed by too many others as tough and apolitical pragmatics. One result of the new pragmatism of neoliberalism is more concern with the scientific and technical training of teachers while denying a more comprehensive preparation because such a preparation always requires a critical understanding of one's role in the world. Thus the pragmatist's proposals always provoke a rupture and a disarticulation from the world in which the specialization or area of study is located. Information and knowledge are thus separated from the social and ethical context in which this information or knowledge appears.

So then, by being disarticulated from your world, you lose the possibility of developing cultural signposts that enable you to understand the world so as to act in it and transform it. Thus the neoliberal pragmatist position works aggressively to provoke a rupture between oneself and one's world while advocating an incredible articulation between oneself and the market. In other words, the focus of education in the neoliberal world really becomes how to become a proficient consumer, how to become a proficient dispenser of knowledge, without asking any ethical questions.

When one accepts the role of being a mere dispenser of knowledge along the lines of the market requirements that view students as mere consumers of knowledge, one becomes entrapped in the very ideological manipulation that denies one the possibility to articulate his or her world as a subject of history and not as a mere object to be consumed and discarded.

Unless they are very careful and very thoughtful, teachers can all too easily adopt the role of dispenser of knowledge. As I said in *Pedagogy of the Oppressed*, they become teachers operating out of a "banking" method of education, making deposits in the minds of their students. What keeps a person, a teacher, alive as a liberatory educator is the political clarity to understand the ideological manipulations that disconfirm human beings as such, the political clarity that would tell us that it is ethically wrong to allow human beings to be dehumanized so that a few can enrich themselves because of market greed. In order to develop this political clarity one has to be motivated and sustained with a strong conviction of history as possibility. One has to believe that if men and women created the ugly world that we are denouncing, then men and women can create a world that is less discriminatory and more humane. Then the teacher who finds herself or himself entrapped by the requirements of a mechanistic curriculum which calls for dispensing more and more content without grounding, needs to revert to her or his conviction that will determine an ethical posture vis-a-vis the curriculum so as to negotiate the context. Another thing to say is that this negotiation is not an individual act. It must be done in a conversation with other teachers who share the same vision of a radically democratic and humane society. As the Chilean poet Pablo Neruda says, "there is no such thing as a lone struggle and a lone hope."

Ethics and the Fear of Ethics

We must ask why so few teacher preparation programs include serious attention to the issue of ethics and why a fundamental focus on ethics is such a small part of today's educational dialogue while methods and statistics play such a large role. There is, today, a deep fear of discussing ethics in any way.

Of course, part of what keeps us from ethical engagement is the fear of imposition. I think basically a lot of the fear may have to do with the belief—perhaps from our days as Sunday School students—that all ethical discussion represents a form of doctrinal imposition. But it is more daunting to confront ethical issues and to dialogue about them to the extent that it also indicts us as teachers and professionals who enjoy certain privileges. We must reexamine and reevaluate our own postures, which may be in direct contradiction with what we depend on as part of our professional identity. Thus it becomes extremely dangerous to engage in a serious ethical reflection, for it will call on us to commit what Amilcar Cabral calls a form of "class suicide." A discussion of ethics involves a willingness to engage in "class and race suicide."

Unfortunately, many progressive educators who are well-intended often misunderstand the theoretical requirements of Cabral's notion of "class suicide" and end up falling into a blind embrace of suicide or martyrdom. In doing this they "suffer" in a process that keeps alive their privilege through a romanticization of the other. This position is in direct contradiction to Cabral's notion. Cabral challenged us to problematize the inner workings of the dominant ideology so as to understand how to struggle against the cruelty of colonialism in order that a radical democracy could be born from the struggle. Thus committing suicide as a blind act would represent a form of fatalism that negates Cabral's belief in history as possibility. It represents a form of radical individualism implicit in "saving my soul" as a martyr as opposed to a radically democratic commitment to continuing struggle in history. And Cabral's notion of class suicide has nothing to do with the mere crossing border from one space to another geographical crossing from oppressor to oppressed. Class suicide never takes place in a mere changing of address. Class suicide is not a matter of being a tourist in suffering communities. Class suicide is a form of Easter; it involves problematicizing a passage through a cultural and ideological context. It is the commitment to meaningful and lasting solidarity with the oppressed that counts.

The Barriers to Ethical Dialogue in Totalitarian and "Democratic" Systems

The question really is not to be free to speak about dialogue, but to fight for the right to participate in a living dialogue. In a totalitarian society it is sometimes possible to speak about progressive education through an authoritarian way. For example, I will never forget that in 1971 I participated in Europe in an international meeting at which there was a professor from the University of Moscow. One of the texts to be discussed in the meeting was a text of mine in which I criticized the attitudes of what I called "Herr Professors," the position of the professor who speaks about dialogue but denies the practice of dialogue. But I remember that the young professor from Moscow, in the discussions, became very angry and he said to me with his finger pointing at me, "Yes, yes I am a Herr Professor." You see, he felt very violated because I was attacking his sense of privilege as one who could dispense the knowledge of a liberation struggle. I did not write the text because of him, but it was as if I had written because of him. I said, "OK, but then because of that you are a reactionary professor, you are an authoritarian professor, and you have nothing to do with the ideals that you speak about in your country, you are a distortion of socialism." In that moment maybe at the University of Moscow he spoke about freedom from imperialism, but he denied ethically his speech about freedom in his practice. So the question for him was how to diminish the distance between what he wrote or said and what he did.

This distortion, this distance or incoherence between the values espoused and the practice of education also happens in the United States due to notions of the market and the willingness to use any level of oppression to maintain, and indeed never question, the status quo. You must also say that in some ways the same thing may happen in an "open democratic society" as in a totalitarian one in which the teacher embraces blindly an empty slogan of "freedom

and justice" for all while constantly violating the very principles of
these very clichés to the extent that they operate blindly through
totalitarian and inflexible structures in such things as schooling. For
example, how many times do teachers in the United States preach
and teach about democracy, solidarity, justice, and equality for all,
on the one hand while, on the other hand, punish any students who
would refuse to say the pledge of allegiance, thus violating the principle of the pledge that he or she is preaching or teaching about?

Can We Print a Dialogue Without, in the Act of Printing, Freezing It and Killing the Dialogue?

This question has been raised by the authors in this volume and it
is, in fact, central to the purpose of *Mentoring the Mentor*. Are the
various authors and editors of this work, in attempting to publish a
dialogue among ourselves, both preserving and destroying the dialogue? I think not. I think also that to worry about freezing the dialogue is to fail to understand that the written language has the
appearance, but only the appearance, of making immobile the
dynamism of orality. In truth the written language does not make
anything immobile, but in certain sense it fixes the force of oral language. It is for this reason that the reading of the written text should
be the reinvention of the oral speech. The pitfall of a linguist is to
believe that writing words is freezing them in time. Writing fixes the
force of the orality in time but the reader, in engaging with that
force, is continually reinventing and redialoguing, and so the text
remains alive and unfrozen.

The question for me, for example, in reading dialogical text is
how do I make myself able to dialogue with the written and thus
seemingly frozen text? When I read and reread Plato's dialogues, I
don't put myself before Plato's dialogues as if I were before a fos-
silized object. I view his dialogues as a discourse that is very much
alive and needs to be reinvented and recreated. It is the same exercise when I read any text written by authors or when I listen to a
friend or colleague with whom I could be speaking. It will be the
same exercise when others read this volume.

I cannot conceive of the possibility that a written dialogue—just because it is fixed in time—ceases being alive or loses its dynamism. The task and the challenge for us readers when dealing with the seemingly fixed and frozen dialogue is to rewrite that text by dialoging with its author via the written text. The key then is not to view the written text as frozen and therefore dated or dead material. The key is to use the text as a vehicle through which one can potentially dialogue with the author and with the potential incompleteness of the ideas. I understand very well that though its initial force may be fixed in time, it is a historical document, emerging from a specific historical context, and that at the same time it is a document that provides the possibility of unveiling in new ways in a different historical time.

The Notion of Completeness, in Written or Oral Communication, Is Itself Part of the Problem

When I say that the written text remains dialogical, I am remaining true to its historicity. But even the notion of completeness has to be problematized. A text is complete in a certain historical moment in that it promotes certainties. When you shift the moment you can begin to see its incompleteness. The reader then has the responsibility for engaging the incompleteness. The incompleteness of the text can be just as important as the completeness in a certain historical moment, for it is the incompleteness that engages the reader in a process of continued reinvention of the text in his or her own historical and cultural context. The reader can approach the text as frozen or as open. A text that is a master work is a text that can transcend its place in time. The notion of a text as frozen because of its lack of orality is a misunderstanding of the nature of the written work. So Plato, for instance, represents a real example of dialogical text that cannot be frozen in time and space. Because if Plato's work was merely a frozen text from the distant past, people would not even know that Plato had existed. In fact Plato is being interpreted and reinterpreted as we move through the centuries.

I don't have any doubt that a particular text, whether it is written in dialogue form or not, is conditioned by special characteristics of time and space. The ideas discussed by a text are ideas that are loaded with history and culture. What can happen in this instance is that as you move this text to another culture or setting or time the ideas may not correspond to the challenge of the new historicity, space, and time. For me, the text continues to be undoubtedly a valid discourse. This is because first the text makes it able for me to understand the relation between the ideas that the text expresses and the time at which these ideas were expressed. Second, because I can continue to be challenged by the ideas even though they may appear to be outdated. In this sense the continuous reinvention of the text means that there is no such thing as immobilization of text. In other words, the contemporary readers also represent a text and they are now interacting with the ideas that are seemingly delineated by a particular history, space, and time. But it is the contemporary reader who gives that mobility to the seemingly frozen text because ideas are never frozen.

Any type of education that is coherently progressive has to discuss not only the text but life itself. The very existence of the "not yet" means that the text can never be seen as something that is paralyzed. The comprehension of life as something that is paralyzed is a necrophylic comprehension. A loving understanding of life is one that sees life as a process taking place and not something that is a priori determined. The text not only speaks of things of life but has a life itself. Thus my position vis-à-vis the text is the loving position of someone who recreates these texts and thus recreates the life in them. You could almost describe much of contemporary education as the opposite; of having a necrophylic comprehension in which the text is frozen and dead.

The Plato scholar Paul Shorey was right when he wrote, "The best writings are only reminders of the discourses that are the true children of the mind." Note he did not say the parents of the mind or the elderly of the mind, but the children, the living and lively offspring of the mind. If that is the case, then we could not possibly think of Plato's written dialogue as a form of death through freezing in the written form. On the contrary, as Shorey says:

And so our final message to Lyusias or to Homer or to any statesman or orator is that if the writer knew the truth about the things of which he spoke and was able to defend it and make his writing seem a poor thing in contrast with his spoken word, then he deserves a higher name than author, orator, or poet. (Paul Shorey, *What Plato Said* [Chicago: University of Chicago Press, 1933, 1965], p. 158.)

What he is saying by this is that the written form capturing the force and life of the dialogical moment provides the possibility of continuity through which readers interact, create, and recreate the original force in a new space and time. This shows you that when we read Plato mechanically our understanding has to be mechanical as well. If we read Plato as a living word, then our understanding can be alive and can continue to grow.

How to Survive and Prevail as a Democratic Teacher/ How to Build a Movement

I think that one of the great difficulties that a teacher with a democratic perspective may have is that he or she may find him or herself alone. It is important to remember that it is not from what is done in the classroom alone that he or she will be able to support the students in reconstructing their position in the world. It is important that we know that the limited time of the classroom represents only a moment of the total social and individual experience of the student. The student wakes up, has his or her first interchange with his or her parents. The socialization he or she receives through the day may represent a negation of the humanistic understanding of life. Students spend a lot of time in front of the TV; they are involved with seeing and experiencing many forms of extreme violence; they experience discrimination—racial, sexual, cultural, gender—all the time; and they come to school. In most cases schools repeat the patterns of negative socialization with respect to humanity. Now comes the important question. What is a teacher to do? What is a teacher to do in order to open himself or herself up toward the reconstruction of the world in a democratic sense? What to do? Many of those with whom I speak are stimulated by these types of questions. I have spoken in the United States, but not only there, of the need that we have as teachers in cases such as I have described to begin to develop what I call the ideological map of the institution.

What does this mean? Developing an ideological map of the institution means that I try to locate in my department or school those who agree with my democratic ideas. I need to have a concrete idea of who my enemies are. I need to know whom I can count on before I can even begin to act as a democratic teacher. When I have the map and I know that I can count on the solidarity of five teachers, for example, and let's say fifteen students, then I can try to call for a first meeting to discuss, very informally, some probable steps to take toward radical democracy. Meeting, perhaps in some corner of the campus, is where I would begin to really entertain some questions with respect to my doubts, with respect to my convictions, my dreams. From this initial meeting we can begin to explore the possibility of establishing and continuing this initial discussion and meeting. In a certain moment it is possible that the five teachers and the fifteen students can now begin to organize an incipient plan of action. After the first experiences, maybe during this time, it may be viable to talk about our goals with some other teachers who are not totally cemented in a negative vision of humanity. Perhaps after some time instead of five teachers we may have twelve teachers. What for me is not possible is isolated work of individuals, particularly those who claim to work critically toward the establishment of a radical democracy. In other words, you cannot individually carry out the demands and requirements of the development of pedagogical spaces that respond to critical and radical democracy as a sole individual. It's impossible. It is precisely because of the individualist nature of many teachers, particularly in North America, that after failing in their individualistic experiment with critical and radical democracy, they claim that some of my proposals are unworkable in the North American context.

For example, when Donaldo Macedo and I are talking in a dialogue we both become more creative. In part this is because of our background as oral individuals who were not socialized in the written text only. What would be really interesting and important is if a

society, through schooling, when reaching the graphic moment—
the written form—would not turn it so as to bureaucratize it. In
other words, when society which is by nature oral, reaches the written stage, it should not freeze orality by bureaucratizing it. Orality
requires solidarity with the Other. Orality is dialogical by its very
nature to the extent that you cannot do it individualistically. Thus
the challenge for schools is to not kill those values of solidarity that
lead to democratic space through a process that freezes the required
dialogical nature of orality through the individualistic apprehension
of reading and writing. This is really fundamental. Students who are
extremely conversant in orality must therefore never be reduced to
one form of thinking that is linear and individualistic. Ironically,
schools do this all the time, reducing students to a nonoral and linear form of reading and thinking. And then these same schools
become frustrated with the difficulty of getting these same students
engaged in dialogical forms because these forms require them to be
resocialized to that which was killed before. All of this difficulty
happens because of the mechanistic nature of what it means to read
and write in modern consumerist societies.

This process reproduces the antidemocratic forces of the so-
called democratic schools. This is very important in that by freezing
the written text we deny the close and intimate interrelationship
between the reading of the word and the reading of the world,
something that I have discussed before. If we view the written text
as providing both possibilities, then the reading of the world cannot
possibly be fixed in time and space because that would be denying
its historicity since the world is never fixed. It is always changing.
Then there is the contradiction in thinking that the world becomes
ahistorical when you write it. This is a fundamental way in which
schools in North America maintain and expand an antidemocratic
system—through distancing students from a frozen written word
and therefore discouraging them from thinking of themselves as
actors in history. Language is first and foremost oral. We don't begin
with writing. History did not begin in a written form, but in words
and actions.

What Is the Role of a Mentor in Supporting the Development of a Democratic Teacher?

This question of the role of a mentor in education and the related question, "can one be a mentor/guide without being an oppressor?", is a basic, fundamental question. In the first place, in thinking radically about the importance of the teacher in the student's life and in thinking of all that the teacher represents, and not only in the scientific and technical training of the student, there is no doubt that the teacher should be a mentor. But for the teacher to become a mentor it is important that he or she challenges the student's creative freedom and that he or she stimulate the construction of the student's autonomy. The contradiction that the teacher must therefore deal with to be an authentic mentor is that he or she needs not to be mentor. What I mean is that to be an authentic mentor, the teacher should not adopt the role of mentor. In other words it is necessary that the teacher understands that the authentic practice of the mentor resides in the fact that the mentor refuses to take control of the life, dreams, and aspirations of the mentee. Because by not doing so we could very easily fall into a type of paternalistic mentorship.

The fundamental task of the mentor is a liberatory task. It is not to encourage the mentor's goals and aspirations and dreams to be reproduced in the mentees, the students, but to give rise to the possibility that the students become the owners of their own history. This is how I understand the need that teachers have to transcend their merely instructive task and to assume the ethical posture of a mentor who truly believes in the total autonomy, freedom, and development of those he or she mentors.

What the true democratic mentor needs to avoid is falling into the liberal pitfalls of viewing students through the orientation of a deficit lens through which the mentor's dreams and aspirations and knowledge are merely and paternalistically transferred to the students as a process through which the mentor clones himself or herself. The student that is cloned couldn't possibly be the image of his or her mentor. At the most he or she would be a poor imitation of Paulo Freire or any mentor.

Another risk that the mentee, the student, could run is having the mentor attempt to transform his or her mentees into his or her workers. For example, the biologist who is a mentor, the physicist or philosopher, the sociologist or the pedagogue who is a mentor can fall into this trap. A true mentor should avoid at all costs transforming his or her mentees into workers who are channeled as objects who in turn will reproduce the work and objectives and aspirations of the scientific endeavor of the mentor. In other words, the ethical posture of the mentor is to never use—which is often done—students to maximize the glory and the aspirations of the mentor. This form of mentorship is not only exploitative; it is fundamentally antidemocratic.

Reinventing Paulo Freire
in a North American—or Any Other—Context

The notion of reinventing Paulo Freire can only imply reinvention in connection with the substantivity of my ideas. That is because if you do not understand the substantivity of my ideas, it is impossible to speak of reinvention. In my particular case, what I would consider as the substantivity of my ideas—but not the totality of my ideas—is that we need to respect the Other. My respect for others represents a form of substantivity in terms of what it means to be in the world. Respect for the Other necessarily implies my refusal to accept any type of discrimination, my radical opposition to racial discrimination, to gender discrimination, to class discrimination, to cultural discrimination, outside of which I would not be able to understand myself. Another substantivity of my ideas is my understanding of history as possibility, therefore my rejection of any fatalistic comprehension or any deterministic view of history. Another aspect of my substantivity is my unconditional love for freedom and my certainty that we can become transformative beings and not adaptive beings, that we can become dialogical beings, that we can also become beings with a capacity for decision making, and that we can also develop the capacity for rupture. Thus it is that I struggle and fight against any system—social, economic, political—that forbids me from being, from asking, from discussing, from intervening, from being a decent human being. I could further develop this description of substantivity that then needs to be reinvented in terms of implementing these commitments in a specific cultural and historical setting. If you understand these things that I have underlined as the substantivity of my ideas that cannot be changed, I can then elaborate what it means to reinvent the substantivity of my ideas that I have just discussed in different moments and conditions.

Reinvention requires of me that I recognize that the historical, political, cultural, and economic conditions of each context present new methodological and tactical requirements, so that it is always necessary to search for the actualization of the substantivity of ideas with every new situation. In other words, the way that I struggle against machismo in Northeast Brazil cannot be possibly the same way that one should fight against machismo in New York City. It may take a different form in terms of tactics and techniques, but it also has to remain true to the substantive idea of fighting against machismo as something unethical and undemocratic. That is what I mean by reinventing me. These words "reinventing Paulo Freire" do no represent mere words in terms of blah, blah, blah. You need to understand the substantivity of the ideas which I have put forth, thus viewing machismo as something that is socially and politically repugnant. This idea, this commitment to ending machismo needs to maintain its force in any context through which I am reinvented, even though the context may require various techniques for struggling against *machismo*.

Therefore, in not being familiar, let us say, with the New York City context, its history, its struggles, its interrelations between men and women, its culture, it would be preposterous of me to provide what many North Americans often so anxiously ask for, recipes in terms of techniques and tactics for action. The only thing that I could offer is to work with North American educators so as to enable them to understand more deeply what it means to struggle against sexism as a substantive object of knowledge. Hence North American educators who dare to be progressive educators, who struggle against let us say sexism or racism or other isms, have the responsibility of analyzing both the possibility and limitations of actions within their own context so as to not sacrifice the force that gave rise to the struggle against sexism, racism, and other isms in the first place. As you can see then, it is not only impossible but a tragedy to reduce my substantive ideas into a mere technique.

I said for the first time in the United States in 1971 or 1972 that I should not be transplanted but reinvented. In 1974, when I wrote *Letters to Guinea Bissau* I explained what I meant by "being reinvented," but I always perceive how difficult it is to be understood regarding this point. For example, I cannot consider the possibility of my being reinvented through an authoritarian practice. Nevertheless the way of being a democratic teacher in Cape Verde is not necessarily the same as the way of being a democratic teacher in Chicago. To reinvent a democratic Cape Verdian educator in Chicago means first of all to maintain a fundamental commitment to being democratic, but secondly it means to search what it means to be democratic given the constraints and opportunities of the specific context. As you can see this is the problem of reinvention.

Perhaps the misunderstanding of what it means to reinvent is caused by the imposition in the United States of a particular notion of what a democracy is. You see, democracy in a Third World country cannot have the same characteristics as democracy in a rich, First World society such as the United States. It has to adopt the character and social and cultural needs of a particular cultural milieu. Thus what needs to be maintained in a democratic practice is the substantivity of democracy, not the surface characteristics of democratic practice.

On the other hand, by this I do not mean that one should fall into the pitfall of a facile cultural relativism; a sort of "everything goes" because the culture determines it. Thus, if a culture is supersexist, and I then claim culture as the rationale to maintain a sexist ideology, because sexism is part of the culture, that goes against my substantive adherence to democratic principles that should inform my vision, my aspirations, my dreams of a "not yet" that is radically democratic.

This concept of reinvention is becoming very clear for me. What

I am saying is that one of the reasons that many progressive and liberal educators in the United States have difficulty in comprehending Freire's concept, what it means to be reinvented, is not necessarily because they are incapable of understanding the concept. It is perhaps because they have only absorbed the substance of my ideas to a certain degree, while remaining ideologically chained to a position that is very anti-Freirian. Thus, by only partially accepting my ideological aspirations, they then develop doubts and questions with respect to specific methods and techniques. In this way they rationalize their total movement away from critically embracing what I represent in terms of theoretical proposals for change and for radical democracy and for history as possibility and for a less discriminatory society and a more humane world.

An honest and critical dialogical moment would require of all participants, and particularly those who perhaps unconsciously resist the major ideology of my proposals, to open up in a dialogue about the possibility of understanding that it may be, in fact, their resistance that prevents them from going forward with clarity with respect to certain positions that I have been talking and writing about for over four decades. It could also be that their resistance is really only minimal and, if this is the situation, such a dialogue would open them up to considering new themes that need to be explored for which I may or may not have answers but that I also believe should be objects of inquiry.

The Search for an Icon Comes Out of a Fear of Democracy

It is important that I say these things, because in accepting Paulo Freire's proposal of dreams for a democratic world, of dreams and aspirations for an antiracist and antisexist society, it does not mean that I do not fight against any movement that would turn me into a guru or an icon, because by accepting the position of iconomic privilege, of guru, I would be sabotaging in a direct way what I think as a thinker for democracy. The idea, then, is not to interact with or engage me and my ideas in bineristic terms—either Paulo Freire the guru or icon or a total rejection of Paulo Freire as proposing ideas that are unworkable in the North American context. The challenge is to engage my theoretical proposals dialogically, and it is through this dialogue that I think we can create possibilities, including the possibility that I can be reinvented in a North American context.

So in Conclusion

My aim here in this response is not to exhaust all of the questions that may be raised in the chapters in this book or by the readers who will engage in dialogue with the written words of this book, but to give examples of how I answer some of the questions. The challenge for the readers is to repeat the questions of the book in order to answer the questions I have not answered, and to do so in their own lives and in their own concrete historical context. These pages can be a pedagogical witness, a series of examples, but never frozen answers. Once again we are in the spirit of our understanding of dialogue and reinvention. The text of this conversation is an example of how we think in all of these dimensions. It is for the reader to reinvent what is here and make it alive in history.

Major Works of Paulo Freire That Are Available in English

Prepared by Elizabeth Wallace

Pedagogy of the Oppressed (New York: Seabury Press, 1970).

Education for Critical Consciousness (New York: Seabury Press, 1973).

Pedagogy in Process: The Letters to Guinea-Bissau (New York: Seabury Press, 1978).

"The People Speak Their Word: Learning to Read and Write in São Tome and Principe." Loretta Slover, trans. *Harvard Educational Review*, vol. 51, February 1981.

The Politics of Education: Culture, Power, and Liberation (South Hadley, Mass.: Bergin & Garvey, 1985).

"Reading the World and Reading the Word: An Interview with Paulo Freire," *Language Arts*, vol. 62, 1985.

Literacy: Reading the Word and the World, with Donaldo Macedo (South Hadley, Mass.: Bergin & Garvey 1987).

Learning to Question: A Pedagogy of Liberation, with A. Faundez (New York: Continuum, 1989).

We Make the Road by Walking: Conversations on Education and Social Change, with Myles Horton; Brenda Bell, John Gaventa, and John Peters, eds. (Philadelphia: Temple University Press, 1990).

Pedagogy of the City (New York: Continuum, 1993).

Pedagogy of Hope: Reliving Pedagogy of the Oppressed (New York: Continuum, 1994).

Paulo Freire on Higher Education: A Dialogue at the National

University of Mexico, with Miguel Escobar, Alfredo L. Fernandez, and Gilberto Guerara-Niebla (Albany, NY: SUNY Press, 1994).

"A Dialogue: Culture, Language, and Race," with Donaldo Macedo, *Harvard Educational Review*, vol. 65, no. 3, (Fall 1995).

Letters to Christina: Reflections on My Life and Work (New York: Routledge, 1996).

GEORGE DEI is a member of the faculty of Sociology at the Ontario Institute for Studies in Education at the University of Toronto.

MICHELLE FINE is a member of the faculty of the Graduate Center, City University of New York, New York City.

MARILYN FRANKENSTEIN is Professor of Applied Language and Mathematics at the College of Public and Community Service, University of Massachusetts, Boston.

JAMES W. FRASER is Professor of History and Education and Director of the Center for Innovation in Urban Education at Northeastern University, Boston, Massachusetts.

PAULO FREIRE, internationally recognized voice for a pedagogy of liberation and hope, teaches at the Catholic University in São Paulo, Brazil.

JAMES PAUL GEE holds the Hiatt Endowed Chair of Education at Clark University, Worcester, Massachusetts.

GLORIA LADSON-BILLINGS is Professor of Education at the University of Wisconsin, Madison.

DONALDO MACEDO is Professor of English and Director of the Bilingual/ESL Program at the University of Massachusetts, Boston.

PETER MCLAREN is a member of the faculty of the Graduate School of Education and Information Studies at the University of California at Los Angeles.

TANYA MCKINNON is a writer and a cultural anthropologist who lives in New York City.

PETER MURRELL is Associate Professor of Education and Director of the Master of Arts in Teaching Program at Northeastern University, Boston, Massachusetts.

RON SCAPP is Director of the Graduate Program in Urban and Multicultural Education at the College of Mount Saint Vincent in the Bronx, New York.

ANITA SHETH is a Graduate Student at the Ontario Institute for Studies in Education at the University of Toronto.

TIM SIEBER is Professor of Anthropology at the University of Massachusetts at Boston.

ASGEDET STEFANOS is a member of the faculty at the College of Public and Community Service, University of Massachusetts at Boston.

WILLIAM T. STOKES is Professor of Education and Director of the Literacy Institute at Lesley College, Cambridge, Massachusetts.

JILL MATTUCK TARULE is Dean of the College of Education and Social Services at the University of Vermont, Burlington.

COUNTERPOINTS

Counterpoints publishes the most compelling and imaginative books being written in education today. Grounded on the theoretical advances in criticalism, feminism and postmodernism in the last two decades of the twentieth century, Counterpoints engages the meaning of these innovations in various forms of educational expression. Committed to the proposition that theoretical literature should be accessible to a variety of audiences, the series insists that its authors avoid esoteric and jargonistic languages that transform educational scholarship into an elite discourse for the initiated. Scholarly work matters only to the degree it affects consciousness and practice at multiple sites. Counterpoints' editorial policy is based on these principles and the ability of scholars to break new ground, to open new conversations, to go where educators have never gone before.

Major Works of Paulo Freire That Are Available in English

Prepared by Elizabeth Wallace

Pedagogy of the Oppressed (New York: Seabury Press, 1970).

Education for Critical Consciousness (New York: Seabury Press, 1973).

Pedagogy in Process: The Letters to Guinea-Bissau (New York: Seabury Press, 1978).

"The People Speak Their Word: Learning to Read and Write in São Tome and Principe." Loretta Slover, trans. *Harvard Educational Review*, vol. 51, February 1981.

The Politics of Education: Culture, Power, and Liberation (South Hadley, Mass.: Bergin & Garvey, 1985).

"Reading the World and Reading the Word: An Interview with Paulo Freire," *Language Arts*, vol. 62, 1985.

Literacy: Reading the Word and the World, with Donaldo Macedo (South Hadley, Mass.: Bergin & Garvey 1987).

Learning to Question: A Pedagogy of Liberation, with A. Faundez (New York: Continuum, 1989).

We Make the Road by Walking: Conversations on Education and Social Change, with Myles Horton; Brenda Bell, John Gaventa, and John Peters, eds. (Philadelphia: Temple University Press, 1990).

Pedagogy of the City (New York: Continuum, 1993).

Pedagogy of Hope: Reliving Pedagogy of the Oppressed (New York: Continuum, 1994).

Paulo Freire on Higher Education: A Dialogue at the National

University of Mexico, with Miguel Escobar, Alfredo L. Fernandez, and Gilberto Guerara-Niebla (Albany, NY: SUNY Press, 1994).

"A Dialogue: Culture, Language, and Race," with Donaldo Macedo, *Harvard Educational Review*, vol. 65, no. 3, (Fall 1995).

Letters to Christina: Reflections on My Life and Work (New York: Routledge, 1996).